S. T COLERIDGE

AN EVALUATION OF HIS POETRY

S.T Coleridge

AN EVALUATION OF HIS POETRY

[A Complete Study Guide including Text, Analysis and Study Questions]

Aditya Nandwani
B.A. English (Hons) , Delhi University;
M.A. (English), IGNOU; Print Journalism (English) YMCA

ANMOL PUBLICATIONS PVT. LTD.
NEW DELHI - 110 002 (INDIA)

ANMOL PUBLICATIONS PVT. LTD.

H.O.: 4374/4B, Ansari Road, Darya Ganj,
New Delhi-110 002 (India)
Ph.: 23278000, 23261597

B.O.: No. 1015, Ist Main Road, BSK IIIrd Stage
IIIrd Phase, IIIrd Block
Bangalore - 560 085 (India)
Visit us at: www.anmolpublications.com

An Evaluation of His Poetry

First Published, 2009

PRINTED IN INDIA

Printed at Mehra Offset Press, Delhi.

Contents

	Preface	*ix*
1.	**Introduction**	**1**
2.	**S.T Coleridge: Biography**	**7**
3.	**Chronology**	**20**
4.	**The Romantic Movement**	**22**
5.	**Coleridge and Romanticism**	**28**
6.	**Selected Poems: Text**	**38**
7.	**Analysis of Selected Poetry**	**105**
8.	**Study Questions**	**132**

Q1. Comment on Coleridge's Use of Precise Observations of the Natural World to Convey Wider Thematic Ideas in His Poetry.
Or
Coleridge's poem revolves around eighteenth century philosophy of a dislocation between man and nature. Discuss
Or
Coleridge's poetry relies entirely on a detailed analysis of nature.Discuss 132

Q2. Analyse Coleridge's Christabel
Or
Evaluate Christabel as a poem of nature
Or
It has been said that "the thing attempted in Christabel is the most difficult in the

whole field of romance: witchery by daylight." Comment 136

Q3. Comment on the major themes in the Rime of Ancient Mariner
Or
The natural world's power in "The Rime of the Ancient Mariner" is unquestionable. Comment.
Or
Rime of Ancient Mariner as a Metaphysical poem. Describe.
Or
How does Coleridge incorporate style of story telling in the Rime of Ancient Marine. 140

Q4. Write a close critical analysis of Coleridge's 'Frost at Midnight' in order to examine the extent to which the poem explores and embodies some of the key concerns of Romanticism.'
Or
Frost at Midnight' is a poem written without calculated adherence to established poetic conventions. Comment. 148

Q5. Comment on the transforming creative self and the hermeneutics Of becoming in Samuel Taylor Coleridge's 'Kubla Khan' and 'Dejection: an Ode.' 153

Q6. These are some of the implications of the word "burst." At one point in The Prelude, Wordsworth describes the bust of Sir Isaac Newton, calling it, "The marble index of a mind forever voyaging through strange seas of thought alone." Certainly that is what Coleridge's poem is about as well. The Mariner is going to travel into strange seas of thought.

Or
Go back to the word "burst." It does suggest birth, but what else? We're talking about going from point A to point B, so why does Coleridge use the word "burst"? It signifies breakage. Romantic poetry is often about boundary breaking.
Or
What else does "burst" suggest? What's the nature of "bursting" into something? Energy . . . violent energy. Think about the structure of this work. The event that really launches the poem, and lies at the heart of the Mariner's journey, is the shooting of the Albatross. So it's not just breaking boundaries: it's an act of violent transgression. And yet this will somehow lead to knowledge and the growth of the poet's mind, to rebirth. That's very Romantic. It is a violation that cannot be undone. In that sense, it is like birth. Once we are born, we are cast out into the world; then the struggle is inevitable. 172

Q7. Critically Analyze Coleridge's "The Rime of Ancient Mariner".
Or
Discuss the various symbols in "The Rime of Ancient Mariner".
Or
What are the various themes in the poem "The Rime of Ancient Mariner". 174

Q8. On the one hand, the shooting of the Albatross may be read as a Romantic version of the myth of the Fall, the act as a symbol of Original Sin. But we can we go deeper.
Or
What might the Albatross symbolize? 182

Q9. How far do you think Kubla Khan is a romantic poem.
Or
How is Kubla Khan different from other poems of Coleridge?
Or
Samuel Taylor Coleridge uses amazingly implicative imagery and allegory to show his romantic ideals of paganism over Christianity. Comment 195

Q10. Evaluate the Symbolism in The Rime of the Ancient Mariner.
Or
To what extent is The Rime of Ancient Mariner a symbolic poem. 204

Q11. Can we say that Coleridge's writing are Explosive in nature? 212

Q12. Critics say that there is poetic failure in Coleridge's 'Kubla Khan'. Do you agree?
Or
The poem celebrates the creative imagination. Do you agree? 223

Q13. Asses Coleridge as a poet.
Or
Comment on Rosseti's statement "the leading point about Coleridge's work is its human love." 240

9. Critical Essays **263**

Bibliography **299**

Preface

Samuel Taylor Coleridge was famous for dreamy and somewhat creepy poems like *The Rime of the Ancient Mariner, Christabel* and *Kubla Khan* (the last of which he allegedly wrote subconsciously during a fever dream). Coleridge and poet William Wordsworth were close pals and their collection of poetry titled *Lyrical Ballads* (1798) was an early pillar of what became known as the Romantic Movement in poetry and art. Coleridge is probably best known for a poem from that collection, *The Rime of the Ancient Mariner,* which describes a sailor who curses himself and his ship by killing an albatross.

The Book provides an in depth analysis of Coleridge' Poetry .With an Introduction to Coleridge the book provides both text and criticism of all the major poems by Coleridge. Hoping that book proves to be a useful study aid for all the students we look forward to your responses.

Author

Chapter 1

Introduction

To comprehend Coleridge's work in any one field, one must also understand his work in the others. This is no small task: Coleridge was enormously learned; his writing seldom accommodates to lesser learning and lesser energies than his own. Furthermore, controversy both obscures and complicates anyone's approach.

Another central controversy that concerns Coleridge is plagiarism. This issue is intimately linked to whether one takes seriously Coleridge's Christianity, and, if so, how one understands his faith. Coleridge believed that God sustains the coherent & reliable relations among consciousness, language, and a genuine, knowable, external reality. This was a mature philosophic conviction, not a conventional piety. His Theo centric context often modifies the definitions and philosophic constructions that he incorporates from Immanuel Kant Friedrich von Schelling and others. As a result, Coleridge's most severe critics accuse him of misunderstanding what he takes or "distorting" it with religious ideas. His apologists, on the other hand, defend the value of his arguments despite this distressingly "mosaic" verbal surface.

Coleridge's work is also controversial because he took important stands on the major western questions concerning language and the possibility of knowledge. According to Coleridge, the accuracy of a statement—the test of its truth, philosophically—depends upon its precise and vivid use of words. His unfinished "Logosophia" was to demonstrate the basis of this extraordinary claim. But the "Logosophia" was to be an imaginative symbolic encounter, not a formal, closed, logical demonstration. Coleridge fully understood that no closed logical system can adequately reflect the character of reality. Because of this insight, Coleridge is sometimes appropriated by post-structuralists whose basic philosophic positions are inimical to his own. In the same way, the "New Criticism" once appropriated Coleridge, despite its antipathy to Coleridge's vision of the moral value of literature.

Coleridge is most famous for his poetry and his literary criticism. Biographia Literaria is a centrally-important inquiry into the nature of literary imagination. Its discussion of William Wordsworth remains a classic, as done in his 1811 lectures on William Shakespeare. His poetic reputation arises primarily from two groups of poems. Pre-eminent are the visionary poems: "The Rime of the Ancient Mariner," "Kubla Khan" and "Christabel". Second are the "conversation" poems: "The Eolian Harp," "This Lime-Tree Bower My Prison," "Frost at Midnight," "The Nightingale" and "Dejection: An Ode". Beneath the psychological power and musicality of his best lines, the careful reader will recognize Coleridge's considerable technical prowess as a poet. Consider, for instance, the spondaic substitutions in the following lines, from "The Eolian Harp":

O! The one Life within us and abroad,
Which meets all motion and becomes its soul,
A light in sound, a sound-like power in light,
Rhythm in all thought, and joyance everywhere—
Methinks, it should have been impossible
Not to love all things in a world so fill'd;
Where the breeze warbles, and the mute still air
Is Music slumbering on her instrument.

In deeply various ways, all Coleridge's work is a celebratory encounter with this "one Life."

Coleridge readily admitted that he demands very much of his readers. Once he called himself a "chamois hunter," who expects that those whom he guides will "cling to the rocks, by the blood of [their] own feet." Any experienced Coleridgean knows just how that feels—and why the journey proves, at last, worth the effort.

"The influence of Coleridge, like that of Bentham, extends far beyond those who share in the peculiarities of his religious or philosophical creed. He has been the great awakener in this country of the spirit of philosophy, within the bounds of traditional opinions. He has been, almost as neither truly as Bentham, 'the great questioner of things established'; for a questioner needs nor necessarily be an enemy."

Samuel Taylor Coleridge was born in Ottery St. Mary, Devonshire, as the youngest son of the vicar of Ottery St Mary. He was the youngest of ten children, adored by his parents. His father, the Reverend John Coleridge, was already fifty-three years old. Ann Bowdon, the daughter of a farmer, his second wife, was forty-five at that time. Later Coleridge described his childhood as full fantasy: "At six years old I remember to have read Belisarius, Robinson Crusoe, and Philip Quarll - and then I found the Arabian Nights' entertainments - one tale of which (the tale of a man who was compelled to seek for a pure virgin) made so deep an impression on me (I had read it in the evening while my mother was mending stockings) that I was haunted by specters whenever I was in the dark - and I distinctly remember the anxious and fearful eagerness with which I used to watch the window in which the books lay - and whenever the sun lay upon them, I would seize it, carry it by the wall, and bask, and read."

After his father's death, Coleridge was sent away to Christ's Hospital School in London. Coleridge studied at Jesus College. He joined in the reformist movement stimulated by the French Revolution, and abandoned his studies in 1793. In desperation, after an unhappy love-affair and pressed by debt, he enlisted in the 15th Light Dragoons under the name of Silas Tomkin Comberbache. Soon he realised that he was unfit for an army career and he was brought out under 'insanity' clause by his brother, Captain James Coleridge. In Cambridge

Coleridge met the radical, future poet laureate Robert Southey in 1794. Coleridge moved with him to Bristol to establish a community, but the plan failed. In 1795 he married the sister of Southey's fiancée Sara Fricker, whom he did not really love.

Coleridge's collection Poems On Various Subjects was published in 1796, and in 1797 appeared POEMS. In the same year he began the publication of a short-lived liberal political periodical The Watchman. He started a close friendship with Dorothy and William Wordsworth, one of the most fruitful creative relationships in English literature. From it resulted Lyrical Ballads, which opened with Coleridge's 'Rime of the Ancient Mariner' and ended with Wordsworth's 'Tintern Abbey'. These poems set a new style by using everyday language and fresh ways of looking at nature. 'The Rime of the Ancient Mariner', a 625-line ballad, is among his essential works. It tells of a sailor who kills an albatross and for that crime against nature endures terrible punishments. The ship upon which the Mariner serves is trapped in a frozen sea. An albatross comes to the aid of the ship; it saves everyone, and stays with the ship until the Mariner shoots it with his crossbow. The motiveless malignity leads to punishment: "And now there came both mist and show, / and it grew wondrous cold; / and ice, mast high, came floating by, / as green as emerald." After a ghost ship passes the crew begins to die but the mariner is eventually rescued. He knows his penance will continue and he is only a machine for dictating always the one story. When Mrs. Barbauld objected to Coleridge that the poem lacked a moral, the poet told her that "in my own judgment the poem had too much; and that the only or chief fault, if I might say so, was the obtrusion of the moral sentiment so openly on the reader as a principle or cause of action in a work of pure imagination."

The brothers Josiah and Thomas Wedge wood granted Coleridge an annuity of 150 pounds, thus enabling him to pursue his literary career. Disenchanted with political developments in France, Coleridge visited Germany in 1798-99 with Dorothy and William Wordsworth, and became interested in the works of Immanuel Kant. He studied philosophy at Göttingen University and mastered the German language. However, he considered his translations of Friedrich von Schiller's plays from the trilogy Wallenstein distasteful. At the end of 1799 Coleridge fell in love with Sara Hutchinson, the sister of Wordsworth's future wife, to whom he devoted his work Dejection: An Ode (1802). During these years Coleridge also began to compile his Notebooks, daily meditations of his life.

Suffering from neuralgic and rheumatic pains, Coleridge had become addicted to opium, freely prescribed by physicians. In 1804 he sailed to Malta in search of better health. Supplied with an ounce of opium and nine ounces of laudanum, he wrote in his journal: "O dear God! Give me strength of soul to make one thorough Trial - If I land at Malta / spite of all horrors to go through one month of unstipulated nature..." He worked two years as secretary to the governor of Malta, and later traveled through Sicily and Italy, returning then to England. In 1809-10 he wrote and edited with Sara Hutchinson the literary and political magazine The Friend. From 1808 to 1818 he gave several lectures, chiefly in London, and was considered the greatest of Shakespearean critics.

According to the poet, he heard the words to his famous 'Kubla Khan' in a dream. "In Xanadu did Kubla Khan / A stately pleasure dome decree: / Where Alph, the sacred river, ran / through caverns measureless to man / Down to a sunless sea. / so twice five miles of fertile ground / with walls and towers were girdled round: / and there were gardens bright with sinuous rills, / Where blossomed many an incense-bearing tree; / and here were forests ancient as the hills / Enfolding sunny spots of greenery." (From Kubla Khan, 1798) 'Christabel' and 'Kubla Khan' circulated many years in oral form before publication, and especially 'Christabel' influenced later the works of Sir Walter Scott and Lord Byron. In the summer of 1797 the author had retired to a lonely farm-house between Porlock and Linton. He had taken anodyne and after three hours sleep he woke up with a clear image of the poem. Disturbed by a visitor, he lost the vision, with the exception of some eight or ten scattered lines and images. Modern scholarship is skeptical of this story, but it reveals Coleridge's interest in the workings of the subconscious.

In 1810 Coleridge's friendship with Wordsworth came to crisis, and the two poets never fully returned to the relationship they had earlier. During the following years, Coleridge lived in London, on the verge of suicide. Remorse, a play which he had written many years earlier, was successfully produced at the Drury Lane theatre in 1813. He received £400, which he spent in a few months. After a physical and spiritual crisis at Greyhound Inn, Bath, he submitted himself to a series of medical régimes to free himself from opium. He found a permanent harbor in High gate in the household of Dr. James Gillman, and enjoyed almost legendary reputation among the younger Romantics. During this time he rarely left the house.

In 1816 the unfinished poems 'Christabel' and 'Kubla Khan' were published, and next year appeared Sibylline Leaves. After 1817 Coleridge devoted himself to theological and politico-sociological works - his final position was that of a Romantic conservative and Christian radical. "Every reform, however necessary, will by weak minds be carried to an excess, that itself will need reforming," he wrote in Biographia Literaria (1817). Coleridge contributed to several magazines, among them Blackwood's Edinburgh Magazine. In 1824 Coleridge was elected a fellow of the Royal Society of Literature. He died in High gate, near London on July 25, 1834. Coleridge's daughter Sara (1802-1852) was also a writer and translator. She published children's verse, Pretty Lessons In Verse For Good Children (1834) and Phantasmion (1837). When her husband died she took up the task of editing her father's works.

Chapter 2

S.T Coleridge: Biography

EARLY LIFE AND EDUCATION

Samuel Taylor Coleridge was born on October 21, 1772 in the rural town of Ottery St Mary, Devonshire. He was the youngest of ten children, and his father, the Reverend John Coleridge, was a well respected vicar. Coleridge suffered from constant ridicule by his older brother Frank, partially due to jealousy, as Samuel was often praised and favoured by his parents. To escape this abuse, he frequently sought refuge at a local library, which led him to discover his passion for poetry.

After the death of his father in 1781, contrary to his desires, he was sent to Christ's Hospital. The school was originally founded in the 16th century in Greyfriars, London and Hertford. [Now a boarding school in West Sussex]. The school was notorious for its unwelcoming atmosphere and strict regimen under The Rev. James Bowyer, many years Head Master of the grammar school, which fostered thoughts of guilt and depression in young Samuel's maturing mind. However, Coleridge seems to have appreciated his teacher, as he wrote in detailed recollections of his schooldays in Biographia Literaria:

I enjoyed the inestimable advantage of a very sensible, though at the same time, a very severe master...At the same time that we were studying the Greek Tragic Poets, he made us read Shakespeare and Milton as lessons: and they were the lessons too, which required most time and trouble to bring up, so as to escape his censure. I learnt from him, that Poetry, even that of the loftiest, and, seemingly, that of the wildest odes, had a logic of its own, as severe as that of science; and more difficult, because more subtle, more complex, and dependent on more, and more fugitive causes....

In our own English compositions (at least for the last three years of our school education) he showed no mercy to phrase, metaphor, or image, unsupported by a sound sense, or where the same sense might have been conveyed with equal force and dignity in plainer words... In fancy I can almost hear him now, exclaiming Harp? Harp? Lyre? Pen and ink, boy, you mean! Muse, boy, Muse? Your Nurse's daughter, you mean! Pierian Spring? Oh aye! The cloister-pump, I suppose! ... Be this as it may, there was one custom of our master's, which I cannot pass over in silence, because I think it ... worthy of imitation. He would often permit our theme exercises, to accumulate, till each lad had four or five to be looked over. Then placing the whole number abreast on his desk, he would ask the writer, why this or that sentence might not have found as appropriate a place under this or that other thesis: and if no satisfying answer could be returned, and two faults of the same kind were found in one exercise, the irrevocable verdict followed, the exercise was torn up, and another on the same subject to be produced, in addition to the tasks of the day.

Throughout life, Coleridge idealized his father as pious and innocent, but his relationship with his mother was more problematic. His childhood was characterized by attention-seeking, which has been linked to his dependent personality as an adult. He was rarely allowed to return home during the school term, and this distance from his family at such a turbulent time proved emotionally damaging. He later wrote of his loneliness at school in the poem Frost at Midnight: "With unclosed lids, already had I dreamt/of my sweet birthplace"

From 1791 until 1794 Coleridge attended Jesus College, Cambridge. In 1792 he won the Browne Gold Medal for an Ode that he wrote on the slave trade. In November, 1793, he left the college and enlisted in the Royal Dragoons, perhaps because of debt or because the girl that he loved, Mary Evans, had rejected him. His brothers arranged for his discharge a few months later (ironically because of supposed insanity) and he was readmitted to Jesus College, though he would never receive a degree from Cambridge.

PANTISOCRACY AND MARRIAGE

At the university he was introduced to political and theological ideas then considered radical, including those of the poet Robert Southey. Coleridge joined Southey in a plan, soon abandoned, to found a utopian commune-like society, called Pantisocracy, in the wilderness of Pennsylvania. In 1795 the two friends married sisters Sarah and Edith Fricker, but Coleridge's marriage proved unhappy. He grew to detest his wife, whom he only married because of social constraints, and eventually divorced her. During and after his failed marriage, he came to love a woman named Sara Hutchinson, who did not share this passion and consequentially caused him much distress. Sara departed for Portugal, but Coleridge remained in Britain. In 1796 he published Poems on Various Subjects.

In 1795 Coleridge met poet William Wordsworth and his sister Dorothy. They became immediate friends.

Around 1796, Coleridge started taking opium as a pain-reliever. His suffering, caused by many ailments, including toothache and facial neuralgia, is mentioned in his own notebook as well as that of Dorothy Wordsworth. There was no stigma associated with taking opium at the time, but also little understanding of the dangers of addiction.

The years 1797 and 1798, during which he lived in Nether Stowey, Somerset, and Wordsworth, having visited him and being enchanted by the surroundings, rented Alfoxton Park, a little over three miles (5 km) away, were among the most fruitful of Coleridge's life. Besides the Rime of The Ancient Mariner, he composed the symbolic poem Kubla Khan, written—Coleridge himself claimed—as a result of an opium dream, in "a kind of a reverie"; and the first part of the narrative poem Christabel. During this period he also produced his much-praised "conversation" poems This Lime-Tree Bower My Prison, Frost at Midnight, and The Nightingale.

In 1798 Coleridge and Wordsworth published a joint volume of poetry, Lyrical Ballads, which proved to be the starting point for the English Romantic Movement. Though the productive Wordsworth contributed more poems to the volume, Coleridge's first version of The Rime of the Ancient Mariner was the longest poem and drew more immediate attention than anything else. In the spring of 1798, Coleridge temporarily took over for Rev. Joshua Toulmin at Taunton's Mary Street Unitarian Chapel while Rev. Toulmin grieved over the drowning death of his daughter Jane. Poetically commenting on the strength of Rev. Toulmin, Coleridge wrote in a 1798 letter to John Prior Estlin.

In the autumn of 1798, Coleridge and Wordsworth left for a stay in Germany; Coleridge soon went his own way and spent much of his time in university towns. During this period he became interested in German philosophy, especially the transcendental idealism of Immanuel Kant, and in the literary criticism of the 18th century dramatist Gotthold Lessing. Coleridge studied German and, after his return to England, translated the dramatic trilogy Wallenstein by the German Classical poet Friedrich Schiller into English.

Coleridge's greatest intellectual debts were first to William Godwin's Political Justice, especially during his Pantisocratic period, and to David Hartley's Observations on Man, which is the source of the psychology which we find in "Frost at Midnight." Hartley argued that we become aware of sensory events as impressions, and that "ideas" are derived by noticing similarities and differences between impressions and then by naming them. Connections resulting from the coincidence of impressions create linkages, so that the occurrence .of one impression triggers those links and calls up the memory of those ideas with which it is associated .Coleridge was critical of the literary taste of his contemporaries, and a literary conservative insofar as he was afraid that the lack of taste in the ever growing masses of literate people would mean a continued desecration of literature itself.

In 1800 he returned to England and shortly thereafter settled with his family and friends at Keswick in the Lake District of Cumberland to be near Grasmere, where Wordsworth had moved. Soon, however, he was beset by marital problems, illnesses, increased opium dependency, tensions with Wordsworth, and a lack of confidence in his poetic powers, all of which fueled the composition of Dejection: An Ode and an intensification of his philosophical studies.

In 1804 he traveled to Sicily and Malta, working for a time as Acting Public Secretary of Malta under the Commissioner, Alexander Ball. He gave this up and returned to England in 1806. Dorothy Wordsworth was shocked at his condition upon his return. From 1807 to 1808, Coleridge returned to Malta and then traveled in Sicily and Italy, in the hope that leaving Britain's damp climate would improve his health and thus enable him to reduce his consumption of opium. Thomas de Quincy alleges in his Recollections of the Lakes and the Lake Poets that it was during this period that Coleridge became a full-blown opium addict, using the drug as a substitute for the lost vigour and creativity of his youth. It has been suggested, however, that this reflects de Quincy's own experiences more than Coleridge's. His opium addiction (he was using as much as two quarts of laudanum a week) now began to take over his life: he separated from his wife in 1808, quarreled with Wordsworth in 1810, lost part of his annuity in 1811, put himself under the care of Dr. Daniel in 1814.Between 1810 and 1820 this "giant among dwarfs", as he was often considered by his contemporaries, gave a series of lectures in London and Bristol – those on Shakespeare renewed interest in the playwright as a model for contemporary writers.

In 1817 Coleridge, with his addiction worsening, his spirits depressed, and his family alienated, took residence in the home of the physician James Gillman, at 3 The Grove, High gate, London, England. In Gillman's home he finished his major prose work, the Biographia Literaria (1815), a volume composed of 23 chapters of autobiographical notes and dissertations on various subjects, including some incisive literary theory and criticism. He composed much poetry here and had many inspirations — a few of them from opium overdose. Perhaps because he conceived such grand projects, he had difficulty carrying them through to completion, and he berated himself for his "indolence." It is unclear whether his growing use of opium was a symptom or a cause of his growing depression. He published other writings while he was living at the Gillman home, notably Sibylline Leaves (1820), Aids to Reflection (1823), and Church and State (1826). He died of a lung disorder including some heart failure from the opium that he was taking in High gate on July 25, 1834.

POETRY

Coleridge is probably best known for his long poems, The Rime of the Ancient Mariner and Christabel. Even those who have never read the Rime have come under its influence: its words have given the English language the metaphor of an albatross around one's neck, the quotation of "water, water everywhere, nor any drop to drink (almost always rendered as "but not a drop to drink")", and the phrase "a sadder and a wiser man (again, usually rendered as "sadder but wiser man")". Christabel is known for its musical rhythm, language, and its Gothic tale.

Kubla Khan, or, A Vision in a Dream, A Fragment, although shorter, is also widely known and loved. It has strange, dreamy imagery and can be read on many levels. Both Kubla Khan and Christabel have an additional "romantic" aura because they were never finished. Stopford Brooke characterized both poems as having no rival due to their "exquisite metrical movement" and "imaginative phrasing." It is one of history's tragedies that Coleridge was interrupted while writing Kubla Khan by a visitor and could not recall any more of the poem afterwards. However, it is now acknowledged that Coleridge had composed previous drafts of Kubla Khan, perhaps a reflection of his desire to flag the 'power' of imagination. Coleridge's shorter, meditative "conversation poems," however, proved to be the most influential of his work. These include both quiet poems like This Lime-Tree Bower My Prison and Frost at Midnight and also strongly emotional poems like Dejection and The Pains of Sleep. Wordsworth immediately adopted the model of these poems, and used it to compose several of his major poems. Via Wordsworth, the conversation poem became a standard vehicle for English poetic expression, and perhaps the most common approach among modern poets. Coleridge's poetry so impressed the parents of British composer Samuel Coleridge-Taylor (1875-1912) that they named him after the poet.

COLERIDGE AND THE INFLUENCE OF THE GOTHIC

Gothic novels like Polidori's The Vampire, Walpole's The Castle of Otranto, Mrs. Radcliff's The Mysteries of Udolpho and The Italian, and Matthew Lewis's The Monk were the best-sellers of the end of the eighteenth century, and thrilled many young women (who were often strictly forbidden to read them). Jane Austen satirized the style mercilessly in Northanger Abbey. Coleridge wrote reviews of Mrs. Radcliff's books and of The Mad Monk among others. He comments in his reviews:

Situations of torment, and images of naked horror, are easily conceived; and a writer in whose works they abound, deserves our gratitude almost equally with him who should drag us by way of sport through a military hospital, or force us to sit at the dissecting-table of a natural philosopher. To trace the nice boundaries, beyond which terror and sympathy are deserted by the pleasurable emotions, - to reach those limits, yet never to pass them, hic labour, hic opus est.

The horrible and the preternatural have usually seized on the popular taste, at the rise and decline of literature. Most powerful stimulants, they can never be required except by the torpor of an unawakened, or the languor of an exhausted, appetite... We trust, however, that satiety will banish what good sense should have prevented; and that, wearied with fiends, incomprehensible characters, with shrieks, murders, and subterraneous dungeons, the public will learn, by the multitude of the manufacturers, with how little expense of thought or imagination this species of composition is manufactured. However, Coleridge used mysterious and demonic elements in poems such as The Rime of the Ancient Mariner (1798), Christabel and Kubla Khan (published 1816 but known in manuscript form before then) and certainly influenced other poets and writers of the time. Poems like these both drew inspiration from and helped to inflame the craze for Gothic romance.

Mary Shelley, who knew Coleridge well, mentions The Rime of the Ancient Mariner twice directly in Frankenstein and some of the descriptions in the novel echo it indirectly. Although William Godwin, her father, disagreed with Coleridge on some important issues, he respected his opinions and Coleridge often visited the Godwins. Mary Shelley later recalled hiding behind the sofa and hearing his voice chanting The Rime of the Ancient Mariner.

COLERIDGE'S FRIENDSHIP WITH WORDSWORTH

It was the genius of Wordsworth—and, with Wordsworth, we must always think of his 'exquisite sister'—that first revealed him to himself. It was in daily intercourse with a stronger spirit than his own—first at Stowey (1797–8), then, more fitfully, in the lake country (1800–3)—that all his enduring poetry was composed. The spell of Wordsworth, however, went far deeper than this. It not only awakened the younger poet to creative energies which had hitherto lain asleep. It was a transforming influence upon his whole cast of thought, upon the whole character of his soul.

His whole nature was roused, for the first time, to a full consciousness of its powers; and powers of which he had hitherto given no suspicion were suddenly called to light. A sense of the beauty of outward things, as deep as

Wordsworth's, but still more delicate and more subtle; a sense of the boundless mystery of life—the inner yet more than the outer life—and a power of interpreting it in terms of thought: these were the two gifts which came to him with this new birth; and, however idly he may have used them, they remained with him to the end. Well might he say that "a new earth and a new heaven" were now "given to him in dower?" For he saw the world with a keener and more radiant vision than had ever been granted to him before; and he saw into it more deeply. In the full sense of the terms, he became, for the first time, both philosopher and poet.

That his use of these magic gifts was not what it might have been is too clear. But it is only just to remember that this applies more to his work as philosopher than as poet. Poetry "comes not with observation." And, if that be true, in a measure, of all poetry, of none is it as true as of that to which the peculiar genius of Coleridge was manifestly ordained. Is it reasonable to suppose that any poet could have gone on living for ever in an air so rarefied as that of The Ancient Mariner, or Kubla Khan, or Christabel? Given circumstances as happy as almost to amount to a miracle, perhaps he might.

But the miracle did not happen to Coleridge; and, even if his will had been as strong as it was weak, there is no warrant that it would have happened. To condemn him on this score, however much he himself would have accepted the condemnation, seems, therefore, unwarrantably harsh. But his other gifts lay in a region more under his control. And, had he been a man of ordinary resolution—above all, had he not let himself become the slave of opium—there was nothing to prevent him from accomplishing a giant's work in philosophy and criticism. In criticism and the theory of criticism, he might have done for his own country the double work which was done for Germany by Lessing and Hegel, and something more besides. In philosophy, he might have recast and even extended the massive fabric of Kant. As it is, in neither field has he left more than a heap of disjointed, but imposing, fragments.

THE FRENCH REVOLUTION

Up to this time, there is nothing beyond the doubtful evidence of a school exercise to show that the revolution in France had roused any deep interest, or even attention, in his mind. Now, under the tenser will of Southey, he became a fiery revolutionist, of a brand, however, peculiarly his own. In hatred of Pitt and the war, he was, no doubt, at one with the other Jacobins of the time. But the Pantisocracy, which the two friends beat out between them, ran decisively athwart the main stream of revolutionary aspirations. It was intended only for the select few; it was no part of a general scheme of social reconstruction.

Again, the "Jacobinism" of Coleridge, though not that of Southey, was always strongly charged with a mystical and religious element, which stands in the sharpest contrast with the purely secular, often atheist, temper more common among the reformers of that day. Lastly—and here, once again, he joins hands with Southey—the whole creed and being of the young convert were drowned in a flood of sentiment which woke in him, for the first time in good earnest, the need of poetic utterance, and which at once sets a barrier between him and most of the leading figures among the rebel band: Godwin, for instance, or Holcroft, or even Thelwall.

It was in pleading the cause of Pantisocracy that he first discovered—to himself, perhaps, as well as to others—his amazing powers of eloquence. His letters of that time are full of boyish delight in the discovery: "Up I arose, terrible in reasoning" is a typical sentence. And, so long as he could convince, or even vanquish, his opponents, it is clear that he did not much trouble himself to put his convictions into act. Even his breach with Southey, who soon became lukewarm in the cause, would seem to have partly sprung from an uneasy sense that he, too, had said more than he was willing or able to make good, and from the consequent impulse, very natural though not very just, to prove that some one else was yet more guilty than himself. Still more ominous, even in an age of overwrought sentiment, is the sentimentalism of his letters.

"Since I quitted this room," he writes on his return from the fateful visit to Oxford, "what and how important events have been evolved! America! Southey! Miss Fricker! Yes, Southey, you are right. Even love is the creature of strong motive. I certainly love her." It is small wondered that the love which began as "the creature of strong motive"—that is, Southey's fiat—should have ended disastrously for both. A year later (October, 1795) the marriage duly took place.

The poetry of these years (1794–6) is a mirror of the man: eloquent, loose-girt, and strongly inclined to preach; in all things, the very reverse of the inspired pieces soon to follow. It is, doubtless, the sincere expression of the generous convictions and aspirations which he held in common with others. But it lacks the individuality which is the soul of poetry; and, only in one passage—some three or four lines of The Eolian Harp 2 —does it offer even a faint promise of the works by which he lives. It is a glorified version of sermons such as Hazlitt heard in the enchanted walls of the Shropshire chapel. It has nothing in common with The Ancient Mariner, or Christabel, or even the ode Dejection.

THE OPIUM HABIT

The opium habit, the beginnings of which go back as far as 1797, seems to have grown upon him during his time at Malta (1804–6); and, by the time he returned to England, the bondage must have been confirmed. Again and again, he strove to throw off the yoke; but only to fall back again more helplessly than before. Degraded in his own eyes, he felt life to be a burden almost too heavy to be borne; and the letters which, now and again, were wrung from him by remorse, are, perhaps, among the most terrible ever written. Two things alone saved him from total shipwreck: the unwearied tenderness of friends, old and new—Poole, Wordsworth, Mrs. Clarkson and the Morgan's; and the innate rectitude, winged by a strong religious impulse, which did not cease to assert itself against reiterated defeat. At length, after ten years of debasement, he nerved himself to seek refuge with James

Gillman, a physician of High gate (1816). And, thanks to the devoted friendship and watchfulness of this man and his wife—he remained their "inmate" till his death—he slowly tore himself loose from the bondage in which he had been held. That he never wholly gave up the drug is tolerably clear. But he so far mastered himself as to take it in rarer and smaller doses; and, for practical purposes, the hard-fought victory was won.

Thus, the last eighteen years of his life were years of inward peace and of fruitful service to others. The old weakness, no doubt, still dogged his steps and prevented the fulfillment of the task—a work on Spiritual Philosophy and half a dozen alternative titles—to which he was conscious of being called. But, in familiar talk, in formal lecturing and even in published writings, this was the richest period of his life; and it left a deep mark upon some of the strongest and most eager spirits of the younger generation.

The victory was won. But the long years of apparently hopeless struggle had left scars which nothing could wholly heal. The prime of his life had been largely wasted. And he had strained the patience of some of his best friends. Josiah Wedgwood had withdrawn, perhaps with undue harshness, his half of the pension that he and his brother had granted in days when nothing seemed beyond the reach of the young poet and thinker. Southey, who had gallantly shouldered the charge of the truant's wife and children, was embittered, if not estranged. Even Wordsworth, by an unguarded utterance made with the best intentions, had caused a breach which could never wholly be made up.

This was probably the deepest sorrow of his life; "all else," he says, "is as a flea-bite." His family life, too—though this was from causes which, in the first instance, at any rate, had little to do with opium—had been entirely broken up. And, though a formal separation was avoided, he never lived with his wife after 1810; and had, in fact, seen as little as he could of her since 1804.

The real secret of the estrangement was that, by temperament, the two were ill sorted with each other. But it is impossible not to feel the deepest sympathy with a woman who battled bravely with the hardships of her lot; and hard to check the suspicion that, but for opium, the difficulties might have been smoothed over. In any case, the breach was a worse thing for Coleridge than he was ever willing to acknowledge. It robbed him of the steadying influences of home life, to which he was by nature peculiarly open. And it left a sting in his conscience which he may have ignored, but which, just for that reason, was never healed.

Chapter 3

Chronology

- 1772 born (Oct. 21) at Ottery St. Mary's, Devonshire.
- 1781 father dies.
- 1782-91 at Christ's Hospital (school). [See Lamb, "Christ's Hospital Five- and-Thirty years ago."]
- 1789 reads Bowles's Sonnets.
- 1790-91 Brother Luke and Sister Ann die.
- 1791-94 at Cambridge.
- 1793 in love with Mary Evans; enlists in the 15th Dragoons.
- 1794 returns to Cambridge; meets Southey. Engaged to Sara Fricker. Meets Godwin. STC and Southey plan a "Pantisocracy."
- 1795 meets Wordsworth. Marries Sara Fricker.
- 1796 Poems on Various Subjects. Son Hartley born. Coleridge moves to Nether Stowey. First takes opium.
- 1796-97 preaching at various Unitarian chapels.
- 1797 with Wordsworth at Nether Stowey. Begins The Ancient Mariner.
- 1798 Lyrical Ballads, with Wordsworth. Wedgwood's give Coleridge £150 annuity. Visits Germany with Wordsworth. Writes "Kubla Khan."
- 1799 meets Sara Hutchinson. Tours the Lake District.
- 1799-1802 writes political leaders for Morning Post.

- 1801 health breaks down; opium again.
- 1802 "Dejection, an Ode." Daughter Sara born.
- 1803 tours Scotland with W. & Dorothy Wordsworth.
- 1804 in Malta and Sicily. Private Secretary to Alex. Ball, High Commissioner at Malta.
- 1805 appointed Acting Public Secretary in Malta.
- 1806 returns to England; D. Wordsworth "shocked" at his condition.
- 1808 separates from wife.
- 1809-10 the Friend.
- 1810 quarrel with Wordsworth. Heavily addicted to opium.
- 1811 Josiah Wedge wood withdraws half STC's annuity.
- 1811-12 Lectures on Shakespeare.
- 1812 reconciled to Wordsworth.
- 1812-13 lectures on Belles Letters.
- 1814 in the care of Dr. Daniel for opium addiction. Lectures in Bristol. Turns from Unitarianism to Anglicanism.
- 1814-16 financial difficulties.
- 1816 settles at High gate with Dr. James Gilman. Christabel and Kubla Khan.
- 1817 Biographia Literaria and Lay Sermons.
- 1819 more Lectures on Shakespeare.
- 1825 Aids to Reflection. Appointed Associate of the Royal Society of Literature, begins receiving £125 annuity.
- 1826-34 "High gate Thursdays."
- 1828 continental tour with Wordsworth.
- 1830 Constitution of Church and State.
- 1834 dies July 25.

Chapter 4

The Romantic Movement

POETRY DEFINED BY ROMANTICS

Though Lord Byron described William Wordsworth as "crazed beyond all hope" and Samuel Taylor Coleridge as "a drunk," the two are exemplary and very important authors of the Romantic period in English literature (648). Together these authors composed a beautiful work of poems entitled Lyrical Ballads. Included in the 1802 work is a very important preface written by William Wordsworth. The preface explains the intention of authors Wordsworth and Coleridge, and more importantly, it includes Wordsworth's personal opinion of the definition and criteria of poetry and of what a poet should be. Although there was some disagreement about the proper diction of a good poem, Coleridge, the lesser represented author of the two in the work, agrees with most of Wordsworth's criteria. He voices his own personal opinions, however, in his Biographia Literaria.

In both Lyrical Ballads and Biographia Literaria the authors' opinions coincide in that the definition and criteria of a poem is to be a structured and carefully planned composition that stirs passionate natural emotions in the reader and that the poet is the force directly responsible for this. To accomplish this, a great poet must possess an intimate knowledge of nature and have close interaction with all aspects of it.

Coleridge states in his Biographia Literaria that "the definition sought for be that of a legitimate poem, must be one the parts of which mutually support and explain each other; all in their proportion harmonizing with and supporting the purpose and known influences of metrical arrangement". This statement illustrates Coleridge's opinion that in order to be a poem, the composition must be properly structured and composed so that all of the sentences create an identifying rhythm while still representing a single purpose. Wordsworth also speaks of the importance of purpose-focused poetry in the Preface to Lyrical Ballads, stating that in order to be a good poem, it must have behind it a "worthy purpose". The two authors believe that a poem must have a definite direction and that the reader should be very clear as to what the poem is actually about. The authors believe that in order for a short metrical composition to be a poem, it must be organized clearly and, according to Wordsworth "also thought long and lovingly about".

Passion and emotion were two subjects that typically characterizes the Romantic period. Exemplifying this, Wordsworth and Coleridge thought that the direct purpose of any poem should be to stir passion in the reader. They thought that a poem should also be a work that stirred the same feeling in the reader every time it is read as if it were being read for the first time; "but that to which we return with the greatest pleasure, possesses the genuine power and claims the name of essential poetry". By this meaning, after a good poem is read once, the reader should have the desire to read it many times. The passion in the reader should also be a pleasurable one, explained by Coleridge as "immediate object pleasure". The pleasure is nicely illustrated by Coleridge in Biographia Literaria in the way he speaks of the pleasure in repeating rhymes. He goes on to identify a passionate pleasure as permanent, "that nothing can permanently please which does not contain in itself the reason why it is so". Wordsworth expands on this by explaining that the passion that is felt by the reader should be of natural descent because they are "the general passions and thoughts and feelings of men" and that "we not only wish to be pleased, but to be pleased in that particular way in which we have been accustomed to be pleased". The pleasures that Wordsworth was referring to man being "accustomed to" are those experiences that are derived from nature. Nature in this sense may be the emotion of an experience with living nature, such as a majestic observance of a mountain, or it may be in the sense of human nature, such as the natural presence of a mother's love. Coleridge explains that "the reader should be carried forward, by the pleasurable activity of the mind excited by the attractions of the journey itself".

Since the purpose of a poem is to stir passion kindred to nature, it is the duty of the poet to convey that feeling and make it immediately apparent in his composition. The poet would therefore have to be capable of being passionate and understanding nature enough to describe it in a sensible literary form. This criterion for a poet is another aspect of which Wordsworth and Coleridge are in agreement. Coleridge says "the poet, described in ideal perfection, brings the whole soul of a man into activity, with the subordination of its faculties to each other," and "diffuses a tone and spirit of unity that blends". This description is of the magnitude of passion that a poet must have in order to reach "the soul," and that passion is intertwined with the soul as an emotion of it. Wordsworth writes of the poet's duty of producing pleasure with a serious overtone, "The poet writes under one restriction only, that of necessity, of giving immediate pleasure to a human being possessed of that information which may be expected of him not as a lawyer, physician, mariner, but as a man". By this statement, Wordsworth is grouping all people together as of mankind, and more specifically as beings of nature. The serious overtone of this statement is elaborated on by Wordsworth in the following paragraph by replacing the description of the poet's obligation to nature as a "restriction" to an "acknowledgement of beauty". This is a point that Coleridge opposes, however, believing that language differs with occupation. To Wordsworth, the poet is a translator that communicates the passion felt by nature to the conscious mind of the reader.

Passion as described by Wordsworth and Coleridge is derived most naturally from "situations from common life". This subject of "common life" in poetry is of particular importance to Wordsworth. Although of much lesser importance to Coleridge, both authors considered this as a one of the criteria of a good poem. Wordsworth chose the subject of common life because it is what he finds to be in closest association with nature. He says "poetry is the image of man and nature" and a "homage paid to the native and naked dignity of man".

To Wordsworth, the most important type of common life was the "low and rustic life because the essential passions of the heart find a better soil in that condition," and the "manners of rural life germinate from those elementary feelings". In other words, this type of man's feelings was more recognizable and more closely connected with the natural, or instinctive, feelings of man. Coleridge, on the other hand, uses the term "ordinary life" in his Biographia Literaria. The different terms indicate the differing feelings of the authors on the subject. The term "ordinary" seems to indicate a more disconnected feeling from nature and seems to be typified more by social standards, while "common" has a much more naturalistic connotation. This point is well supported in a PMLA article on Coleridge by addressing the use of the Latin phrase lingua communist...

Some critics argue that, rather than diction, this disagreement was over "dramatic method" but this may be incorrect. Their idea about diction is where the controversy between Coleridge and Wordsworth occurred, which stems from their differing views on "common" versus "ordinary" life. William Wordsworth thought that the poem should speak directly from common life "by fitting to metrical arrangement a selection of the real language of men in a state of vivid sensation". It is in this context that he describes his idea of proper poetic diction, which was the complete opposite of what was considered proper in the late 1700's. He in fact says of his own works' diction "found in these volumes little of what is usually called poetic diction". The diction of a poem is not bound by a set of rules or binding for every poetic composition according to Wordsworth. In his opinion, it is necessary for a poet to choose his own diction because a poet is a "man speaking to men". The language of common life is the language of nature as well, so it is the best way to describe the feelings of nature. Coleridge, on the other hand, has a more formal idea of what the diction of a poem should be. He says, "My own differences from certain supposed parts of Mr. Wordsworth's theory ground themselves on the proper diction for poetry from the mouths of men in real life under natural feelings". Coleridge doesn't believe that common language can be applied to a wide enough public, or that certain classes wouldn't understand it. He says, "My objection is this rule is applicable only to certain classes of poetry," and "either need not or ought not to be practiced". He also explains that the common language varies with location, occupation, and culture. Coleridge thought that the proper diction of a poem could not be produced from the vocabulary of common language and had "no place in the consciousness of an uneducated man". Most critics, such as David Joplin, agree that this opposition in opinion arises from Coleridge's more formal idea of poetry.

The second topic in which Coleridge disagrees with Wordsworth is on the application of prose to poetry. He directly addresses this matter in Biographia Literaria by quoting from Wordsworth's Preface, "between the language of prose and that of metrical composition, there neither is, nor can be any essential difference." "It is against these exclusively that my opposition is directed". Their disagreement on the concept of poetry and prose is in the purpose of each of the methods. Coleridge says that a poem is "opposed to the works of science by proposing for its immediate object of pleasure". In this statement "works of science" is in reference to prose, where Coleridge is quoted in the Oxford English Dictionary as 'The definition of good prose is – proper words in their proper places. Wordsworth says that metre is the only thing separating a "good poem" from "good prose . Coleridge however elaborates on the distinction between poem and prose by explaining the emotional purposes of each, "it is discriminated by proposing itself such delight from the whole, as from each component part". This means that in order for the work to be poetry, it must produce natural and passionate feelings from reading the whole, but must also do so simply by reading a small part of the poem. To Coleridge, poetry is different from prose in that, prose does not produce a fraction of the emotions that are produced by a poem, and therefore does not deserve to be called poetry.

Oxford gives the definition of prose as an ordinary form of written or spoken language without metrical structure. However, to capture the language spoken by men was the chief objective in Wordsworth's poetry. When Wordsworth says, "no essential difference between the language of prose and of metrical composition", he is speaking of the ordinary language spoken by men. The distinction between poetry and prose discussed by the authors is in agreement that a poem is something better than a work of prose. Coleridge sys this by completely separating the definitions of the two while Wordsworth blends the two terms together by saying "poems will be found to be strictly the language of prose, when prose is well written".

Coleridge and Wordsworth create a definition and criteria for a poem that becomes representative for the ideology of the Romantic era. They thought that a poem should be a careful composition resulting from the passionate feelings that are experienced through nature. They are in agreement on the criteria of a poem being that it must evoke the emotion of passion each time it is written and that it must be written about nature, whether of Earth or of the human experience. The two also believe it is the poet's responsibility to put these emotions into words by being knowledgeable about poetry and, most importantly, having a truly intimate interaction between nature and his own mind. The two poets did seem to disagree on the actual proper structure of a poem, however, they both agreed on a basic purpose and technique that brought about an entirely new kind of poem in the beginning of the nineteenth century.

Chapter 5

Coleridge and Romanticism

Coleridge re-states the main Romantic views on poetry. He wants poetry to be based on genius and originality, and to deal with its subject matter in such a way that its language will be organically linked to it; or rather, that the subject-matter is co-extensive with the poem: "to the truly great poets . . . there is a reason assignable not only for every word, but for the position of every word." Coleridge is the major English exponent of organics as a metaphor for the work of art; he opposes organic form and mechanic form in the same way as the German romantics (Herder, Schlegel). Imagination produces organic forms, fancy merely mechanic forms. "The work of art must grow organically from within itself. Its principles of order are finally internal and not imposed from without". There are rules in the work of art, Coleridge admits as he criticizes the neo-classicists, but they are not imposed mechanically. The order of the work of art is like that of a living body: each part is connected to the whole, and each is at once end and means.

The true ground of the mistake lies in the confounding mechanical regularity with organic form. The form is mechanic, when on any given material we impress a predetermined form, not necessarily arising out of the properties of the material; as when to a mass of wet clay we give whatever shape we wish it to retain when hardened. The organic form, on the other hand, is innate; it shapes, as it develops itself form within, and the fullness of its development is one and the same with the perfection of its outward form. Such as the life is, such is the form. .

Coleridge opposes in this way, like Schelling or Goethe, symbol to allegory.

Just as he opposes the rules of drama, in his Biographia Literaria he opposes that conception of poetry inherited from the eighteenth century: he is against the closed couplet, and favours lines running into each other and the use of plain words whenever possible. There is no question of "poetic diction" as something which can be isolated from the poems themselves. This was the defect of the poetry of the previous century for Coleridge: it presented "not so much of poetic thoughts as thoughts translated into the language of poetry" .

The effect of a good poem, Coleridge says, is to make us see life anew, to remove "the film of familiarity" which sets at length on all our thoughts and perceptions. An imaginative poem is characterized by its "awakening the mind's attention form the lethargy of custom and directing it to the loveliness and the wonders of the world before us". This freshness of perception can never be achieved with a poetic diction which is old-fashioned, well-known; clichés and hackneyed expressions rather have the opposite effect, they dull our perception. However, as it happened with Wordsworth, Coleridge lays the stress not so much on novelty as on quality of expression; badness comes not so much from repetition as from intrinsic faults.

But Coleridge's attitude to poetic language is not the same as Wordsworth's. He will criticize Wordsworth's primitivistic assumptions as well as the implications which derived from them with respect to poetic language. Coleridge does not share Wordsworth's faith in the intrinsic virtues of the cottagers and country life. He believes in the value of culture and education, rather than in "untutored minds" in contact with nature. He points out that Wordsworth's definition of "the language of real life" was equivocal: on one hand, he identified it with the language of the lower classes; on the other, that language was to be a "selection." In fact, he says, if you "select" from a particularity (language of peasants) what you obtain is a generality (language of men): "I adopt with full faith the principle of Aristotle that poetry as poetry is essentially ideal, that it avoids and excludes all accident, that its apparent individualities of rank, character, or occupation must be representative of a class". Language, for Coleridge, does not spring immediately from nature in the way Wordsworth would have it: it is the product of a whole society, and it has a long history, in which the role of the learned is fundamental.

Even allowing that the same words can be used in prose and in poetry, Coleridge claims, and the "poetic manner of combining words" is not that of prose. Coleridge identifies badness in poetry as faults of logic, psychology, good sense and taste: in general, faults against the rules of the Imagination. The criterion to define badness is not to be found in the opposition between the hackneyed and the new. The same is true for Wordsworth, although he complains that some themes and expressions beautiful in themselves could no longer be used because of their having been so drawn upon by bad poets. Today we tend rather to lay the stress upon this idea, following T.S. Eliot: "It is as wasteful for a poet to do what has been done already, as for a biologist to rediscover Mendel's theories."

The Hour of Romance

Of his place in the poetic movement of his time there is no need to speak at length. It was the hour of romance. And, of all that is purest and most ethereal in the romantic spirit, his poetry is the most finished the supreme, embodiment. No doubt, some of the strands which went to make up the intricate web of the romantic tissue appear but faintly, if at all, in the poetry of Coleridge. Medievalism, which plays a large part in the work of Scott and others, is to Coleridge commonly no more than a vague atmosphere, such as would give the needful sense of remoteness and supply the fit setting for the marvelous which it is his purpose to hint at or openly display. Once only does he go palpably beyond this: in the shadowy picture of

The chamber carved so curiously,
Carved with figures strange and sweet,
For a lady's chamber meet.

But, even these touches of medievalism are studiously vague; nor are the allusions to trial by combat which follow in the second part of Christabel any more precise. Contrast these with the description of Madeline's chamber in The Eve of Saint Agnes or of the feudal castle and the moss-troopers in The Lady of the Last Minstrel; and we have the measure of the gulf which parts Coleridge from other romantic poets in this matter. Of the historic instinct, strong both in Scott and Byron, Coleridge, in truth, was defiantly destitute.

"Of all the men I ever knew, Wordsworth himself not excepted," he writes, "I have the faintest pleasure in things contingent and transitory.... Nay, it goes to a disease with me. As I was gazing at a wall in Caravan Castle, I wished the guide fifty miles off that was telling me, In this chamber the Black Prince was born—or whoever it was," he adds, as well he might. It is true that, when the first cantos of Childe Harold appeared, he had the courage to assert: "It is exactly on the plan that I myself had not only conceived six years ago, but have the whole scheme drawn out in one of my old memorandum books." But this was a pure delusion, of the same kind as that which led him to declare he had conceived a poem, with Michael Scott for hero, much superior to Goethe's Faust; with this difference, that, whereas Faust lay within his field of vision, Childe Harold, or any other poem that should make appeal to "the sense of a former world," after the manner of Byron, assuredly did not.

It was in the subtler, more spiritual, regions of romance that Coleridge found his home. As to his treatment of the marvelous, ever "the main region of his song," little need be added to what has been said already. In one form or another, the theme never ceased to haunt his mind during the brief flowering time of his genius; and The Ancient Mariner, Christabel and The Three Graves stand for three quite distinct modes of approaching it. In The Ancient Mariner, the poet openly proclaims his marvels, and exults in them. In Christabel, they are thrown into the background, and conveyed to our mind rather by subtle suggestion than direct assertion. Finally, in The Three Graves, neither incidents nor persons have, in themselves, anything of the marvelous; it appears solely in the withering blight brought by a mother's curse upon three innocent lives. It is here that Coleridge most nearly approaches the field and method of Wordsworth; whose Peter Bell—in another way, perhaps, The Thorn—offers a curious analogy with this powerful but, as usual, unfinished poem. In the homelier region, he was, manifestly, less at ease than among the marvels and subtleties of the two other poems; and it is rather there that the secret of his unique genius must be sought.

Two things, in particular, may be noted. The indirectness by which the elusive touches of Christabel are made to work their cumulative effect may be contrasted with the directness of the method employed by Keats in his treatment of a like theme, the transformation of a serpent into the guise of a woman, in Lamia. But it is more important to bear in mind that, if Coleridge is haunted by the marvelous, it is less for its own sake than as a symbol of the abiding mystery which he, like Wordsworth, found everywhere in life, within man and around him; a sign of the spiritual presence which, in his faith, bound "man and bird and beast" in one mystical body and fellowship; a token of the love which is the life of all creation, and which is revealed to us in "the blue sky bent over all." It is this faith which gives a deeper meaning to these fairy creations than they bear upon the surface, and which raises the closing verses of The Ancient Mariner from the mere irrelevant appendage they have seemed to some critics, to an expression of the thought that lies at the core of the whole poem. And, if this be true, his well-known retort to Mrs. Barbauld—"Madam, the fault of the poem is that it has too much moral"—would take a wider significance than has commonly been supposed. Only, the self-depreciation of the poet must not be taken more seriously than it deserves

Definition of a poem

For Coleridge, metre is the proper form for poetry. It favours, when it is successful, the most perfect blend of content and form; it must be adequate to the content of the poem and become one with its meaning. The role of metre is to intensify the attention of the reader to every element in the poem, as well as to the whole. Metre tends to increase the vivacity and susceptibility both of the general feelings and of the attention. This effect it produces by the continual excitement of surprise, and by the quick reciprocation of curiosity still gratified and still re-excited, which are too slight indeed to be at any one moment objects of distinct consciousness, yet become considerable in their aggregate influence.

However, it is not a necessary element for poetry: only the most suitable form. And this is so because the language of poetry is not the same as the language of prose, even if its vocabulary is the same. It is peculiar to the Romantic era that poetry is defined not only with respect to science, but also with respect to other kinds of literature. Coleridge points out that poetry does not equal rhythmical language nor does it equal literature.

A poem is that species of composition which is opposed to works of science by proposing for its immediate object pleasure, not truth; and from all other species (having this object in common with it) it is discriminated by proposing to itself such delight from the whole as is compatible with a distinct gratification from each component part . . . one the parts of which mutually support and explain each other , all in their proportion harmonizing with, and supporting the purpose and known influences of metrical arrangement.

The communication of pleasure, Coleridge affirms, is the only legitimate way for a poet to moralize his readers.

We may note that Coleridge has defined the whole of the poem as a system, a structure. This is only possible not merely through Wordsworth's orderly mind feeling spontaneously, but through reflection, consciousness and hard work.

In poetry, in which every line, every phrase, may pass the ordeal of deliberation and deliberate choice, it is possible, and barely possible, to attain that ultimatum which I have ventured to propose as the infallible test of a blameless style, namely its untranslatable ness in words of the same language without injury to the meaning, Be it observed, however, that I include in the meaning of a word not only its correspondent object, but likewise all the associations which it recalls. For language is framed to convey not the object alone, but likewise the character, mood and intentions of the person who is representing it.

The same could be said of imagery. Together with dramatization, Coleridge points out the importance of imagery as an element which is used by the "invisible" author in directing the response of the reader. Imagery is significant and becomes alive when it is modified by a predominant passion, or when it has the virtue of reducing multiplicity to unity, or succession to an instant; or when a humour and an intellectual life is transferred to it from the poet's own spirit. That is, when it has an experiential, subjective and perceptual value, "when it moulds and colours itself to the circumstances, passion or character present and foremost in the mind". The guiding spirit of the imagery may be the author in an immediate way, or the author through his characters. This is the difference between Shakespeare and Milton: "All things and modes of action shape themselves anew in the being of Milton; while Shakespeare becomes all things, yet for ever remaining himself".

This new view of the relationship between the poet and his language will inspire many studies of the poets' imagery in the twentieth century, from Caroline Spurgeon's study of Shakespeare's imagery as a means of characterization and creation of atmosphere to Charles Mauron's "psycho criticism," which analyses the mind of the poet on the basis of his "obsessive metaphors." This new perspective becomes possible after Coleridge and other romantic: let us note that language for Coleridge is no longer a mere means to communicate things or concepts: it is more like a tool which shapes reality. Likewise, we find a new definition of metaphor in Coleridge: it is a thought of its own, which creates a new meaning, and not a dress or cloak for a pre-existing thought.

In seeming paradox with his organic conception of the poem, Coleridge affirms that a poem of any length neither can be, nor ought to be, all poetry. Yet if a harmonious whole is to be produced, the remaining parts must be preserved in keeping with the poetry; and this can be no otherwise affected than by such a studied selection and artificial arrangement as will partake of one, though not a peculiar, property of poetry. And this again can be no other than the property of exciting a more continuous and equal attention than the language of prose aims at, whether colloquial or written.

Coleridge

The Poetry of Nature

This was the golden age of "the poetry of nature"; and Coleridge may claim his place in it with the best. It is a place entirely to him; and it depends upon two qualities. The first is a faculty of minute and subtle observation, which he may have learned, in the first instance, from Wordsworth, but which he fostered to a degree of delicacy to which neither Wordsworth himself, nor, perhaps, any other "worshipper of nature," Keats excepted, ever quite attained. The "creaking of the rook's wing" and the branchless ash, Unsunned and damp, whose few poor yellow leaves

Ne'er tremble in the gale, yet tremble still,

Fanned by the waterfall, in this lime-tree bower, my prison, and that "peculiar tint of yellow-green" which marks the sunset sky in the ode Dejection, together with whole poems such as The Nightingale, bears witness to this extraordinary power. And, if more were wanted, it is supplied in abundance, though rather as raw material than as poetic creation, by the notes written when he was once more in constant communion with Wordsworth (1803), and published in the book which, of all others, throws most light upon the secret springs of his genius, Nor does this command of minute detail in any sense bar the way to an equal mastery of broad, general effects. What picture was ever painted with broader brush than that of the ice-fields or the tropical ocean in The Ancient Mariner? What general effect was ever caught more precisely than that of the moon-light "steeping in silent ness the steady weathercock" of the same poem, or of April as the month "of dark brown gardens and of peeping flowers" in the ode Dejection? It may be doubted whether full justice has even yet been done to this side of the poet's genius.

Yet, even this quality, great though it is, would have availed little, if it had not gone hand in hand with one of a very different order. With such a store of observed images at his command, there must have been a constant temptation to lavish it at every turn. Nothing is more surprising than the reserve, the sleepless sense of poetic fitness, with which it is employed by Coleridge.

Even this, indeed, does not give us the whole truth. It is not only that such images recur seldom; but that, when they do, they are lifted into a rarer atmosphere, a more remote region, than that of mere outward vision. In all his greater poems—The Ancient Mariner, perhaps, alone excepted—we are made to feel, and we should hardly have entered into their spirit unless we did feel, that the outer world is presented to us not directly, but through a veil of mystery, which softens all that is harsh in outline or colour; by a kind of second sight, which rather recalls objects, once familiar, to the memory, than offers their actual image to the eye.

"Sir George Beaumont," he notes in Anima Poetæ, "found great advantage in learning to draw from nature through gauze spectacles." And, with a success which we may be very sure Sir George never approached, he seems to have applied a like process to the forms of nature, as reflected in his poetry. Not that his eye was ever shut even to the crudest effects of the "inanimate cold world."

The very chemists' jars of "blue and green vitriol," as reflected in the stagnant reaches of a London canal, win an entry in his note-book. But when they appear in his poetry, it is—or, did dates allow, it would be—as the "witch's oils" that "burnt green and blue and white" around the waterlogged vessel in the "charmed water" of the tropical sea. Nothing, in short, that he found in the outer world attained its rightful value for him until, "by sublimation strange," it had passed into the "realm of shadows" which Schiller conceived to be the true region both of poetry and of action.

Chapter 6

Selected Poems: Text

A Mathematical Problem

This is now—this was erst,
Proposition the first—and Problem the first.

I

On a given finite Line
Which must no way incline;
To describe an equi—
—lateral Tri—
—A, N, G, L, E.
Now let A. B.
Be the given line
Which must no way incline;
The great Mathematician
Makes this Requisition,
That we describe an Equi—
—lateral Tri—
—angle on it:
Aid us, Reason—aid us, Wit!

II

From the centre A. at the distance A. B.
Describe the circle B. C. D.
At the distance B. A. from B. the centre
The round A. C. E. to describe boldly venture.

(Third Postulate see.)
And from the point C.
In which the circles make a pother
Cutting and slashing one another,
Bid the straight lines a journeying go,
C. A., C. B. those lines will show.
To the points, which by A. B. are reckon'd,
And postulate the second
For Authority ye know.
A. B. C.
Triumphant shall be
An Equilateral Triangle,
Not Peter Pindar carp, not Zoilus can wrangle.

III

Because the point A. is the centre
Of the circular B. C. D.
And because the point B. is the centre
Of the circular A. C. E.
A. C. to A. B. and B. C. to B. A.
Harmoniously equal for ever must stay;
Then C. A. and B. C.
Both extend the kind hand
To the basis, A. B.
Unambitiously join'd in Equality's Band.
But to the same powers, when two powers are equal,
My mind forbodes the sequel;
My mind does some celestial impulse teach,
And equalises each to each.
Thus C. A. with B. C. strikes the same sure alliance,
That C. A. and B. C. had with A. B. before;
And in mutual affiance,
None attempting to soar
Above another,
The unanimous three
C. A. and B. C. and A. B.
All are equal, each to his brother,
Preserving the balance of power so true:

Ah! the like would the proud Autocratorix do!
At taxes impending not Britain would tremble,
Nor Prussia struggle her fear to dissemble;
Nor the Mah'met-sprung Wight,
The great Mussulman
Would stain his Divan
With Urine the soft-flowing daughter of Fright.

IV

But rein your stallion in, too daring Nine!
Should Empires bloat the scientific line?
Or with dishevell'd hair all madly do ye run
For transport that your task is done?
For done it is—the cause is tried!
And Proposition, gentle Maid,
Who soothly ask'd stern Demonstration's aid,
Has prov'd her right, and A. B. C.
Of Angles three
Is shown to be of equal side;
And now our weary steed to rest in fine,
'Tis rais'd upon A. B. the straight, the given line.

The Æolian Harp

My pensive SARA ! thy soft cheek reclined
Thus on mine arm, most soothing sweet it is
To sit beside our Cot, our Cot o'ergrown
With white-flower'd Jasmin, and the broad-leav'd Myrtle,
(Meet emblems they of Innocence and Love !)
And watch the clouds, that late were rich with light,
Slow saddenning round, and mark the star of eve
Serenely brilliant (such should Wisdom be)
Shine opposite ! How exquisite the scents
Snatch'd from yon bean-field ! and the world so hush'd !
The stilly murmur of the distant Sea
Tells us of silence.
And that simplest Lute,
Plac'd length-ways in the clasping casement, hark !

How by the desultory breeze caress'd,
Like some coy maid half-yielding to her lover,
It pours such sweet upbraiding, as must needs
Tempt to repeat the wrong ! And now, its strings
Boldlier swept, the long sequacious notes
Over delicious surges sink and rise,
Such a soft floating witchery of sound
As twilight Elfins make, when they at eve
Voyage on gentle gales from Faery-Land,
Where Melodies round honey-dropping flowers,
Footless and wild, like birds of Paradise,
Nor pause, nor perch, hovering on untam'd wing !
O ! the one Life within us and abroad,
Which meets all motion and becomes its soul,
A light in sound, a sound-like power in light,
Rhythm in all thought, and joyance every where—
Methinks, it should have been impossible
Not to love all things in a world so fill'd ;
Where the breeze warbles, and the mute still air
Is Music slumbering on her instrument.
And thus, my Love ! as on the midway slope

Of yonder hill I stretch my limbs at noon,
Whilst thro' my half-clos'd eye-lids I behold
The sunbeams dance, like diamonds, on the main,
And tranquil muse upon tranquility ;
Full many a thought uncall'd and undetain'd,
And many idle flitting phantasies,
Traverse my indolent and passive brain,
As wild and various, as the random gales
That swell and flutter on this subject Lute !

And what if all of animated nature
Be but organic Harps diversly fram'd,
That tremble into thought, as o'er them sweeps
Plastic and vast, one intellectual breeze,
At once the Soul of each, and God of all ?

But thy more serious eye a mild reproof
Darts, O belovéd Woman ! nor such thoughts
Dim and unhallow'd dost thou not reject,
And biddest me walk humbly with my God.
Meek Daughter in the Family of Christ !

Well hast thou said and holily disprais'd
These shapings of the unregenerate mind ;
Bubbles that glitter as they rise and break
On vain Philosophy's aye-babbling spring.
For never guiltless may I speak of him,
The Incomprehensible ! save when with awe
I praise him, and with Faith that inly feels ;
Who with his saving mercies healéd me,
A sinful and most miserable man,
Wilder'd and dark, and gave me to possess
Peace, and this Cot, and thee, heart-honour'd Maid !

Reflections on Having Left a Place of Retirement

Low was our pretty Cot : our tallest Rose
Peep'd at the chamber-window. We could hear
At silent noon, and eve, and early morn,
The Sea's faint murmur. In the open air
Our Myrtles blossom'd; and across the porch
Thick Jasmins twined : the little landscape round
Was green and woody, and refresh'd the eye.
It was a spot which you might aptly call
The Valley of Seclusion ! Once I saw
(Hallowing his Sabbath-day by quiteness)
A wealthy son of Commerce saunter by,
Bristowa's citizen : methought, it calm'd
His thirst of idle gold, and made him muse
With wiser feelings : for he paus'd, and look'd
With a pleas'd sadness, and gaz'd all around,
Then eyed our Cottage, and gaz'd round again,
And sigh'd, and said, it was a Blesséd Place.
And we were bless'd. Oft with patient ear
Long-listening to the viewless sky-lark's note

(Viewless, or haply for a moment seen
Gleaming on sunny wings) in whisper'd tones
I said to my Belovéd, 'Such, sweet Girl !
The inobtrusive song of Happiness,
Unearthly minstrelsy ! then only heard
When the Soul seeks to hear ; when all is hush'd,
And the Heart listens !'
But the time, when first

From that low Dell, steep up the stony Mount
I climb'd with perilous toil and reach'd the top,
Oh ! what a goodly scene ! Here the bleak mount,
The bare bleak mountain speckled thin with sheep ;
Grey clouds, that shadowing spot the sunny fields ;
And river, now with bushy rocks o'er-brow'd,
Now winding bright and full, with naked banks ;
And seats, and lawns, the Abbey and the wood,
And cots, and hamlets, and faint city-spire ;
The Channel there, the Islands and white sails,
Dim coasts, and cloud-like hills, and shoreless Ocean—
It seem'd like Omnipresence ! God, methought,
Had build him there a Temple : the whole World
Seem'd imag'd in its vast circumference :
No wish profan'd my overwhelméd heart.
Blest hour ! It was a luxury,—to be !
Ah ! quiet Dell ! dear Cot, and Mount sublime !

I was constrain'd to quit you. Was it right,
While my unnumber'd brethren toil'd and bled,
That I should dream away the entrusted hours
On rose-leaf beds, pampering the coward heart
With feelings all too delicate for use ?
Sweet is the tear that from some Howard's eye
Drops on the cheek of one he lifts from earth :
And he that works me good with unmov'd face,
Does it but half : he chills me while he aids,
My benefactor, not my brother man !
Yet even this, this cold beneficience
Praise, praise it, O my Soul ! oft as thou scann'st

The sluggard Pity's vision-weaving tribe !
Who sigh for Wretchedness, yet shun the Wretched,
Nursing in some delicious solitude
Their slothful loves and dainty sympathies !
I therefore go, and join head, heart, and hand,
Active and firm, to fight the bloodless fight
Of Science, Freedom, and the Truth in Christ.
Yet oft when after honourable toil
Rests the tir'd mind, and waking loves to dream,
My spirit shall revisit thee, dear Cot !
Thy Jasmin and thy window-peeping Rose,
And Myrtles fearless of the mild sea-air.
And I shall sigh fond wishes—sweet Abode !
Ah !—had none greater ! And that all had such !
It might be so—but the time is not yet.
Speed it, O Father ! Let thy Kingdom come !

On a Ruined House in a Romantic Country

And this reft house is that the which he built,
Lamented Jack ! And here his malt he pil'd,
Cautious in vain ! These rats that squeak so wild,
Squeak, not unconscious of their father's guilt.
Did ye not see her gleaming thro' the glade ?
Belike, 'twas she, the maiden all forlorn.
What though she milk no cow with crumpled horn,
Yet aye she haunts the dale where erst she stray'd ;
And aye beside her stalks her amorous knight !
Still on his thighs their wonted brogues are worn,
And thro' those brogues, still tatter'd and betorn,
His hindward charms gleam an unearthly white ;
As when thro' broken clouds at night's high noon
Peeps in fair fragments forth the full-orb'd harvest-moon !

This Lime-Tree Bower my Prison

Well, they are gone, and here must I remain,
This lime-tree bower my prison ! I have lost
Beauties and feelings, such as would have been
Most sweet to my remembrance even when age

Had dimm'd mine eyes to blindness ! They, meanwhile,
Friends, whom I never more may meet again,
On springy heath, along the hill-top edge,
Wander in gladness, and wind down, perchance,
To that still roaring dell, of which I told ;
The roaring dell, o'erwooded, narrow, deep,
And only speckled by the mid-day sun ;
Where its slim trunk the ash from rock to rock
Flings arching like a bridge ;—that branchless ash,
Unsunn'd and damp, whose few poor yellow leaves
Ne'er tremble in the gale, yet tremble still,
Fann'd by the water-fall ! and there my friends
Behold the dark green file of long lank weeds,
That all at once (a most fantastic sight !)
Still nod and drip beneath the dripping edge
Of the blue clay-stone.

Now, my friends emerge

Beneath the wide wide Heaven—and view again
The many-steepled tract magnificent
Of hilly fields and meadows, and the sea,
With some fair bark, perhaps, whose sails light up
The slip of smooth clear blue betwixt two Isles
Of purple shadow ! Yes ! they wander on
In gladness all ; but thou, methinks, most glad,
My gentle-hearted Charles ! for thou hast pined
And hunger'd after Nature, many a year,
In the great City pent, winning thy way
With sad yet patient soul, through evil and pain
And strange calamity ! Ah ! slowly sink
Behind the western ridge, thou glorious Sun !
Shine in the slant beams of the sinking orb,
Ye purple heath-flowers ! richlier burn, ye clouds !
Live in the yellow light, ye distant groves !
And kindle, thou blue Ocean ! So my friend
Struck with deep joy may stand, as I have stood,
Silent with swimming sense ; yea, gazing round

On the wide landscape, gaze till all doth seem
Less gross than bodily ; and of such hues
As veil the Almighty Spirit, when yet he makes
Spirits perceive his presence.
A delight

Comes sudden on my heart, and I am glad
As I myself were there ! Nor in this bower,
This little lime-tree bower, have I not mark'd
Much that has sooth'd me. Pale beneath the blaze
Hung the transparent foliage ; and I watch'd
Some broad and sunny leaf, and lov'd to see
The shadow of the leaf and stem above
Dappling its sunshine ! And that walnut-tree
Was richly ting'd, and a deep radiance lay
Full on the ancient ivy, which usurps
Those fronting elms, and now, with blackest mass
Makes their dark branches gleam a lighter hue
Through the late twilight : and though now the bat
Wheels silent by, and not a swallow twitters,
Yet still the solitary humble-bee
Sings in the bean-flower ! Henceforth I shall know
That Nature ne'er deserts the wise and pure ;
No plot so narrow, be but Nature there,
No waste so vacant, but may well employ
Each faculty of sense, and keep the heart
Awake to Love and Beauty ! and sometimes
'Tis well to be bereft of promis'd good,
That we may lift the soul, and contemplate
With lively joy the joys we cannot share.
My gentle-hearted Charles ! when the last rook
Beat its straight path across the dusky air
Homewards, I blest it ! deeming its black wing
(Now a dim speck, now vanishing in light)
Had cross'd the mighty Orb's dilated glory,
While thou stood'st gazing ; or, when all was still,
Flew creeking o'er thy head, and had a charm
For thee, my gentle-hearted Charles, to whom
No sound is dissonant which tells of Life.

The Dungeon

And this place our forefathers made for man !
This is the process of our Love and Wisdom,
To each poor brother who offends against us—
Most innocent, perhaps—and what if guilty ?
Is this the only cure ? Merciful God !
Each pore and natural outlet shrivell'd up
By Ignorance and parching Poverty,
His energies roll back upon his heart,
And stagnate and corrupt ; till chang'd to poison,
They break out on him, like a loathsome plague-spot ;
Then we call in our pamper'd mountebanks—
And this is their best cure ! uncomforted
And friendless Solitude, Groaning and Tears,
And savage Faces, at the clanking hour,
Seen through the steams and vapour of his dungeon,
By the lamp's dismal twilight ! So he lies
Circled with evil, till his very soul
Unmoulds its essence, hopelessly deform'd
By sights of ever more deformity !

With other ministrations thou, O Nature !
Healest thy wandering and distemper'd child :
Thou pourest on him thy soft influences,
Thy sunny hues, fair forms, and breathing sweets,
Thy melodies of woods, and winds, and waters,
Till he relent, and can no more endure
To be a jarring and a dissonant thing,
Amid this general dance and minstrelsy ;
But, bursting into tears, wins back his way,
His angry spirit heal'd and harmoniz'd
By the benignant touch of Love and Beauty

The Rime of the Ancient Mariner

PART I

An ancient Mariner meeteth three Gallants bidden to a wedding-feast, and detaineth one.

It is an ancient Mariner,
And he stoppeth one of three.
'By thy long beard and glittering eye,
Now wherefore stopp'st thou me ?
The Bridegroom's doors are opened wide,
And I am next of kin ;
The guests are met, the feast is set :
May'st hear the merry din.'

He holds him with his skinny hand,
'There was a ship,' quoth he.
'Hold off ! unhand me, grey-beard loon !'
Eftsoons his hand dropt he.

The Wedding-Guest is spell-bound by the eye of the old seafaring man, and constrained to hear his tale.

He holds him with his glittering eye—
The Wedding-Guest stood still,
And listens like a three years' child :
The Mariner hath his will.
The Wedding-Guest sat on a stone :
He cannot choose but hear ;
And thus spake on that ancient man,
The bright-eyed Mariner.

'The ship was cheered, the harbour cleared,
Merrily did we drop
Below the kirk, below the hill,
Below the lighthouse top.

The Mariner tells how the ship sailed southward with a good wind and fair weather, till it reached the Line.

The Sun came up upon the left,
Out of the sea came he !
And he shone bright, and on the right
Went down into the sea.
Higher and higher every day,
Till over the mast at noon—'
The Wedding-Guest here beat his breast,
For he heard the loud bassoon.

The Wedding-Guest heareth the bridal music ; but the Mariner continueth his tale.

The bride hath paced into the hall,
Red as a rose is she ;
Nodding their heads before her goes
The merry minstrelsy.
The Wedding-Guest he beat his breast,
Yet he cannot choose but hear ;
And thus spake on that ancient man,
The bright-eyed Mariner.

The ship driven by a storm toward the south pole.
'And now the STORM-BLAST came, and he
Was tyrannous and strong :
He struck with his o'ertaking wings,
And chased us south along.
With sloping masts and dipping prow,
As who pursued with yell and blow
Still treads the shadow of his foe,
And forward bends his head,
The ship drove fast, loud roared the blast,
The southward aye we fled.

And now there came both mist and snow,
And it grew wondrous cold :
And ice, mast-high, came floating by,
As green as emerald.

The land of ice, and of fearful sounds where no living thing was to be seen.

And through the drifts the snowy clifts
Did send a dismal sheen :
Nor shapes of men nor beasts we ken—
The ice was all between.
The ice was here, the ice was there,
The ice was all around :
It cracked and growled, and roared and howled,
Like noises in a swound !

Till a great sea-bird, called the Albatross, came through the snow-fog, and was received with great joy and hospitality.

At length did cross an Albatross,
Thorough the fog it came ;
As if it had been a Christian soul,
We hailed it in God's name.
It ate the food it ne'er had eat,
And round and round it flew.
The ice did split with a thunder-fit ;
The helmsman steered us through !

And lo ! the Albatross proveth a bird of good omen, and followeth the ship as it returned northward through fog and floating ice.

And a good south wind sprung up behind ;
The Albatross did follow,
And every day, for food or play,
Came to the mariner's hollo !
In mist or cloud, on mast or shroud,
It perched for vespers nine ;
Whiles all the night, through fog-smoke white,
Glimmered the white Moon-shine.'

The ancient Mariner inhospitably killeth the pious bird of good omen.

'God save thee, ancient Mariner !
From the fiends, that plague thee thus !—
Why look'st thou so ?'—With my cross-bow
I shot the ALBATROSS.

PART II

The Sun now rose upon the right :
Out of the sea came he,
Still hid in mist, and on the left
Went down into the sea.
And the good south wind still blew behind,
But no sweet bird did follow,
Nor any day for food or play
Came to the mariners' hollo !

His shipmates cry out against the ancient Mariner, for killing the bird of good luck.

And I had done an hellish thing,
And it would work 'em woe :
For all averred, I had killed the bird
That made the breeze to blow.
Ah wretch ! said they, the bird to slay,
That made the breeze to blow !

But when the fog cleared off, they justify the same, and thus make themselves accomplices in the crime.

Nor dim nor red, like God's own head,
The glorious Sun uprist :
Then all averred, I had killed the bird
That brought the fog and mist.
'Twas right, said they, such birds to slay,
That bring the fog and mist.

The fair breeze continues ; the ship enters the Pacific Ocean, and sails northward, even till it reaches the Line.

The fair breeze blew, the white foam flew,
The furrow followed free ;
We were the first that ever burst
Into that silent sea.
The ship hath been suddenly becalmed.
Down dropt the breeze, the sails dropt down,
'Twas sad as sad could be ;
And we did speak only to break
The silence of the sea !
All in a hot and copper sky,
The bloody Sun, at noon,
Right up above the mast did stand,
No bigger than the Moon.

Day after day, day after day,
We stuck, nor breath nor motion ;
As idle as a painted ship
Upon a painted ocean.

And the Albatross begins to be avenged.

Water, water, every where,
And all the boards did shrink ;
Water, water, every where,
Nor any drop to drink.
The very deep did rot : O Christ !
That ever this should be !
Yea, slimy things did crawl with legs
Upon the slimy sea.

About, about, in reel and rout
The death-fires danced at night ;
The water, like a witch's oils,
Burnt green, and blue and white.

A Spirit had followed them ; one of the invisible inhabitants of this planet, neither departed souls nor angels ; concerning whom the learned Jew, Josephus, and the Platonic Constantinopolitan, Michael Psellus, may be consulted. They are very numerous, and there is no climate or element without one or more.

And some in dreams assuréd were
Of the Spirit that plagued us so ;
Nine fathom deep he had followed us
From the land of mist and snow.
And every tongue, through utter drought,
Was withered at the root ;
We could not speak, no more than if
We had been choked with soot.

The shipmates, in their sore distress, would fain throw the whole guilt on the ancient Mariner : in sign whereof they hang the dead sea-bird round his neck.

Ah ! well a-day ! what evil looks
Had I from old and young !
Instead of the cross, the Albatross
About my neck was hung.

PART III

There passed a weary time. Each throat
Was parched, and glazed each eye.

A weary time ! a weary time !
How glazed each weary eye,
When looking westward, I beheld
A something in the sky.

The ancient Mariner beholdeth a sign in the element afar off.

At first it seemed a little speck,
And then it seemed a mist ;
It moved and moved, and took at last
A certain shape, I wist.
A speck, a mist, a shape, I wist !
And still it neared and neared :
As if it dodged a water-sprite,
It plunged and tacked and veered.

At its nearer approach, it seemeth him to be a ship ; and at a dear ransom he freeth his speech from the bonds of thirst.

With throats unslaked, with black lips baked,
We could nor laugh nor wail ;
Through utter drought all dumb we stood !
I bit my arm, I sucked the blood,
And cried, A sail ! a sail !
A flash of joy ;
With throats unslaked, with black lips baked,
Agape they heard me call :
Gramercy ! they for joy did grin,
And all at once their breath drew in,
As they were drinking all.

And horror follows. For can it be a ship that comes onward without wind or tide ?

See ! see ! (I cried) she tacks no more !
Hither to work us weal ;
Without a breeze, without a tide,
She steadies with upright keel !
The western wave was all a-flame.
The day was well nigh done !
Almost upon the western wave

Rested the broad bright Sun ;
When that strange shape drove suddenly
Betwixt us and the Sun.

It seemeth him but the skeleton of a ship.
And straight the Sun was flecked with bars,
(Heaven's Mother send us grace !)
As if through a dungeon-grate he peered
With broad and burning face.

And its ribs are seen as bars on the face of the setting Sun.

Alas ! (thought I, and my heart beat loud)
How fast she nears and nears !
Are those her sails that glance in the Sun,
Like restless gossameres ?

The Spectre-Woman and her Death-mate, and no other on board the skeleton ship.

And those her ribs through which the Sun
Did peer, as through a grate ?
And is that Woman all her crew ?
Is that a Death ? and are there two ?
Is Death that woman's mate ?
[first version of this stanza through the end of Part III]
Like vessel, like crew !

Her lips were red, her looks were free,
Her locks were yellow as gold :
Her skin was as white as leprosy,
The Night-mare Life-in-death was she,
Who thicks man's blood with cold.

Death and Life-in-Death have diced for the ship's crew, and she (the latter) winneth the ancient Mariner.

The naked hulk alongside came,
And the twain were casting dice ;
'The game is done ! I've won ! I've won !'
Quoth she, and whistles thrice.
No twilight within the courts of the Sun.
The Sun's rim dips ; the stars rush out :

At one stride comes the dark ;
With far-heard whisper, o'er the sea,
Off shot the spectre-bark.
At the rising of the Moon,
We listened and looked sideways up !
Fear at my heart, as at a cup,
My life-blood seemed to sip !
The stars were dim, and thick the night,
The steerman's face by his lamp gleamed white ;
From the sails the dew did drip—
Till clomb above the eastern bar
The hornéd Moon, with one bright star
Within the nether tip.
One after another,
One after one, by the star-dogged Moon,
Too quick for groan or sigh,
Each turned his face with a ghastly pang,
And cursed me with his eye.
His shipmates drop down dead.
Four times fifty living men,
(And I heard nor sigh nor groan)
With heavy thump, a lifeless lump,
They dropped down one by one.
But Life-in-Death begins her work on the ancient Mariner.
The souls did from their bodies fly,—
They fled to bliss or woe !
And every soul, it passed me by,
Like the whizz of my cross-bow !

PART IV

The Wedding-Guest feareth that a Spirit is talking to him ;
'I fear thee, ancient Mariner !
I fear thy skinny hand !
And thou art long, and lank, and brown,
As is the ribbed sea-sand.
(Coleridge's note on above stanza)
I fear thee and thy glittering eye,
And thy skinny hand, so brown.'—
Fear not, fear not, thou Wedding-Guest !
This body dropt not down.

But the ancient Mariner assureth him of his bodily life, and proceedeth to relate his horrible penance.

Alone, alone, all, all alone,
Alone on a wide wide sea !
And never a saint took pity on
My soul in agony.
He despiseth the creatures of the calm,
The many men, so beautiful !
And they all dead did lie :
And a thousand thousand slimy things
Lived on ; and so did I.
And envieth that they should live, and so many lie dead.
I looked upon the rotting sea,
And drew my eyes away ;
I looked upon the rotting deck,
And there the dead men lay.
I looked to heaven, and tried to pray ;
But or ever a prayer had gusht,
A wicked whisper came, and made
My heart as dry as dust.

I closed my lids, and kept them close,
And the balls like pulses beat ;
For the sky and the sea, and the sea and the sky
Lay like a load on my weary eye,
And the dead were at my feet.

But the curse liveth for him in the eye of the dead men.
The cold sweat melted from their limbs,
Nor rot nor reek did they :
The look with which they looked on me
Had never passèd away.
An orphan's curse would drag to hell
A spirit from on high ;
But oh ! more horrible than that
Is the curse in a dead man's eye !
Seven days, seven nights, I saw that curse,
And yet I could not die.

In his loneliness and fixedness he yearneth towards the journeying Moon, and the stars that still sojourn, yet still move onward ; and every where the blue sky belongs to them, and is their appointed rest, and their native country and their own natural homes, which they enter unannounced, as lords that are certainly expected and yet there is a silent joy at their arrival.

The moving Moon went up the sky,
And no where did abide :
Softly she was going up,
And a star or two beside—
Her beams bemocked the sultry main,
Like April hoar-frost spread ;
But where the ship's huge shadow lay,
The charméd water burnt alway
A still and awful red.

By the light of the Moon he beholdeth God's creatures of the great calm.

Beyond the shadow of the ship,
I watched the water-snakes :
They moved in tracks of shining white,
And when they reared, the elfish light
Fell off in hoary flakes.
Within the shadow of the ship
I watched their rich attire :
Blue, glossy green, and velvet black,
They coiled and swam ; and every track
Was a flash of golden fire.

Their beauty and their happiness.
He blesseth them in his heart.

O happy living things ! no tongue
Their beauty might declare :
A spring of love gushed from my heart,
And I blessed them unaware :
Sure my kind saint took pity on me,
And I blessed them unaware.
The spell begins to break.
The self-same moment I could pray ;
And from my neck so free

The Albatross fell off, and sank
Like lead into the sea.

PART V

Oh sleep ! it is a gentle thing,
Beloved from pole to pole !
To Mary Queen the praise be given !
She sent the gentle sleep from Heaven,
That slid into my soul.

By grace of the holy Mother, the ancient Mariner is refreshed with rain.

The silly buckets on the deck,
That had so long remained,
I dreamt that they were filled with dew ;
And when I awoke, it rained.
My lips were wet, my throat was cold,
My garments all were dank ;
Sure I had drunken in my dreams,
And still my body drank.

I moved, and could not feel my limbs :
I was so light—almost
I thought that I had died in sleep,
And was a blesséd ghost.

He heareth sounds and seeth strange sights and commotions in the sky and the element.

And soon I heard a roaring wind :
It did not come anear ;
But with its sound it shook the sails,
That were so thin and sere.
The upper air burst into life !
And a hundred fire-flags sheen,
To and fro they were hurried about !
And to and fro, and in and out,
The wan stars danced between.

And the coming wind did roar more loud,
And the sails did sigh like sedge ;

And the rain poured down from one black cloud ;
The Moon was at its edge.

The thick black cloud was cleft, and still
The Moon was at its side :
Like waters shot from some high crag,
The lightning fell with never a jag,
A river steep and wide.

The bodies of the ship's crew are inspired, and the ship moves on ;

The loud wind never reached the ship,
Yet now the ship moved on !
Beneath the lightning and the Moon
The dead men gave a groan.
They groaned, they stirred, they all uprose,
Nor spake, nor moved their eyes ;
It had been strange, even in a dream,
To have seen those dead men rise.

The helmsman steered, the ship moved on ;
Yet never a breeze up-blew ;
The mariners all 'gan work the ropes,
Where they were wont to do ;
They raised their limbs like lifeless tools—
We were a ghastly crew.

The body of my brother's son
Stood by me, knee to knee :
The body and I pulled at one rope,
But he said nought to me.

But not by the souls of the men, nor by dæmons of earth or middle air, but by a blessed troop of angelic spirits, sent down by the invocation of the guardian saint:

'I fear thee, ancient Mariner !'
Be calm, thou Wedding-Guest !
'Twas not those souls that fled in pain,
Which to their corses came again,
But a troop of spirits blest :

For when it dawned—they dropped their arms,
And clustered round the mast ;
Sweet sounds rose slowly through their mouths,
And from their bodies passed.

Around, around, flew each sweet sound,
Then darted to the Sun ;
Slowly the sounds came back again,
Now mixed, now one by one.

Sometimes a-dropping from the sky
I heard the sky-lark sing ;
Sometimes all little birds that are,
How they seemed to fill the sea and air
With their sweet jargoning !

And now 'twas like all instruments,
Now like a lonely flute ;
And now it is an angel's song,
That makes the heavens be mute.

It ceased ; yet still the sails made on
A pleasant noise till noon,
A noise like of a hidden brook
In the leafy month of June,
That to the sleeping woods all night
Singeth a quiet tune.

Additional stanzas, dropped after the first edition.
Till noon we quietly sailed on,
Yet never a breeze did breathe :
Slowly and smoothly went the ship,
Moved onward from beneath.

The lonesome Spirit from the south-pole carries on the ship as far as the Line, in obedience to the angelic troop, but still requireth vengeance.

Under the keel nine fathom deep,
From the land of mist and snow,
The spirit slid : and it was he
That made the ship to go.
The sails at noon left off their tune,

And the ship stood still also.
The Sun, right up above the mast,
Had fixed her to the ocean :
But in a minute she 'gan stir,
With a short uneasy motion—
Backwards and forwards half her length
With a short uneasy motion.

Then like a pawing horse let go,
She made a sudden bound :
It flung the blood into my head,
And I fell down in a swound.

The Polar Spirit's fellow-dæmons, the invisible inhabitants of the element, take part in his wrong ; and two of them relate, one to the other, that penance long and heavy for the ancient Mariner hath been accorded to the Polar Spirit, who returneth southward.

How long in that same fit I lay,
I have not to declare ;
But ere my living life returned,
I heard and in my soul discerned
Two voices in the air.
'Is it he ?' quoth one, 'Is this the man ?
By him who died on cross,
With his cruel bow he laid full low
The harmless Albatross.

The spirit who bideth by himself
In the land of mist and snow,
He loved the bird that loved the man
Who shot him with his bow.'

The other was a softer voice,
As soft as honey-dew :
Quoth he, 'The man hath penance done,
And penance more will do.'

PART VI

FIRST VOICE

'But tell me, tell me ! speak again,
Thy soft response renewing—

What makes that ship drive on so fast ?
What is the ocean doing ?'

SECOND VOICE
'Still as a slave before his lord,
The ocean hath no blast ;
His great bright eye most silently
Up to the Moon is cast—
If he may know which way to go ;
For she guides him smooth or grim.
See, brother, see ! how graciously
She looketh down on him.'

The Mariner hath been cast into a trance ; for the angelic power causeth the vessel to drive northward faster than human life could endure.

FIRST VOICE
'But why drives on that ship so fast,
Without or wave or wind ?'

SECOND VOICE
'The air is cut away before,
And closes from behind.

Fly, brother, fly ! more high, more high !
Or we shall be belated :
For slow and slow that ship will go,
When the Mariner's trance is abated.'

The supernatural motion is retarded ; the Mariner awakes, and his penance begins anew.

I woke, and we were sailing on
As in a gentle weather :
'Twas night, calm night, the moon was high ;
The dead men stood together.
All stood together on the deck,
For a charnel-dungeon fitter :
All fixed on me their stony eyes,
That in the Moon did glitter.

The pang, the curse, with which they died,
Had never passed away :

I could not draw my eyes from theirs,
Nor turn them up to pray.

The curse is finally expiated.
And now this spell was snapt : once more
I viewed the ocean green,
And looked far forth, yet little saw
Of what had else been seen—
Like one, that on a lonesome road
Doth walk in fear and dread,
And having once turned round walks on,
And turns no more his head ;
Because he knows, a frightful fiend
Doth close behind him tread.

But soon there breathed a wind on me,
Nor sound nor motion made :
Its path was not upon the sea,
In ripple or in shade.

It raised my hair, it fanned my cheek
Like a meadow-gale of spring—
It mingled strangely with my fears,
Yet it felt like a welcoming.

Swiftly, swiftly flew the ship,
Yet she sailed softly too :
Sweetly, sweetly blew the breeze—
On me alone it blew.

And the ancient Mariner beholdeth his native country.
Oh ! dream of joy ! is this indeed
The light-house top I see ?
Is this the hill ? is this the kirk ?
Is this mine own countree ?
We drifted o'er the harbour-bar,
And I with sobs did pray—
O let me be awake, my God !
Or let me sleep alway.

The harbour-bay was clear as glass,
So smoothly it was strewn !

And on the bay the moonlight lay,
And the shadow of the Moon.

[Additional stanzas, dropped after the first edition.]
The rock shone bright, the kirk no less,
That stands above the rock :
The moonlight steeped in silentness
The steady weathercock.
The angelic spirits leave the dead bodies,
And the bay was white with silent light,
Till rising from the same,
Full many shapes, that shadows were,
In crimson colours came.
And appear in their own forms of light.
A little distance from the prow
Those crimson shadows were :
I turned my eyes upon the deck—
Oh, Christ ! what saw I there !
Each corse lay flat, lifeless and flat,
And, by the holy rood !
A man all light, a seraph-man,
On every corse there stood.

This seraph-band, each waved his hand :
It was a heavenly sight !
They stood as signals to the land,
Each one a lovely light ;

This seraph-band, each waved his hand,
No voice did they impart—
No voice ; but oh ! the silence sank
Like music on my heart.
But soon I heard the dash of oars,
I heard the Pilot's cheer ;
My head was turned perforce away
And I saw a boat appear.

Additional stanza, dropped after the first edition.
The Pilot and the Pilot's boy,
I heard them coming fast :
Dear Lord in Heaven ! it was a joy

The dead men could not blast.
I saw a third—I heard his voice :
It is the Hermit good !
He singeth loud his godly hymns
That he makes in the wood.
He'll shrieve my soul, he'll wash away
The Albatross's blood.

PART VII

The Hermit of the Wood,
This Hermit good lives in that wood
Which slopes down to the sea.
How loudly his sweet voice he rears !
He loves to talk with marineres
That come from a far countree.
He kneels at morn, and noon, and eve—
He hath a cushion plump :
It is the moss that wholly hides
The rotted old oak-stump.

The skiff-boat neared : I heard them talk,
'Why, this is strange, I trow !
Where are those lights so many and fair,
That signal made but now ?'

Approacheth the ship with wonder.
'Strange, by my faith !' the Hermit said—
'And they answered not our cheer !
The planks looked warped ! and see those sails,
How thin they are and sere !
I never saw aught like to them,
Unless perchance it were
Brown skeletons of leaves that lag
My forest-brook along ;
When the ivy-tod is heavy with snow,
And the owlet whoops to the wolf below,
That eats the she-wolf's young.'

'Dear Lord ! it hath a fiendish look—
(The Pilot made reply)
I am a-feared'—'Push on, push on !'
Said the Hermit cheerily.

The boat came closer to the ship,
But I nor spake nor stirred ;
The boat came close beneath the ship,
And straight a sound was heard.

The ship suddenly sinketh.
Under the water it rumbled on,
Still louder and more dread :
It reached the ship, it split the bay ;
The ship went down like lead.
The ancient Mariner is saved in the Pilot's boat.
Stunned by that loud and dreadful sound,
Which sky and ocean smote,
Like one that hath been seven days drowned
My body lay afloat ;
But swift as dreams, myself I found
Within the Pilot's boat.
Upon the whirl, where sank the ship,
The boat spun round and round ;
And all was still, save that the hill
Was telling of the sound.

I moved my lips—the Pilot shrieked
And fell down in a fit ;
The holy Hermit raised his eyes,
And prayed where he did sit.

I took the oars : the Pilot's boy,
Who now doth crazy go,
Laughed loud and long, and all the while
His eyes went to and fro.
'Ha ! ha !' quoth he, 'full plain I see,
The Devil knows how to row.'

And now, all in my own countree,
I stood on the firm land !
The Hermit stepped forth from the boat,
And scarcely he could stand.

The ancient Mariner earnestly entreateth the Hermit to shrieve him ; and the penance of life falls on him.

'O shrieve me, shrieve me, holy man !'
The Hermit crossed his brow.
'Say quick,' quoth he, 'I bid thee say—
What manner of man art thou ?'
Forthwith this frame of mine was wrenched
With a woful agony,
Which forced me to begin my tale ;
And then it left me free.

And ever and anon through out his future life an agony constraineth him to travel from land to land ;

Since then, at an uncertain hour,
That agony returns :
And till my ghastly tale is told,
This heart within me burns.
I pass, like night, from land to land ;
I have strange power of speech ;
That moment that his face I see,
I know the man that must hear me :
To him my tale I teach.

What loud uproar bursts from that door !
The wedding-guests are there :
But in the garden-bower the bride
And bride-maids singing are :
And hark the little vesper bell,
Which biddeth me to prayer !

O Wedding-Guest ! this soul hath been
Alone on a wide wide sea :
So lonely 'twas, that God himself
Scarce seeméd there to be.

O sweeter than the marriage-feast,
'Tis sweeter far to me,
To walk together to the kirk
With a goodly company !—

To walk together to the kirk,
And all together pray,
While each to his great Father bends,

Old men, and babes, and loving friends
And youths and maidens gay !

And to teach, by his own example, love and reverence to all things that God made and loveth.

Farewell, farewell ! but this I tell
To thee, thou Wedding-Guest !
He prayeth well, who loveth well
Both man and bird and beast.
He prayeth best, who loveth best
All things both great and small ;
For the dear God who loveth us,
He made and loveth all.

The Mariner, whose eye is bright,
Whose beard with age is hoar,
Is gone : and now the Wedding-Guest
Turned from the bridegroom's door.

He went like one that hath been stunned,
And is of sense forlorn :
A sadder and a wiser man,
He rose the morrow morn.

Christabel

PART I

'Tis the middle of night by the castle clock,
And the owls have awakened the crowing cock ;
Tu—whit !— — Tu—whoo !
And hark, again ! the crowing cock,
How drowsily it crew.
Sir Leoline, the Baron rich,
Hath a toothless mastiff bitch ;
From her kennel beneath the rock
She maketh answer to the clock,
Four for the quarters, and twelve for the hour ;
Ever and aye, by shine and shower,
Sixteen short howls, not over loud ;
Some say, she sees my lady's shroud.

Is the night chilly and dark ?
The night is chilly, but not dark.
The thin gray cloud is spread on high,
It covers but not hides the sky.
The moon is behind, and at the full ;
And yet she looks both small and dull.
The night is chill, the cloud is gray :
'Tis a month before the month of May,
And the Spring comes slowly up this way.

The lovely lady, Christabel,
Whom her father loves so well,
What makes her in the wood so late,
A furlong from the castle gate ?
She had dreams all yesternight
Of her own betrothéd knight ;
And she in the midnight wood will pray
For the weal of her lover that's far away.

She stole along, she nothing spoke,
The sighs she heaved were soft and low,
And naught was green upon the oak
But moss and rarest misletoe :
She kneels beneath the huge oak tree,
And in silence prayeth she.

The lady sprang up suddenly,
The lovely lady, Christabel !
It moaned as near, as near can be,
But what it is she cannot tell.—
On the other side it seems to be,
Of the huge, broad-breasted, old oak tree.

The night is chill ; the forest bare ;
Is it the wind that moaneth bleak ?
There is not wind enough in the air
To move away the ringlet curl
From the lovely lady's cheek—
There is not wind enough to twirl
The one red leaf, the last of its clan,
That dances as often as dance it can,

Hanging so light, and hanging so high,
On the topmost twig that looks up at the sky.

Hush, beating heart of Christabel !
Jesu, Maria, shield her well !
She folded her arms beneath her cloak,
And stole to the other side of the oak.

What sees she there ?
There she sees a damsel bright,
Dressed in a silken robe of white,
That shadowy in the moonlight shone :
The neck that made that white robe wan,
Her stately neck, and arms were bare ;
Her blue-veined feet unsandal'd were ;
And wildly glittered here and there
The gems entangled in her hair.
I guess, 'twas frightful there to see
A lady so richly clad as she—
Beautiful exceedingly !
Mary mother, save me now !
(Said Christabel,) And who art thou ?

The lady strange made answer meet,
And her voice was faint and sweet :—
Have pity on my sore distress,
I scarce can speak for weariness :
Stretch forth thy hand, and have no fear !
Said Christabel, How camest thou here ?
And the lady, whose voice was faint and sweet,
Did thus pursue her answer meet :—

My sire is of a noble line,
And my name is Geraldine :
Five warriors seized me yestermorn,
Me, even me, a maid forlorn :
They choked my cries with force and fright,
And tied me on a palfrey white.
The palfrey was as fleet as wind,
And they rode furiously behind.

They spurred amain, their steeds were white :
And once we crossed the shade of night.
As sure as Heaven shall rescue me,
I have no thought what men they be ;
Nor do I know how long it is
(For I have lain entranced, I wis)
Since one, the tallest of the five,
Took me from the palfrey's back,
A weary woman, scarce alive.
Some muttered words his comrades spoke :
He placed me underneath this oak ;
He swore they would return with haste ;
Whither they went I cannot tell—
I thought I heard, some minutes past,
Sounds as of a castle bell.
Stretch forth thy hand (thus ended she),
And help a wretched maid to flee.

Then Christabel stretched forth her hand,
And comforted fair Geraldine :
O well, bright dame ! may you command
The service of Sir Leoline ;
And gladly our stout chivalry
Will he send forth and friends withal
To guide and guard you safe and free
Home to your noble father's hall.

She rose : and forth with steps they passed
That strove to be, and were not, fast.
Her gracious stars the lady blest,
And thus spake on sweet Christabel :
All our household are at rest,
The hall is silent as the cell ;
Sir Leoline is weak in health,
And may not well awakened be,
But we will move as if in stealth,
And I beseech your courtesy,
This night, to share your couch with me.

They crossed the moat, and Christabel
Took the key that fitted well ;
A little door she opened straight,
All in the middle of the gate ;
The gate that was ironed within and without,
Where an army in battle array had marched out.
The lady sank, belike through pain,
And Christabel with might and main
Lifted her up, a weary weight,
Over the threshold of the gate :
Then the lady rose again,
And moved, as she were not in pain.

So free from danger, free from fear,
They crossed the court : right glad they were.
And Christabel devoutly cried
To the Lady by her side,
Praise we the Virgin all divine
Who hath rescued thee from thy distress !
Alas, alas ! said Geraldine,
I cannot speak for weariness.
So free from danger, free from fear,
They crossed the court : right glad they were.

Outside her kennel, the mastiff old
Lay fast asleep, in moonshine cold.
The mastiff old did not awake,
Yet she an angry moan did make !
And what can ail the mastiff bitch ?
Never till now she uttered yell
Beneath the eye of Christabel.
Perhaps it is the owlet's scritch :
For what can aid the mastiff bitch ?

They passed the hall, that echoes still,
Pass as lightly as you will !
The brands were flat, the brands were dying,
Amid their own white ashes lying ;
But when the lady passed, there came
A tongue of light, a fit of flame ;

And Christabel saw the lady's eye,
And nothing else saw she thereby,
Save the boss of the shield of Sir Leoline tall,
Which hung in a murky old niche in the wall.
O softly tread, said Christabel,
My father seldom sleepeth well.

Sweet Christabel her feet doth bare,
And jealous of the listening air
They steal their way from stair to stair,
Now in glimmer, and now in gloom,
And now they pass the Baron's room,
As still as death, with stifled breath !
And now have reached her chamber door ;
And now doth Geraldine press down
The rushes of the chamber floor.

The moon shines dim in the open air,
And not a moonbeam enters here.
But they without its light can see
The chamber carved so curiously,
Carved with figures strange and sweet,
All made out of the carver's brain,
For a lady's chamber meet :
The lamp with twofold silver chain
Is fastened to an angel's feet.

The silver lamp burns dead and dim ;
But Christabel the lamp will trim.
She trimmed the lamp, and made it bright,
And left it swinging to and fro,
While Geraldine, in wretched plight,
Sank down upon the floor below.

O weary lady, Geraldine,
I pray you, drink this cordial wine !
It is a wine of virtuous powers ;
My mother made it of wild flowers.

And will your mother pity me,
Who am a maiden most forlorn ?

Christabel answered—Woe is me !
She died the hour that I was born.
I have heard the gray-haired friar tell
How on her death-bed she did say,
That she should hear the castle-bell
Strike twelve upon my wedding-day.
O mother dear ! that thou wert here !
I would, said Geraldine, she were !

But soon with altered voice, said she—
'Off, wandering mother ! Peak and pine !
I have power to bid thee flee.'
Alas ! what ails poor Geraldine ?
Why stares she with unsettled eye ?
Can she the bodiless dead espy ?
And why with hollow voice cries she,
'Off, woman, off ! this hour is mine—
Though thou her guardian spirit be,
Off, woman. off ! 'tis given to me.'

Then Christabel knelt by the lady's side,
And raised to heaven her eyes so blue—
Alas ! said she, this ghastly ride—
Dear lady ! it hath wildered you !
The lady wiped her moist cold brow,
And faintly said, ''Tis over now !'

Again the wild-flower wine she drank :
Her fair large eyes 'gan glitter bright,
And from the floor whereon she sank,
The lofty lady stood upright :
She was most beautiful to see,
Like a lady of a far countrée.

And thus the lofty lady spake—
'All they who live in the upper sky,
Do love you, holy Christabel !
And you love them, and for their sake
And for the good which me befel,
Even I in my degree will try,
Fair maiden, to requite you well.

But now unrobe yourself ; for I
Must pray, ere yet in bed I lie.'

Quoth Christabel, So let it be !
And as the lady bade, did she.
Her gentle limbs did she undress
And lay down in her loveliness.

But through her brain of weal and woe
So many thoughts moved to and fro,
That vain it were her lids to close ;
So half-way from the bed she rose,
And on her elbow did recline
To look at the lady Geraldine.

Beneath the lamp the lady bowed,
And slowly rolled her eyes around ;
Then drawing in her breath aloud,
Like one that shuddered, she unbound
The cincture from beneath her breast :
Her silken robe, and inner vest,
Dropt to her feet, and full in view,
Behold ! her bosom, and half her side
A sight to dream of, not to tell !
O shield her ! shield sweet Christabel !

Yet Geraldine nor speaks nor stirs ;
Ah ! what a stricken look was hers !
Deep from within she seems half-way
To lift some weight with sick assay,
And eyes the maid and seeks delay ;
Then suddenly as one defied
Collects herself in scorn and pride,
And lay down by the Maiden's side !—
And in her arms the maid she took,

Ah wel-a-day !

And with low voice and doleful look
These words did say :
'In the touch of this bosom there worketh a spell,
Which is lord of thy utterance, Christabel !

Thou knowest to-night, and wilt know to-morrow
This mark of my shame, this seal of my sorrow ;

But vainly thou warrest,
For this is alone in
Thy power to declare,
That in the dim forest
Thou heard'st a low moaning,

And found'st a bright lady, surpassingly fair ;
And didst bring her home with thee in love and in charity,
To shield her and shelter her from the damp air.'

THE CONCLUSION TO PART I

It was a lovely sight to see
The lady Christabel, when she
Was praying at the old oak tree.

Amid the jaggéd shadows
Of mossy leafless boughs,
Kneeling in the moonlight,
To make her gentle vows ;

Her slender palms together prest,
Heaving sometimes on her breast ;
Her face resigned to bliss or bale—
Her face, oh call it fair not pale,
And both blue eyes more bright than clear.
Each about to have a tear.
With open eyes (ah, woe is me !)
Asleep, and dreaming fearfully,
Fearfully dreaming, yet, I wis,
Dreaming that alone, which is—
O sorrow and shame ! Can this be she,
The lady, who knelt at the old oak tree ?
And lo ! the worker of these harms,
That holds the maiden in her arms,
Seems to slumber still and mild,
As a mother with her child.

A star hath set, a star hath risen,
O Geraldine ! since arms of thine

Have been the lovely lady's prison.
O Geraldine ! one hour was thine—
Thou'st had thy will ! By tairn and rill,
The night-birds all that hour were still.
But now they are jubilant anew,
From cliff and tower, tu—whoo ! tu—whoo !
Tu—whoo ! tu—whoo ! from wood and fell !

And see ! the lady Christabel
Gathers herself from out her trance ;
Her limbs relax, her countenance
Grows sad and soft ; the smooth thin lids
Close o'er her eyes ; and tears she sheds—
Large tears that leave the lashes bright !
And oft the while she seems to smile
As infants at a sudden light !

Yea, she doth smile, and she doth weep,
Like a youthful hermitess,
Beauteous in a wilderness,
Who, praying always, prays in sleep.
And, if she move unquietly,
Perchance, 'tis but the blood so free
Comes back and tingles in her feet.
No doubt, she hath a vision sweet.
What if her guardian spirit 'twere,
What if she knew her mother near ?
But this she knows, in joys and woes,
That saints will aid if men will call :
For the blue sky bends over all !

PART II

Each matin bell, the Baron saith,
Knells us back to a world of death.
These words Sir Leoline first said,
When he rose and found his lady dead :
These words Sir Leoline will say
Many a morn to his dying day !
And hence the custom and law began
That still at dawn the sacristan,

Who duly pulls the heavy bell,
Five and forty beads must tell
Between each stroke—a warning knell,
Which not a soul can choose but hear
From Bratha Head to Wyndermere.

Saith Bracy the bard, So let it knell !
And let the drowsy sacristan
Still count as slowly as he can !
There is no lack of such, I ween,
As well fill up the space between.
In Langdale Pike and Witch's Lair,
And Dungeon-ghyll so foully rent,
With ropes of rock and bells of air
Three sinful sextons' ghosts are pent,
Who all give back, one after t'other,
The death-note to their living brother ;
And oft too, by the knell offended,
Just as their one ! two ! three ! is ended,
The devil mocks the doleful tale
With a merry peal from Borrowdale.

The air is still ! through mist and cloud
That merry peal comes ringing loud ;
And Geraldine shakes off her dread,
And rises lightly from the bed ;
Puts on her silken vestments white,
And tricks her hair in lovely plight,
And nothing doubting of her spell
Awakens the lady Christabel.
'Sleep you, sweet lady Christabel ?
I trust that you have rested well.'

And Christabel awoke and spied
The same who lay down by her side—
O rather say, the same whom she
Raised up beneath the old oak tree !
Nay, fairer yet ! and yet more fair !
For she belike hath drunken deep
Of all the blessedness of sleep !

And while she spake, her looks, her air
Such gentle thankfulness declare,
That (so it seemed) her girded vests
Grew tight beneath her heaving breasts.
'Sure I have sinn'd !' said Christabel,
'Now heaven be praised if all be well !'
And in low faltering tones, yet sweet,
Did she the lofty lady greet
With such perplexity of mind
As dreams too lively leave behind.

So quickly she rose, and quickly arrayed
Her maiden limbs, and having prayed
That He, who on the cross did groan,
Might wash away her sins unknown,
She forthwith led fair Geraldine
To meet her sire, Sir Leoline.

The lovely maid and the lady tall
Are pacing both into the hall,
And pacing on through page and groom,
Enter the Baron's presence-room.

The Baron rose, and while he prest
His gentle daughter to his breast,
With cheerful wonder in his eyes
The lady Geraldine espies,
And gave such welcome to the same,
As might beseem so bright a dame !

But when he heard the lady's tale,
And when she told her father's name,
Why waxed Sir Leoline so pale,
Murmuring o'er the name again,
Lord Roland de Vaux of Tryermaine ?

Alas ! they had been friends in youth ;
But whispering tongues can poison truth ;
And constancy lives in realms above ;
And life is thorny ; and youth is vain ;
And to be wroth with one we love,

Doth work like madness in the brain.
And thus it chanced, as I divine,
With Roland and Sir Leoline.
Each spake words of high disdain
And insult to his heart's best brother :
They parted—ne'er to meet again !
But never either found another
To free the hollow heart from paining—
They stood aloof, the scars remaining,
Like cliffs which had been rent asunder ;
A dreary sea now flows between ;—
But neither heat, nor frost, nor thunder,
Shall wholly do away, I ween,
The marks of that which once hath been.

Sir Leoline, a moment's space,
Stood gazing on the damsel's face :
And the youthful Lord of Tryermaine
Came back upon his heart again.

O then the Baron forgot his age,
His noble heart swelled high with rage ;
He swore by the wounds in Jesu's side,
He would proclaim it far and wide
With trump and solemn heraldry,
That they, who thus had wronged the dame,
Were base as spotted infamy !
'And if they dare deny the same,
My herald shall appoint a week,
And let the recreant traitors seek
My tourney court—that there and then
I may dislodge their reptile souls
From the bodies and forms of men !'
He spake : his eye in lightning rolls !
For the lady was ruthlessly seized ; and he kenned
In the beautiful lady the child of his friend !

And now the tears were on his face,
And fondly in his arms he took

Fair Geraldine, who met the embrace,
Prolonging it with joyous look.
Which when she viewed, a vision fell
Upon the soul of Christabel,
The vision of fear, the touch and pain !
She shrunk and shuddered, and saw again—
(Ah, woe is me ! Was it for thee,
Thou gentle maid ! such sights to see ?)

Again she saw that bosom old,
Again she felt that bosom cold,
And drew in her breath with a hissing sound :
Whereat the Knight turned wildly round,
And nothing saw, but his own sweet maid
With eyes upraised, as one that prayed.

The touch, the sight, had passed away,
And in its stead that vision blest,
Which comforted her after-rest.
While in the lady's arms she lay,
Had put a rapture in her breast,
And on her lips and o'er her eyes
Spread smiles like light !

With new surprise,

'What ails then my belovéd child ?'
The Baron said—His daughter mild
Made answer, 'All will yet be well !'
I ween, she had no power to tell
Aught else : so mighty was the spell.
Yet he, who saw this Geraldine,
Had deemed her sure a thing divine :
Such sorrow with such grace she blended,
As if she feared she had offended
Sweet Christabel, that gentle maid !
And with such lowly tones she prayed,
She might be sent without delay
Home to her father's mansion.

'Nay !

Nay, by my soul !' said Leoline.
'Ho ! Bracy the bard, the charge be thine !

Go thou, with music sweet and loud,
And take two steeds with trappings proud,
And take the youth whom thou lov'st best
To bear thy harp, and learn thy song,
And clothe you both in solemn vest,
And over the mountains haste along,
Lest wandering folk, that are abroad,
Detain you on the valley road.
'And when he has crossed the Irthing flood,
My merry bard ! he hastes, he hastes
Up Knorren Moor, through Halegarth Wood,
And reaches soon that castle good
Which stands and threatens Scotland's wastes.

'Bard Bracy ! bard Bracy ! your horses are fleet,
Ye must ride up the hall, your music so sweet,
More loud than your horses' echoing feet !
And loud and loud to Lord Roland call,
Thy daughter is safe in Langdale hall !
Thy beautiful daughter is safe and free—
Sir Leoline greets thee thus through me !
He bids thee come without delay
With all thy numerous array
And take thy lovely daughter home :
And he will meet thee on the way
With all his numerous array
White with their panting palfreys' foam :
And, by mine honour ! I will say,
That I repent me of the day
When I spake words of fierce disdain
To Roland de Vaux of Tryermaine !—
—For since that evil hour hath flown,
Many a summer's sun hath shone ;
Yet ne'er found I a friend again
Like Roland de Vaux of Tryermaine.'

The lady fell, and clasped his knees,
Her face upraised, her eyes o'erflowing ;
And Bracy replied, with faltering voice,

His gracious hail on all bestowing !—
'Thy words, thou sire of Christabel,
Are sweeter than my harp can tell ;
Yet might I gain a boon of thee,
This day my journey should not be,
So strange a dream hath come to me,
That I had vowed with music loud
To clear yon wood from thing unblest,
Warned by a vision in my rest !
For in my sleep I saw that dove,
That gentle bird, whom thou dost love,
And call'st by thy own daughter's name—
Sir Leoline ! I saw the same
Fluttering, and uttering fearful moan,
Among the green herbs in the forest alone.
Which when I saw and when I heard,
I wonder'd what might ail the bird ;
For nothing near it could I see,
Save the grass and herbs underneath the old tree.

'And in my dream methought I went
To search out what might there be found ;
And what the sweet bird's trouble meant,
That thus lay fluttering on the ground.
I went and peered, and could descry
No cause for her distressful cry ;
But yet for her dear lady's sake
I stooped, methought, the dove to take,
When lo ! I saw a bright green snake
Coiled around its wings and neck.
Green as the herbs on which it couched,
Close by the dove's its head it crouched ;
And with the dove it heaves and stirs,
Swelling its neck as she swelled hers !
I woke ; it was the midnight hour,
The clock was echoing in the tower ;
But though my slumber was gone by,
This dream it would not pass away—

It seems to live upon my eye !
And thence I vowed this self-same day,
With music strong and saintly song
To wander through the forest bare,
Lest aught unholy loiter there.'

Thus Bracy said : the Baron, the while,
Half-listening heard him with a smile ;
Then turned to Lady Geraldine,
His eyes made up of wonder and love ;
And said in courtly accents fine,
'Sweet maid, Lord Roland's beauteous dove,
With arms more strong than harp or song,
Thy sire and I will crush the snake !'
He kissed her forehead as he spake,
And Geraldine in maiden wise,
Casting down her large bright eyes,
With blushing cheek and courtesy fine
She turned her from Sir Leoline ;
Softly gathering up her train,
That o'er her right arm fell again ;
And folded her arms across her chest,
And couched her head upon her breast,
And looked askance at Christabel— —
Jesu, Maria, shield her well !

A snake's small eye blinks dull and shy ;
And the lady's eyes they shrunk in her head,
Each shrunk up to a serpent's eye,
And with somewhat of malice, and more of dread,
At Christabel she looked askance !—
One moment—and the sight was fled !
But Christabel in dizzy trance
Stumbling on the unsteady ground
Shuddered aloud, with a hissing sound ;
And Geraldine again turned round,
And like a thing, that sought relief,
Full of wonder and full of grief,

She rolled her large bright eyes divine
Wildly on Sir Leoline.

The maid, alas ! her thoughts are gone,
She nothing sees—no sight but one !
The maid, devoid of guile and sin,
I know not how, in fearful wise,
So deeply had she drunken in
That look, those shrunken serpent eyes,
That all her features were resigned
To this sole image in her mind :
And passively did imitate
That look of dull and treacherous hate !
And thus she stood, in dizzy trance,
Still picturing that look askance
With forced unconscious sympathy
Full before her father's view— —
As far as such a look could be
In eyes so innocent and blue !

And when the trance was o'er, the maid
Paused awhile, and inly prayed :
Then falling at the Baron's feet,
'By my mother's soul do I entreat
That thou this woman send away !'
She said : and more she could not say :
For what she knew she could not tell,
O'er-mastered by the mighty spell.

Why is thy cheek so wan and wild,
Sir Leoline ? Thy only child
Lies at thy feet, thy joy, thy pride,
So fair, so innocent, so mild ;
The same, for whom thy lady died !
O by the pangs of her dear mother
Think thou no evil of thy child !
For her, and thee, and for no other,
She prayed the moment ere she died :
Prayed that the babe for whom she died,
Might prove her dear lord's joy and pride !

That prayer her deadly pangs beguiled,
Sir Leoline !
And wouldst thou wrong thy only child,
Her child and thine ?
Within the Baron's heart and brain
If thoughts, like these, had any share,
They only swelled his rage and pain,
And did but work confusion there.
His heart was cleft with pain and rage,
His cheeks they quivered, his eyes were wild,
Dishonoured thus in his old age ;
Dishonoured by his only child,
And all his hospitality
To the wronged daughter of his friend
By more than woman's jealousy
Brought thus to a disgraceful end—
He rolled his eye with stern regard
Upon the gentle ministrel bard,
And said in tones abrupt, austere—
'Why, Bracy ! dost thou loiter here ?
I bade thee hence !' The bard obeyed ;
And turning from his own sweet maid,
The agéd knight, Sir Leoline,
Led forth the lady Geraldine !

THE CONCLUSION TO PART II

A little child, a limber elf,
Singing, dancing to itself,
A fairy thing with red round cheeks,
That always finds, and never seeks,
Makes such a vision to the sight
As fills a father's eyes with light ;
And pleasures flow in so thick and fast
Upon his heart, that he at last
Must needs express his love's excess
With words of unmeant bitterness.
Perhaps 'tis pretty to force together
Thoughts so all unlike each other ;

To mutter and mock a broken charm,
To dally with wrong that does no harm.
Perhaps 'tis tender too and pretty
At each wild word to feel within
A sweet recoil of love and pity.
And what, if in a world of sin
(O sorrow and shame should this be true !)
Such giddiness of heart and brain
Comes seldom save from rage and pain,
So talks as it's most used to do.

France : An Ode [Excerpt]

O Liberty ! with profitless endeavour
Have I pursued thee, many a weary hour ;
But thou nor swell'st the victor's strain, nor ever
Didst breathe thy soul in forms of human power.

Alike from all, howe'er they praise thee,
(Nor prayer, nor boastful name delays thee)
Alike from Priestcraft's harpy minions,
And factious Blasphemy's obscener slaves,
Thou speedest on thy subtle pinions,

The guide of homeless winds, and playmate of the waves !
And there I felt thee !—on that sea-cliff's verge,

Whose pines, scarce travelled by the breeze above,

Had made one murmur with the distant surge !
Yes, while I stood and gazed, my temples bare,
And shot my being through earth, sea, and air,

Possessing all things with intensest love,
O Liberty ! my spirit felt thee there

Kubla Khan

In Xanadu did Kubla Khan
A stately pleasure-dome decree :
Where Alph, the sacred river, ran
Through caverns measureless to man

Down to a sunless sea.

So twice five miles of fertile ground
With walls and towers were girdled round :
And there were gardens bright with sinuous rills,
Where blossomed many an incense-bearing tree ;
And here were forests ancient as the hills,
Enfolding sunny spots of greenery.
But oh ! that deep romantic chasm which slanted
Down the green hill athwart a cedarn cover !
A savage place ! as holy and enchanted
As e'er beneath a waning moon was haunted
By woman wailing for her demon-lover !
And from this chasm, with ceaseless turmoil seething,
As if this earth in fast thick pants were breathing,
A mighty fountain momently was forced :
Amid whose swift half-intermitted burst
Huge fragments vaulted like rebounding hail,
Or chaffy grain beneath the thresher's flail :
And 'mid these dancing rocks at once and ever
It flung up momently the sacred river.
Five miles meandering with a mazy motion
Through wood and dale the sacred river ran,
Then reached the caverns measureless to man,
And sank in tumult to a lifeless ocean :
And 'mid this tumult Kubla heard from far
Ancestral voices prophesying war !

The shadow of the dome of pleasure
Floated midway on the waves ;
Where was heard the mingled measure
From the fountain and the caves.

It was a miracle of rare device,
A sunny pleasure-dome with caves of ice !
A damsel with a dulcimer
In a vision once I saw :
It was an Abyssinian maid,
And on her dulcimer she played,
Singing of Mount Abora.
Could I revive within me

Her symphony and song,
To such a deep delight 'twould win me,

That with music loud and long,
I would build that dome in air,
That sunny dome ! those caves of ice !
And all who heard should see them there,
And all should cry, Beware ! Beware !
His flashing eyes, his floating hair !
Weave a circle round him thrice,
And close your eyes with holy dread,
For he on honey-dew hath fed,
And drunk the milk of Paradise.

Fears in Solitude

A green and silent spot, amid the hills,
A small and silent dell ! O'er stiller place
No singing sky-lark ever poised himself.
The hills are heathy, save that swelling slope,
Which hath a gay and gorgeous covering on,
All golden with the never-bloomless furze,
Which now blooms most profusely : but the dell,
Bathed by the mist, is fresh and delicate
As vernal corn-field, or the unripe flax,
When, through its half-transparent stalks, at eve,
The level sunshine glimmers with green light.
Oh ! 'tis a quiet spirit-healing nook !
Which all, methinks, would love ; but chiefly he,
The humble man, who, in his youthful years,
Knew just so much of folly, as had made
His early manhood more securely wise !
Here he might lie on fern or withered heath,
While from the singing lark (that sings unseen
The minstrelsy that solitude loves best),
And from the sun, and from the breezy air,
Sweet influences trembled o'er his frame ;
And he, with many feelings, many thoughts,
Made up a meditative joy, and found
Religious meanings in the forms of Nature !

And so, his senses gradually wrapt
In a half sleep, he dreams of better worlds,
And dreaming hears thee still, O singing lark,
That singest like an angel in the clouds !
My God ! it is a melancholy thing

For such a man, who would full fain preserve
His soul in calmness, yet perforce must feel
For all his human brethren—O my God !
It weighs upon the heart, that he must think
What uproar and what strife may now be stirring
This way or that way o'er these silent hills—
Invasion, and the thunder and the shout,
And all the crash of onset ; fear and rage,
And undetermined conflict—even now,
Even now, perchance, and in his native isle :
Carnage and groans beneath this blessed sun !
We have offended, Oh ! my countrymen !
We have offended very grievously,
And been most tyrannous. From east to west
A groan of accusation pierces Heaven !
The wretched plead against us ; multitudes
Countless and vehement, the sons of God,
Our brethren ! Like a cloud that travels on,
Steamed up from Cairo's swamps of pestilence,
Even so, my countrymen ! have we gone forth
And borne to distant tribes slavery and pangs,
And, deadlier far, our vices, whose deep taint
With slow perdition murders the whole man,
His body and his soul ! Meanwhile, at home,
All individual dignity and power
Engulfed in Courts, Committees, Institutions,
Associations and Societies,
A vain, speach-mouthing, speech-reporting Guild,
One Benefit-Club for mutual flattery,
We have drunk up, demure as at a grace,
Pollutions from the brimming cup of wealth ;
Contemptuous of all honourable rule,
Yet bartering freedom and the poor man's life

For gold, as at a market ! The sweet words
Of Christian promise, words that even yet
Might stem destruction, were they wisely preached,
Are muttered o'er by men, whose tones proclaim
How flat and wearisome they feel their trade :
Rank scoffers some, but most too indolent
To deem them falsehoods or to know their truth.
Oh ! blasphemous ! the Book of Life is made
A superstitious instrument, on which
We gabble o'er the oaths we mean to break ;
For all must swear—all and in every place,
College and wharf, council and justice-court ;
All, all must swear, the briber and the bribed,
Merchant and lawyer, senator and priest,
The rich, the poor, the old man and the young ;
All, all make up one scheme of perjury,
That faith doth reel ; the very name of God
Sounds like a juggler's charm ; and, bold with joy,
Forth from his dark and lonely hiding-place,
(Portentious sight !) the owlet Atheism,
Sailing on obscene wings athwart the noon,
Drops his blue-fringéd lids, and holds them close,
And hooting at the glorious sun in Heaven,
Cries out, 'Where is it ?'
Thankless too for peace,

(Peace long preserved by fleets and perilous seas).
Secure from actual warfare, we have loved
To swell the war-whoop, passionate for war !
Alas ! for ages ignorant of all
Its ghastlier workings, (famine or blue plague,
Battle, or siege, or flight through wintry snows,)
We, this whole people, have been clamorous
For war and bloodshed ; animating sports,
The which we pay for as a thing to talk of,
Spectators and not combatants ! No guess
Anticipative of a wrong unfelt,
No speculation on contingency,
However dim and vague, too vague and dim

To yield a justifying cause ; and forth,
(Stuffed out with big preamble, holy names,
And adjurations of the God in Heaven,)
We send our mandates for the certain death
Of thousands and ten thousands ! Boys and girls,
And women, that would groan to see a child
Pull off an insect's wing, all read of war,
The best amusement for our morning meal !
The poor wretch, who has learnt his only prayers
From curses, and who knows scarcely words enough
To ask a blessing from his Heavenly Father,
Becomes a fluent phraseman, absolute
And technical in victories and defeats,
And all our dainty terms for fratricide ;
Terms which we trundle smoothly o'er our tongues
Like mere abstractions, empty sounds to which
We join no feeling and attach no form !
As if the soldier died without a wound ;
As if the fibres of this godlike frame
Were gored without a pang ; as if the wretch,
Who fell in battle, doing bloody deeds,
Passed off to Heaven, translated and not killed ;
As though he had no wife to pine for him,
No God to judge him ! Therefore, evil days
Are coming on us, O my countrymen !
And what if all-avenging Providence,
Strong and retributive, should make us know
The meaning of our words, force us to feel
The desolation and the agony
Of our fierce doings ?
Spare us yet awhile,

Father and God ! O ! spare us yet awhile !
Oh ! let not English women drag their flight
Fainting beneath the burthen of their babes,
Of the sweet infants, that but yesterday
Laughed at the breast ! Sons, brothers, husbands, all
Who ever gazed with fondness on the forms
Which grew up with you round the same fire-side,

And all who ever heard the sabbath-bells
Without the infidel's scorn, make yourselves pure !
Stand forth ! be men ! repel an impious foe,
Impious and false, a light yet cruel race,
Who laugh away all virtue, mingling mirth
With deeds of murder ; and still promising
Freedom, themselves too sensual to be free,
Poison life's amities, and cheat the heart
Of faith and quiet hope, and all that soothes,
And all that lifts the spirit ! Stand we forth ;
Render them back upon the insulted ocean,
And let them toss as idly on its waves
As the vile sea-weed, which some mountain-blast
Swept from our shores ! And oh ! may we return
Not with a drunken triumph, but with fear,
Repenting of the wrongs with which we stung
So fierce a foe to frenzy !
I have told,

O Britons ! O my brethren ! I have told
Most bitter truth, but without bitterness.
Nor deem my zeal or factious or mistimed ;
For never can true courage dwell with them,
Who, playing tricks with conscience, dare not look
At their own vices. We have been too long
Dupes of a deep delusion ! Some, belike,
Groaning with restless enmity, expect
All change from change of constituted power ;
As if a Government had been a robe,
On which our vice and wretchedness were tagged
Like fancy-points and fringes, with the robe
Pulled off at pleasure. Fondly these attach
A radical causation to a few
Poor drudges of chastising Providence,
Who borrow all their hues and qualities
From our own folly and rank wickedness,
Which gave them birth and nursed them. Others, meanwhile,
Dote with a mad idolatry ; and all

Who will not fall before their images,
And yield them worship, they are enemies
Even of their country !
Such have I been deemed—

But, O dear Britain ! O my Mother Isle !
Needs must thou prove a name most dear and holy
To me, a son, a brother, and a friend,
A husband, and a father ! who revere
All bonds of natural love, and find them all
Within the limits of thy rocky shores.
O native Britain ! O my Mother Isle !
How shouldst thou prove aught else but dear and holy
To me, who from thy lakes and mountain-hills,
Thy clouds, thy quiet dales, thy rocks and seas,
Have drunk in all my intellectual life,
All sweet sensations, all ennobling thoughts,
All adoration of God in nature,
All lovely and all honourable things,
Whatever makes this mortal spirit feel
The joy and greatness of its future being ?
There lives nor form nor feeling in my soul
Unborrowed from my country ! O divine
And beauteous island ! thou hast been my sole
And most magnificent temple, in the which
I walk with awe, and sing my stately songs,
Loving the God that made me !—
May my fears,

My filial fears, be vain ! and may the vaunts
And menace of the vengeful enemy
Pass like the gust, that roared and died away
In the distant tree : which heard, and only heard
In this low dell, bowed not the delicate grass.
But now the gentle dew-fall sends abroad

The fruit-like perfume of the golden furze :
The light has left the summit of the hill,
Though still a sunny gleam lies beautiful,
Aslant the ivied beacon. Now farewell,

Farewell, awhile, O soft and silent spot !
On the green sheep-track, up the heathy hill,
Homeward I wind my way ; and lo ! recalled
From bodings that have well-nigh wearied me,
I find myself upon the brow, and pause
Startled ! And after lonely sojourning
In such a quiet and surrounded nook,
This burst of prospect, here the shadowy main,
Dim tinted, there the mighty majesty
Of that huge amphitheatre of rich
And elmy fields, seems like society—
Conversing with the mind, and giving it
A livelier impulse and a dance of thought !
And now, belovéd Stowey ! I behold
Thy church-tower, and, methinks, the four huge elms
Clustering, which mark the mansion of my friend ;
And close behind them, hidden from my view,
Is my own lowly cottage, where my babe
And my babe's mother dwell in peace ! With light
And quickened footsteps thitherward I tend,
Remembering thee, O green and silent dell !
And grateful, that by nature's quietness
And solitary musings, all my heart
Is softened, and made worthy to indulge
Love, and the thoughts that yearn for human kind.

Dejection: An Ode

I

Well ! If the Bard was weather-wise, who made
The grand old ballad of Sir Patrick Spence,
This night, so tranquil now, will not go hence
Unroused by winds, that ply a busier trade
Than those which mould yon cloud in lazy flakes,
Or the dull sobbing draft, that moans and rakes

Upon the strings of this Æolian lute,
Which better far were mute.
For lo ! the New-moon winter-bright !
And overspread with phantom light,
(With swimming phantom light o'erspread
But rimmed and circled by a silver thread)
I see the old Moon in her lap, foretelling
The coming-on of rain and squally blast.

And oh ! that even now the gust were swelling,
And the slant night-shower driving loud and fast !

Those sounds which oft have raised me, whilst they awed,
And sent my soul abroad,
Might now perhaps their wonted impulse give,
Might startle this dull pain, and make it move and live !

II

A grief without a pang, void, dark, and drear,
A stifled, drowsy, unimpassioned grief,
Which finds no natural outlet, no relief,
In word, or sigh, or tear—
O Lady ! in this wan and heartless mood,
To other thoughts by yonder throstle woo'd,

All this long eve, so balmy and serene,
Have I been gazing on the western sky,
And its peculiar tint of yellow green :

And still I gaze—and with how blank an eye !
And those thin clouds above, in flakes and bars,
That give away their motion to the stars ;
Those stars, that glide behind them or between,
Now sparkling, now bedimmed, but always seen :
Yon crescent Moon, as fixed as if it grew
In its own cloudiess, starless lake of blue ;
I see them all so excellently fair,
I see, not feel, how beautiful they are !

III

My genial spirits fail ;
And what can these avail
To lift the smothering weight from off my breast ?
It were a vain endeavour,
Though I should gaze for ever
On that green light that lingers in the west :
I may not hope from outward forms to win
The passion and the life, whose fountains are within.

IV

O Lady ! we receive but what we give,
And in our life alone does Nature live :
Ours is her wedding-garment, ours her shroud !
And would we aught behold, of higher worth,
Than that inanimate cold world allowed
To the poor loveless ever-anxious crowd,
Ah ! from the soul itself must issue forth
A light, a glory, a fair luminous cloud
Enveloping the Earth—
And from the soul itself must there be sent
A sweet and potent voice, of its own birth,
Of all sweet sounds the life and element !

V

O pure of heart ! thou need'st not ask of me
What this strong music in the soul may be !
What, and wherein it doth exist,
This light, this glory, this fair luminous mist,
This beautiful and beauty-making power.
Joy, virtuous Lady ! Joy that ne'er was given,
Save to the pure, and in their purest hour,
Life, and Life's effluence, cloud at once and shower,
Joy, Lady ! is the spirit and the power,
Which wedding Nature to us gives in dower

A new Earth and new Heaven,
Undreamt of by the sensual and the proud—
Joy is the sweet voice, Joy the luminous cloud—
We in ourselves rejoice !

And thence flows all that charms or ear or sight,
All melodies the echoes of that voice,
All colours a suffusion from that light.

VI

There was a time when, though my path was rough,
This joy within me dallied with distress,
And all misfortunes were but as the stuff
Whence Fancy made me dreams of happiness :

For hope grew round me, like the twining vine,
And fruits, and foliage, not my own, seemed mine.
But now afflictions bow me down to earth :
Nor care I that they rob me of my mirth ;
But oh ! each visitation
Suspends what nature gave me at my birth,
My shaping spirit of Imagination.

For not to think of what I needs must feel,
But to be still and patient, all I can ;
And haply by abstruse research to steal
From my own nature all the natural man—
This was my sole resource, my only plan :
Till that which suits a part infects the whole,
And now is almost grown the habit of my soul.

VII

Hence, viper thoughts, that coil around my mind,
Reality's dark dream !
I turn from you, and listen to the wind,
Which long has raved unnoticed. What a scream
Of agony by torture lengthened out

That lute sent forth ! Thou Wind, that rav'st without,
Bare crag, or mountain-tairn, or blasted tree,

Or pine-grove whither woodman never clomb,
Or lonely house, long held the witches' home,

Methinks were fitter instruments for thee,
Mad Lutanist ! who in this month of showers,
Of dark-brown gardens, and of peeping flowers,
Mak'st Devils' yule, with worse than wintry song,
The blossoms, buds, and timorous leaves among.

Thou Actor, perfect in all tragic sounds !
Thou mighty Poet, e'en to frenzy bold !

What tell'st thou now about ?
'Tis of the rushing of an host in rout,
With groans, of trampled men, with smarting wounds—
At once they groan with pain, and shudder with the cold !
But hush ! there is a pause of deepest silence !

And all that noise, as of a rushing crowd,
With groans, and tremulous shudderings—all is over—
It tells another tale, with sounds less deep and loud !
A tale of less affright,
And tempered with delight,
As Otway's self had framed the tender lay,—

'Tis of a little child
Upon a lonesome wild,

Not far from home, but she hath lost her way :
And now moans low in bitter grief and fear,
And now screams loud, and hopes to make her mother hear.

VIII

'Tis midnight, but small thoughts have I of sleep :
Full seldom may my friend such vigils keep !
Visit her, gentle Sleep ! with wings of healing,
And may this storm be but a mountain-birth,
May all the stars hang bright above her dwelling,
Silent as though they watched the sleeping Earth !
With light heart may she rise,
Gay fancy, cheerful eyes,

Joy lift her spirit, joy attune her voice ;
To her may all things live, from the pole to pole,
Their life the eddying of her living soul !
O simple spirit, guided from above,
Dear Lady ! friend devoutest of my choice,
Thus may'st thou ever, evermore rejoice.

To William Wordsworth

Friend of the Wise ! and Teacher of the Good !
Into my heart have I received that Lay
More than historic, that prophetic Lay
Wherein (high theme by thee first sung aright)
Of the foundations and the building up
Of a Human Spirit thou hast dared to tell
What may be told, to the understanding mind
Revealable ; and what within the mind
By vital breathings secret as the soul
Of vernal growth, oft quickens in the heart
Thoughts all too deep for words !—
Theme hard as high !

Of smiles spontaneous, and mysterious fears
(The first-born they of Reason and twin-birth),
Of tides obedient to external force,
And currents self-determined, as might seem,
Or by some inner Power ; of moments awful,
Now in thy inner life, and now abroad,
When power streamed from thee, and thy soul received
The light reflected, as a light bestowed—
Of fancies fair, and milder hours of youth,
Hyblean murmurs of poetic thought
Industrious in its joy, in vales and glens
Native or outland, lakes and famous hills !
Or on the lonely high-road, when the stars
Were rising ; or by secret mountain-streams,
The guides and the companions of thy way !
Of more than Fancy, of the Social Sense
Distending wide, and man beloved as man,

Where France in all her towns lay vibrating
Like some becalméd bark beneath the burst
Of Heaven's immediate thunder, when no cloud
Is visible, or shadow on the main.
For thou wert there, thine own brows garlanded,
Amid the tremor of a realm aglow,
Amid the mighty nation jubilant,
When from the general heart of human kind
Hope sprang forth like a full-born Diety !
—Of that dear Hope afflicted and struck down,
So summoned homeward, thenceforth calm and sure
From the dread watch-tower of man's absolute self,
With light unwaning on her eyes, to look
Far on—herself a glory to behold,
The Angel of the vision ! Then (last strain)
Of Duty, chosen Laws controlling choice,
Action and Joy !—An Orphic song indeed,
A song divine of high and passionate thoughts
To their own music chaunted !

O great Bard !

Ere yet that last strain dying awed the air,
With stedfast eye I viewed thee in the choir
Of ever-enduring men. The truly great
Have all one age, and from one visible space
Shed influence ! They, both in power and act,
Are permanent, and Time is not with them,
Save as it worketh for them, they in it.
Nor less a sacred Roll, than those of old,
And to be placed, as they, with gradual fame
Among the archives of mankind, thy work
Makes audible a linkéd lay of Truth,
Of Truth profound a sweet continuous lay,
Not learnt, but native, her own natural notes !
Ah ! as I listened with a heart forlorn,
The pulses of my being beat anew :
And even as Life returns upon the drowned,
Life's joy rekindling roused a throng of pains—
Keen pangs of Love, awakening as a babe

Turbulent, with an outcry in the heart ;
And Fears self-willed, that shunned the eye of Hope ;
And Hope that scarce would know itself from Fear ;
Sense of past Youth, and Manhood come in vain,
And Genius given, and Knowledge won in vain ;
And all which I had culled in wood-walks wild,
And all which patient toil had reared, and all,
Commune with thee had opened out—but flowers
Strewed on my corse, and borne upon my bier,
In the same coffin, for the self-same grave !
That way no more ! and ill beseems it me,

Who came a welcomer in herald's guise,
Singing of Glory, and Futurity,
To wander back on such unhealthful road,
Plucking the poisons of self-harm ! And ill
Such intertwine beseems triumphal wreaths
Strew'd before thy advancing !
Nor do thou,
Sage Bard ! impair the memory of that hour
Of thy communion with my nobler mind
By pity or grief, already felt too long !
Nor let my words import more blame than needs.
The tumult rose and ceased : for Peace is nigh
Where Wisdom's voice has found a listening heart.
Amid the howl of more than wintry storms,
The Halcyon hears the voice of vernal hours
Already on the wing.

Eve following eve,
Dear tranquil time, when the sweet sense of Home
Is sweetest ! moments for their own sake hailed
And more desired, more precious, for thy song,
In silence listening, like a devout child,
My soul lay passive, by thy various strain
Driven as in surges now beneath the stars,
With momentary stars of my own birth,
Fair constellated foam, still darting off

Into the darkness ; now a tranquil sea,
Outspread and bright, yet swelling to the moon.
And when—O Friend ! my comforter and guide !
Strong in thyself, and powerful to give strength !—
Thy long sustainéd Song finally closed,
And thy deep voice had ceased—yet thou thyself
Wert still before my eyes, and round us both
That happy vision of belovéd faces—
Scarce conscious, and yet conscious of its close
I sate, my being blended in one thought
(Thought was it ? or aspiration ? or resolve ?)
Absorbed, yet hanging still upon the sound—
And when I rose, I found myself in prayer.

Youth and Age

Verse, a Breeze 'mid blossoms straying,
Where hope clung feeding, like a bee—
Both were mine ! Life went a-maying

With Nature, Hope, and Poesy,
When I was young !
When I was young ?—Ah, woful When !
Ah ! for the Change 'twixt Now and Then !
This breathing House not built with hands,
This body that does me grievous wrong,
O'er æry Cliffs and glittering Sands,
How lightly then it flashed along :—
Like those trim skiffs, unknown of yore,
On winding lakes and rivers wide,
That ask no aid of Sail or Oar,
That fear no spite of Wind or Tide !
Nought cared this Body for wind or weather
When Youth and I lived in't together.
Flowers are lovely ; Love is flower-like ;
Friendship is a sheltering tree ;
O ! the Joys, that came down shower-like,
of Friendship, Love, and Liberty,

Ere I was old !
Ere I was old ? Ah woful ERE,
Which tells me, Youth's no longer here !
O Youth! for years so many and sweet,
'Tis known, that Thou and I were one,
I'll think it but a fond conceit—
It cannot be that Thou art gone !
Thy Vesper-bell hath not yet toll'd :—
And thou wert aye a Masker bold !
What strange Disguise hast now put on,
To make believe, that thou art gone ?
I see these Locks in silvery slips,
This drooping Gait, this altered Size :
But Springtide blossoms on thy Lips,
And Tears take sunshine from thine eyes !
Life is but Thought : so think I will
That Youth and I are House-mates still.
Dew-drops are the gems of morning,
But the tears of mournful eve !
Where no hope is, life's a warning
That only serves to make us grieve,
When we are old :
That only serves to make us grieve
With oft and tedious taking-leave,
Like some poor nigh-related guest,
That may not rudely be dismist ;
Yet hath outstay'd his welcome while,
And tells the jest without the smile.

revisited his memories of childhood in order to soothe his feelings and provoke his imagination. Coleridge, on the other hand, was raised in London, "pent 'mid cloisters dim," and questions Wordsworth's easy identification of childhood with a kind of automatic, original happiness; instead, in this poem he says that, as a child, he "saw naught lovely but the stars and sky" and seems to feel the lingering effects of that alienation. In this poem, we see how the pain of this alienation has strengthened Coleridge's wish that his child enjoy an idyllic Wordsworthian upbringing "by lakes and sandy shores, beneath the crags / Of ancient mountain, and beneath the clouds..." Rather than seeing the link between childhood and nature as an inevitable, Coleridge seems to perceive it as a fragile, precious, and extraordinary connection, one of which he himself was deprived.

In expressing its central themes, "Frost at Midnight" relies on a highly personal idiom whereby the reader follows the natural progression of the speaker's mind as he sits up late one winter night thinking. His idle observation gives the reader a quick impression of the scene, from the "silent ministry" of the frost to the cry of the owl and the sleeping child. Coleridge uses language that indicates the immediacy of the scene to draw in the reader; for instance, the speaker cries "Hark!" upon hearing the owl, as though he were surprised by its call. The objects surrounding the speaker become metaphors for the work of the mind and the imagination, so that the fluttering film on the fire grate plunges him into the recollection of his childhood. His memory of feeling trapped in the schoolhouse naturally brings him back into his immediate surroundings with a surge of love and sympathy for his son. His final meditation on his son's future becomes mingled with his Romantic interpretation of nature and its role in the child's imagination, and his consideration of the objects of nature brings him back to the frost and the icicles, which, forming and shining in silence, mirror the silent way in which the world works upon the mind; this revisitation of winter's frosty forms brings the poem full circle.

"Kubla Khan"

Summary

The speaker describes the "stately pleasure-dome" built in Xanadu according to the decree of Kubla Khan, in the place where Alph, the sacred river, ran "through caverns measureless to man / Down to a sunless sea." Walls and towers were raised around "twice five miles of fertile ground," filled with beautiful gardens and forests. A "deep romantic chasm" slanted down a green hill, occasionally spewing forth a violent and powerful burst of water, so great that it flung boulders up with it "like rebounding hail." The river ran five miles through the woods, finally sinking "in tumult to a lifeless ocean." Amid that tumult, in the place "as holy and enchanted / As e'er beneath a waning moon was haunted / By woman wailing to her demon-lover," Kubla heard "ancestral voices" bringing prophesies of war. The pleasure-dome's shadow floated on the waves, where the mingled sounds of the fountain and the caves could be heard. "It was a miracle of rare device," the speaker says, "A sunny pleasure-dome with caves of ice!"

The speaker says that he once saw a "damsel with a dulcimer," an Abyssinian maid who played her dulcimer and sang "of Mount Abora." He says that if he could revive "her symphony and song" within him, he would rebuild the pleasure-dome out of music, and all who heard him would cry "Beware!" of "His flashing eyes, his floating hair!" The hearers would circle him thrice and close their eyes with "holy dread," knowing that he had tasted honeydew, "and drunk the milk of Paradise."

Form

The chant-like, musical incantations of "Kubla Khan" result from Coleridge's masterful use of iambic tetrameter and alternating rhyme schemes. The first stanza is written in tetrameter with a rhyme scheme of ABAABCCDEDE, alternating between staggered rhymes and couplets. The second stanza expands into tetrameter and follows roughly the same rhyming pattern, also expanded— ABAABCCD DFFGGHIIHJJ. The third stanza tightens into tetrameter and rhymes ABABCC. The fourth stanza continues the tetrameter of the third and rhymes ABCCBDEDEFGFFFGHHG.

Commentary

Along with "The Rime of the Ancient Mariner," "Kubla Khan" is one of Coleridge's most famous and enduring poems. The story of its composition is also one of the most famous in the history of English poetry. As the poet explains in the short preface to this poem, he had fallen asleep after taking "an anodyne" prescribed "in consequence of a slight disposition" (this is a euphemism for opium, to which Coleridge was known to be addicted). Before falling asleep, he had been reading a story in which Kubla Khan commanded the building of a new palace; Coleridge claims that while he slept, he had a fantastic vision and composed simultaneously—while sleeping—some two or three hundred lines of poetry, "if that indeed can be called composition in which all the images rose up before him as things, with a parallel production of the correspondent expressions, without any sensation or conscious effort."

Waking after about three hours, the poet seized a pen and began writing furiously; however, after copying down the first three stanzas of his dreamt poem—the first three stanzas of the current poem as we know it—he was interrupted by a "person on business from Porlock," who detained him for an hour. After this interruption, he was unable to recall the rest of the vision or the poetry he had composed in his opium dream. It is thought that the final stanza of the poem, thematizing the idea of the lost vision through the figure of the "damsel with a dulcimer" and the milk of Paradise, was written post-interruption. The mysterious person from Porlock is one of the most notorious and enigmatic figures in Coleridge's biography; no one knows who he was or why he disturbed the poet or what he wanted or, indeed, whether any of Coleridge's story is actually true. But the person from Porlock has become a metaphor for the malicious interruptions the world throws in the way of inspiration and genius, and "Kubla Khan," strange and ambiguous as it is, has become what is perhaps the definitive statement on the obstruction and thwarting of the visionary genius.

Regrettably, the story of the poem's composition, while thematically rich in and of itself, often overshadows the poem proper, which is one of Coleridge's most haunting and beautiful. The first three stanzas are products of pure imagination: The pleasure-dome of Kubla Khan is not a useful metaphor for anything in particular (though in the context of the poem's history, it becomes a metaphor for the unbuilt monument of imagination); however, it is a fantastically prodigious descriptive act.

The poem becomes especially evocative when, after the second stanza, the meter suddenly tightens; the resulting lines are terse and solid, almost beating out the sound of the war drums ("The shadow of the dome of pleasure / Floated midway on the waves...").

The fourth stanza states the theme of the poem as a whole (though "Kubla Khan" is almost impossible to consider as a unified whole, as its parts are so sharply divided). The speaker says that he once had a vision of the damsel singing of Mount Abora; this vision becomes a metaphor for Coleridge's vision of the 300-hundred-line masterpiece he never completed.

The speaker insists that if he could only "revive" within him "her symphony and song," he would recreate the pleasure-dome out of music and words, and take on the persona of the magician or visionary. His hearers would recognize the dangerous power of the vision, which would manifest itself in his "flashing eyes" and "floating hair." But, awestruck, they would nonetheless dutifully take part in the ritual, recognizing that "he on honey-dew hath fed, / And drunk the milk of Paradise."

"Dejection: An Ode"

Summary

The speaker recalls a poem that tells the tale of Sir Patrick Spence: In this poem, the moon takes on a certain strange appearance that presages the coming of a storm. The speaker declares that if the author of the poem possessed a sound understanding of weather, then a storm will break on this night as well, for the moon looks now as it did in the poem. The speaker wishes ardently for a storm to erupt, for the violence of the squall might cure his numb feeling. He says that he feels only a "dull pain," "a grief without a pang"—a constant deadening of all his feelings. Speaking to a woman whom he addresses as "O Lady," he admits that he has been gazing at the western sky all evening, able to see its beauty but unable fully to feel it. He says that staring at the green sky will never raise his spirits, for no "outward forms" can generate feelings: Emotions can only emerge from within.

According to the speaker, "we receive but what we give": the soul itself must provide the light by which we may hope to see nature's true beauty--a beauty not given to the common crowd of human beings ("the poor loveless ever-anxious crowd"). Calling the Lady "pure of heart," the speaker says that she already knows about the light and music of the soul, which is Joy. Joy, he says, marries us to nature, thereby giving us "a new Earth and new Heaven, / Undreamt of by the sensual and the proud."

The speaker insists that there was a time when he was full of hope, when every tribulation was simply the material with which "fancy made me dreams of happiness." But now his afflictions press him to the earth; he does not mind the decline of his mirth, but he cannot bear the corresponding degeneration of his imagination, which is the source of his creativity and his understanding of the human condition, that which enables him to construct "from my own nature all the natural man." Hoping to escape the "viper thoughts" that coil around his mind, the speaker turns his attention to the howling wind that has begun to blow. He thinks of the world as an instrument played by a musician, who spins out of the wind a "worse than wintry song." This melody first calls to mind the rush of an army on the field; quieting, it then evokes a young girl, lost and alone.

It is midnight, but the speaker has "small thoughts" of sleep. However, he hopes that his friend the Lady will be visited by "gentle Sleep" and that she will wake with joyful thoughts and "light heart." Calling the Lady the "friend devoutest of my choice," the speaker wishes that she might "ever, evermore rejoice."

Form

The long ode stanzas of "Dejection" are metered in iambic lines ranging in length from trimeter to pentameter. The rhymes alternate between bracketed rhymes (ABBA) and couplets (CC) with occasional exceptions.

Commentary

In this poem, Coleridge continues his sophisticated philosophical exploration of the relationship between man and nature, positing as he did in "The Nightingale" that human feelings and the forms of nature are essentially separate. Just as the speaker insisted in the earlier poem that the nightingale's song should not be called melancholy simply because it sounded so to a melancholy poet, he insists here that the beauty of the sky before the storm does not have the power to fill him with joy, for the source of human feeling is within. Only when the individual has access to that source, so that joy shines from him like a light, is he able to see the beauty of nature and to respond to it. (As in "Frost in Midnight," the city-raised Coleridge insists on a sharper demarcation between the mind and nature than the country-raised Wordsworth would ever have done.)

Coleridge blames his desolate numbness for sapping his creative powers and leaving him without his habitual method of understanding human nature. Despite his insistence on the separation between the mind and the world, Coleridge nevertheless continues to find metaphors for his own feelings in nature: His dejection is reflected in the gloom of the night as it awaits the storm.

"Dejection" was written in 1802 but was originally drafted in the form of a letter to Sara Hutchinson, the woman Coleridge loved. The much longer original version of the poem contained many of the same elements as "The Nightingale" and "Frost at Midnight," including the same meditation on his children and their natural education. This version also referred explicitly to "Sara" (replaced in the later version by "Lady") and "William" (a clear reference to Wordsworth). Coleridge's strict revision process shortened and tightened the poem, depersonalizing it, but the earlier draft hints at just how important the poem's themes were to Coleridge personally and indicates that the feelings expressed were the poet's true beliefs about his own place in the world.

A side note: The story of Sir Patrick Spence, to which the poet alludes in the first stanza, is an ancient Scottish ballad about a sailor who drowns with a boatload of Scottish noblemen, sailing on orders from the king but against his own better judgment. It contains lines that refer to the moon as a predictor of storms, which Coleridge quotes as an epigraph for his ode: "Late, late yestreen I saw the new Moon / With the old Moon in her arms; / And I fear, I fear, my Master dear! / We shall have a deadly storm."

The Rime of Ancient Mariner

In the poem's first line, we meet its protagonist, "an ancient Mariner." He stops one of three people on their way to a wedding celebration. The leader of the group, the Wedding Guest, tries to resist being stopped by the strange old man with the "long grey beard and glittering eye." He explains that he is on his way to enjoy the wedding merriment; he is the closest living relative to the groom, and the festivities have already begun. Still, the Ancient Mariner takes his hand and begins his story. The Wedding Guest has no choice but to sit down on a rock to listen.

The Ancient Mariner explains that one clear and bright day, he set out sail on a ship full of happy seamen. They sailed along smoothly until they reached the equator. Suddenly, the sounds of the wedding interrupt the Ancient Mariner's story. The Wedding Guest beats his chest impatiently as the blushing bride enters the reception hall and music plays. However, he is compelled to continue listening to the Ancient Mariner, who goes on with his tale. As soon as the ship reached the equator, a terrible storm hit and forced the ship southwards. The wind blew with such force that the ship pitched down in the surf as though it were fleeing an enemy. Then the sailors reached a calm patch of sea that was "wondrous cold", full of snow and glistening green icebergs as tall as the ship's mast. The sailors were the only living things in this frightening, enclosed world where the ice made terrible groaning sounds that echoed all around. Finally, an Albatross emerged from the mist, and the sailors revered it as a sign of good luck, as though it were a "Christian soul" sent by God to save them. No sooner than the sailors fed the Albatross did the ice break apart, allowing the captain to steer out of the freezing world. The wind picked up again, and continued for nine days. All the while, the Albatross followed the ship, ate the food the sailors gave it, and played with them. At this point, the Wedding Guest notices that the Ancient Mariner looks at once grave and crazed. He exclaims: "God save thee, ancient Mariner! / From the fiends that plague thee thus!- / Why lookst thou so?" The Ancient Mariner responds that he shot the Albatross with his crossbow.

Analysis

In editions where it is included, the Latin epigraph serves as a semi-thesis for the poem. It is a Latin quote from Burnet's "Archaeologiae Philosophicae" (1692), which Coleridge translates as follows:

I readily believe that there are more invisible than visible Natures in the universe. But who will explain for us the family of all these beings, and the ranks and relations and distinguishing features and functions of each? What do they do? What places do they inhabit? The human mind has always sought the knowledge of these things, but never attained it. Meanwhile I do not deny that it is helpful sometimes to contemplate in the mind, as on a tablet, the image of a greater and better world, lest the intellect, habituated to the petty things of daily life, narrow itself and sink wholly into trivial thoughts. But at the same time we must be watchful for the truth and keep a sense of proportion, so that we may distinguish the certain from the uncertain, day from night.

Burnet, who authored the original quote, begins by acknowledging that "invisible natures" such as spirits, ghosts, and angels exist; moreover, there are more of them than their readily-perceivable counterparts such as humans and animals. However, "invisible natures" are difficult to classify, because people perceive them only occasionally. Burnet asserts that while it is important to strive to understand the ethereal and ideal, one must stay grounded in the temporal, imperfect world. By maintaining a balance between these two worlds, one avoids becoming too idealistic or too hopeless, and can eventually reach the truth. By prefacing "The Rime of the Ancient Mariner" with this quote, Coleridge asks the reader to pay careful attention to the near-constant interactions between the spiritual and temporal worlds in the poem. Like the Ancient Mariner, the reader must navigate these interactions and worlds in order to understand the truth ingrained in the poem. The Ancient Mariner as a character can be identified with a number of archetypes: the wise man, the writer, the traitor, and more. The epigraph suggests that regardless of with whom the reader associates the Ancient Mariner, there is great importance in the way in which he manages (or fails) to balance the spiritual and temporal worlds.

From the Ancient Mariner's first interaction with the Wedding Guest, we know there is more to him than the fact that he appears unnaturally old. He has a "glittering eye" that immediately unnerves the Wedding Guest, who presumes he is mad and calls him a "grey-beard loon." Yet there is more to his "glittering eye" than mere madness, as he is able to compel the Wedding Guest to listen to his story with the fascination of a three-year-old child. Although he is clearly human, the Ancient Mariner seems to have a touch of the otherworldly in him.

Throughout Part 1, the temporal world interjects itself into the storytelling haze in which the Ancient Mariner captures the Wedding Guest and reader. For example, just as the Ancient Mariner begins his tale, the joyful sound of a bassoon at the wedding reception distracts the Wedding Guest. He "beat[s] his breast" in frustration that he is missing the festivities. In light of Burnet's quote, one can say that the temporal world with its "petty" pleasures tempts the Wedding Guest. He is of that world - indeed he is next of kin to the bridegroom and therefore intimate with the festival's worldly joy. Meanwhile, the Ancient Mariner cannot enjoy the temporal world because he is condemned to perpetually relive the story of his past.

In the Ancient Mariner's story itself, the spiritual and temporal worlds are confounded the moment the sailors cross the equator. Suddenly the natural world - which is closely connected to the spiritual world - makes the sailors lose control of their course. The storm drives them into an icy world that is called "the land of mist and snow" throughout the rest of the poem. The word "rime" can mean "ice", and can also be interpreted as an alternate spelling of the word "rhyme." Therefore, as much as the poem is the rhymed story of the Ancient Mariner, it is also the tale of the "land of mist and snow": the "rime", where the Ancient Mariner's troubles begin. By calling the poem "The Rime of the Ancient Mariner," Coleridge equates the "rhyme" or tale with the actual "rime" or icy world. As we learn at the story's end, the Ancient Mariner is condemned to feel perpetual pangs of terror that force him to tell his "rhyme," a fate just as confining and terrifying as the "rime" itself is initially for the sailors.

Summary and Analysis of Part 2

The ship sailed northward into the Pacific Ocean, and although the sun shone during the day and the wind remained strong, the mist held fast. The other sailors were angry with the Ancient Mariner for killing the Albatross, which they believed had saved them from the icy world by summoning the wind: "Ah wretch! Said they, the bird to slay / That made the breeze to blow!" Then the mist disappeared and the sun shone particularly brightly, "like God's own head." The sailors suddenly changed their opinion. They decided that the Albatross must have brought the must, and praise the Ancient Mariner for having killed it and rid them of the mist: "Twas right, said they, such birds to slay, / That bring the fog and mist."

The ship sailed along merrily until it entered an uncharted part of the ocean, and the wind disappeared. The ship could not move, and sat "As idle as a painted ship / Upon a painted ocean." Then the sun became unbearably hot just as the sailors ran out of water, leading up to the most famous lines in the poem: "Water, water, every where, / And all the boards did shrink; / Water, water, every where, / Nor any drop to drink." The ocean became a horrifying place; the water churned with "slimy" creatures, and at night, eerie fires seemed to burn on the ocean's surface. Some of the sailors dreamed that an evil spirit had followed them from the icy world, and they all suffered from a thirst so terrible that they could not speak. To brand the Ancient Mariner for his crime and place the guilt on him and him alone, the sailors hung the Albatross's dead carcass around his neck.

Analysis

Coleridge introduces the idea of responsibility in Part 2. The sailors have an urge to pin whatever happens to them on the Ancient Mariner, since he killed the Albatross for no good reason. It seems more important to them to make him claim responsibility for their fate than what their fate actually is; first, they curse him for making the wind disappear, and then they praise him for making the mist disappear. Coleridge may be poking fun at allegory in this section. He told reviewers after the poem's release that he did not intend for it to have a moral, even though when reading the poem, one is hard-pressed not to discern a moral message. By having the sailors switch from blame to praise and back to blame again, Coleridge mocks those quick to judge. To go back to the preface, the sailors represent those too eager to discern the "certain" from the "uncertain", preferring to see things in black-and-white terms.

The major theme of liminality emerges more fully in Part 2. In literature - and especially Romantic literature - a liminal space is where plot twists occur or things begin to go awry. The Romantic hero, although he begins confident and with a clear mission, stumbles into a bewildering space where he struggles, and from which he emerges wizened and saddened. Traditionally these places are borderlines, such as the edge of a forest or a shoreline. Recall from Part 1 that the ship's course is sunny and smooth until it crosses the equator and the storm begins.

The equator is the boundary between the earth's hemispheres, and is therefore an extreme example of a liminal space. The icy world or "rime" itself is also a compelling liminal space. At first it seems to be the epitome of the temporal; there are no visible creatures there besides the sailors, whose senses it assaults with huge icy forms, terrifying sounds, and bewildering echoes. But it is equally a spiritual place, the dwelling of a very powerful spirit who wreaks havoc on the sailors to punish the Ancient Mariner for killing its beloved Albatross. The icy world represents a tenuous balance between the temporal and spiritual. The physicality of the icy world represents its tenuousness; in it, water exists in all its three phases: ice, water, and mist. The boundaries between the temporal and the spiritual, what Burnet calls the "certain and uncertain" in the epigraph, are as indistinct there as the physical state of water. It is not necessarily the loudness, coldness, or desolateness of the icy world that makes it so terrifying. Rather, it is the fact that nothing there is easily definable. In light of the epigraph, it represents the balance that one must seek between the "certain and uncertain," which will ultimately lead to the truth. However, the icy world as a symbol suggests that this path to enlightenment is equally fascinating and terrifying.

The most famous lines in "The Rime of the Ancient Mariner" are unquestionably: "Water, water, every where, / Nor any drop to drink." The sailors are punished for the Ancient Mariner's mistake with deprivation made worse by the fact that what they need so badly - water - is all around them, but is entirely undrinkable. Since the poem's publication, these lines have come into common usage to refer to situations in which one is surrounded by the thing one desires, but is denied it nevertheless.

In light of the epigraph, the Ancient Mariner shoots the Albatross because he, like humans throughout time, wants to learn about the spiritual world. The Albatross is an animal, but it is akin to a spirit, and its murder wreaks spiritual havoc on the sailors. We are given no reason why the Ancient Mariner shoots the Albatross, and he does so without premeditation. It is as though he needs to bring the beauty of the spiritual world (embodied in the Albatross) down to the temporal world in order to understand it. He takes the bird out of the air and onto the deck, where it proves to be mortal indeed. After that, the spiritual world begins to punish the Ancient Mariner and the other sailors by making all elements of the temporal world painful. They are thirsty and sunburned, cannot sail for lack of wind, and are threatened by creatures and strange lights in the water. The sailors add to the Ancient Mariner's physical punishment when they hang the Albatross around his neck, giving him a physical burden to remind him of the spiritual burden of sin he carries. They too punish him physically for his spiritual depravity.

Summary and Analysis of Part 3

The sailors were trapped in their ship on the windless ocean for some time, and eventually became delirious with thirst. One day, the Ancient Mariner noticed something approaching from the West. As it moved closer, the sailors realised it was a ship, but no one could cry out because their throats were dry and their lips badly sunburned. The Ancient Mariner bit his own arm and sipped the blood so that he could wet his mouth enough to cry out: "A sail! A sail!" Mysteriously, the approaching ship managed to turn its course to them, even though there was still no wind. Suddenly, it crossed the path of the setting sun, and its masts made the sun look as though it was imprisoned, "As if through a dungeon-grate he peered." The Ancient Mariner's initial joy turned to dread as he noticed that the ship was approaching menacingly quickly, and had sails that looked like cobwebs. The ship came near enough for the Ancient Mariner to see who manned it: Death, embodied in a naked man, and The Night-mare Life-in-Death, embodied in a naked woman.

The latter was eerily beautiful, with red lips, golden hair, and skin "as white as leprosy." Death and Life-in-Death were gambling with dice for the Ancient Mariner's soul, and Life-in-Death won. She whistled three times just as the last of the sun sank into the ocean; night fell in an instant, and the ghost ship sped away, though its crew's whispers could be heard long after it was out of sight. The crescent moon rose above the ship with "one bright star" just inside its bottom rim, and all at once, the sailors turned towards the Ancient Mariner and cursed him with their eyes. Then all two hundred of them dropped dead without a sound. The Ancient Mariner watched each sailor's soul zoom out of his body like the arrow he shot at the Albatross: "And every soul, it passed me by, / Like the whiz of my cross-bow!"

Analysis

In Part 3, the poem becomes more fantastical as the spiritual world continues to punish the Ancient Mariner and his fellow sailors. Although later in the poem Coleridge reveals that a specific spirit is responsible for their demise, it seems as though the spiritual world as a whole is punishing the men, using the natural world as its weapon: the wind refuses to blow, the ocean churns with dreadful creatures, and the sun's relentless heat chars the men. The ghost ship, however, is separate from the natural world - it sails without wind, and its inhabitants are spirits. Death and Life-in-Death are allegorical figures who become frighteningly real for the sailors, especially the Ancient Mariner, whose soul Life-in-Death "wins", thereby dooming him to a fate worse than death. Even those sailors whose souls go to hell seem freer than the Ancient Mariner; while their souls fly unencumbered out of their bodies, he is destined to be trapped in his indefinitely - a living hell.

Life-in-Death, who takes on the form of an alluring naked woman, represents perpetual temptation. Because she wins the Ancient Mariner's soul, he is doomed to die only when he has paid his due...perhaps never. As we learn later, the Ancient Mariner is cursed to continually feel the agonizing compulsion to tell his tale to others; although telling the tale allows him temporary relief, he may never be free. First, he and the sailors are denied the satisfaction of drinking; now the Ancient Mariner will be denied the satisfaction of being able to die. His spirit is trapped in his own body, in an excruciating state of limbo - the realm of Life-in-Death. His "glittering eye" suggests more than madness; it is also a synecdoche representing his soul, which longs to be released from living death. It yearns to fly out of his body like the two hundred other sailors' souls did. In fact, when the sailors' souls are released, they fly past the Ancient Mariner with the same sound as the arrow he shot at the Albatross. Initially, the Ancient Mariner is relieved to have survived his shipmates, but in retrospect the sound tantalizes him, as it reminds him that his impulsive sin is the reason for his torture.

Part 3 introduces the theme of imprisonment. As we have said, the Ancient Mariner is doomed to be trapped in a state of deathlike life; his own immortal body is his prison. The ship itself is a prison for the sailors when there is no wind to carry it. Even before the ghost ship comes near enough for the Ancient Mariner to see its crew, it seems to imprison the very sun with its masts. This symbolizes Death and Life-in-Death's level of power; they have so much sway over the natural world and its inhabitants that they can jail the sun itself. The natural world seems to have this power, as well: the sailors are trapped in the "rime" by impenetrable ice until the Albatross sets them free. For this reason, many have interpreted the Albatross as Christ, and the Ancient Mariner as the archetypal sinner.

The Albatross has the power to guide the sailors just as Christ has the ability to guide men's souls to heaven. By sinning on impulse, the Ancient Mariner ruins his chances at salvation, and is condemned to the eternal limbo of Life-in-Death. This interpretation implies that every time a person sins, he destroys his relationship with Christ and his chances of reaching heaven, and must redeem himself through acts of atonement. Just as people wear crucifixes around their necks to remind them of Christ's sacrifice and their responsibility to him, the sailors hang the Albatross around the Ancient Mariner's neck to remind him of his sin.

Summary and Analysis of Part 4

The Wedding Guest proclaims that he fears the Ancient Mariner because he is unnaturally skinny, so tanned and wrinkled that he resembles the sand, and possesses a "glittering eye." The Ancient Mariner assures him that he has not returned from the dead; he is the only sailor who did not die on his ship, but rather drifted in lonely, scorching agony. His only living company was the plethora of "slimy" creatures in the ocean.

He tried to pray, but could produce only a muffled curse. For seven days and nights the Ancient Mariner remained alone on the ship. The dead sailors, who miraculously did not rot, continued to curse him with their open eyes. Only the sight of beautiful water snakes frolicking beside the boat lifted the Ancient Mariner's spirits. They cheered him so much that he blessed them "unawares"; finally, he was able to pray. At that very moment, the Albatross fell off his neck and sank heavily into the ocean.

Analysis

As the Ancient Mariner drifts on the ocean, the natural world becomes more threatening. His surroundings - the ship, the ocean, and the creatures within it - are "rotting" in the heat and sun, but he is the one who is rotten on the inside. Meanwhile the sailors' corpses refuse to rot, and their open eyes curse him continuously, giving the Ancient Mariner a visible manifestation of the living death that awaits him. He will age, but his body will never rot enough to release his soul; his eye will glitter forever with the horror of damnation. As the Ancient Mariner floats, he becomes delirious, unable to escape his overwhelming loneliness even by sleeping: "I closed my lids, and kept them close, / And the balls like pulses beat; / For the sky and the sea, and the sea and the sky / Lay like a load on my weary eye..." His depravity has even denied him the comfort of prayer.

Ironically, it is the "slimy", "rotten" creatures themselves that finally comfort the Ancient Mariner and allow him to pray. Until this moment, Coleridge's imagery has underscored the overbearing nature of the Ancient Mariner's environment: it is hot, salty, pungent, and "rotten." However, his surroundings - and the imagery that accompanies them - turn cool in the moonlight. Coleridge compares the moonlight to a gentle frost, connecting it to the serenity of the "rime": "[The moon's] beams bemocked the sultry main, / Like April hoar-frost spread." Aglow in the moonlight, the sea creatures begin frolicking, rather than churning nastily; creatures of a beautiful, supernatural world, they "moved in tracks of shining white, / And when they reared, the elfish light / Fell off in hoary flakes...I watched their rich attire; / Blue, glossy green, and velvet black, / They coiled and swam; and every track / Was a flash of golden fire." Whereas Coleridge's descriptions of the ghost ship, sun, and sailors are replete with spare, harsh imagery, he describes the water-snakes in decadent, lush terms. Only when the Ancient Mariner is able to appreciate the beauty of the natural world is he granted the ability to pray - and, it is implied, eventually redeem himself. Earlier in the work, the desiccated setting represented the Ancient Mariner's moral drought, but the moment he begins to view the natural world benevolently, his spiritual thirst is quenched: "A spring of love gushed from my heart." As a sign that his burden has been lifted, the Albatross - the burden of sin - falls from his neck: it is no longer his cross to bear.

Summary and Analysis of Part 5

After praying, the Ancient Mariner thanked the Virgin Mary for finally allowing him to sleep. He dreamed that the buckets on the ship were filled with dew, and awoke to the sound of the falling rain. He drank and drank after so many days of thirst, and became so lightheaded that he thought he was a ghost. Suddenly he heard a loud wind far off, and the sky lit up with darting "fire-flags" that could be interpreted as lightning, aurora borealis, or "St. Elmo's Fire" (electricity visible in the atmosphere that sailors consider a sign of bad luck). The rain poured from a single cloud, as did an unbroken stream of lightning. The ship began to sail, although there was still no wind. Just then, all the dead men stood up and went about their jobs as a mute, ghostly crew.

The Wedding Guest proclaims again: "I fear thee, Ancient Mariner!" but the Ancient Mariner quickly assures him that the dead sailors were not evil. At dawn, they even gathered around the mast and sang so beautifully that they sounded like an orchestra. When they stopped singing, the ship's sails sang instead. The ship sailed on miraculously in the absence of wind, moved instead by the spirit that had followed it from the icy world. Once the ship reached the equator and the sun was directly overhead, it stopped moving and the sails stopped singing. Then it began to rock back and forth uneasily until it suddenly jolted, causing the Ancient Mariner to faint. He lay for an indeterminate period of time on the ship's deck, during which he heard two voices. The first voice swore on Christ that he was the man who betrayed the Albatross that loved him, and that the spirit from the icy world also loved the Albatross: "The spirit who bideth by himself / In the land of mist and snow, / He loved the bird that loved the man / Who shot him with his bow." The second voice, softer than the first, declared that the Ancient Mariner would continue to pay for his crime: "The man hath penance done, / And penance more will do."

Analysis

Until the end of Part 5, it seems as though the Ancient Mariner is redeemed. Not only is he allowed to sleep, but it finally rains, and his thirst is quenched. Since physical drought and thirst have represented the Ancient Mariner's moral depravity up until this point, it is implied that the abundant rain symbolizes his redemption. According to a Christian interpretation, the rain signifies that he is being baptized anew as a righteous servant of Christ who respects God's creatures. Even though terrifying things continue to happen all around him - a storm, lightning, thunder - the Ancient Mariner is awed by them, instead of fearful of them. The natural world is no less forceful or imposing than it was previously, but it is now benevolent. Part 5 also sees an end to the Ancient Mariner's loneliness, as the sailors 'awaken' to sail the ship; they and the ship itself sing beautiful music, and some spiritual force moves the ship along its course even though the air is still. Again, only when the ship crosses a boundary - the equator - does confusion return; the Ancient Mariner is knocked unconscious, and the reader begins to doubt whether he will actually be redeemed.

The voices confirm that it is indeed a specific spirit punishing the Ancient Mariner. The text's suggestions of sin, baptism, redemption, and other Christian themes shifts towards a more pagan understanding of the story's moral intricacies. A spirit that inhabits the icy world of the "rime" loved the Albatross - perhaps kept it as a pet - and is making the Ancient Mariner pay for murdering it. In the 1817 version of the poem, we are told that the two voices that the Ancient Mariner hears are spirits. Perhaps they are kin to the spirit that is punishing the Ancient Mariner, or are even taking part in his punishment. It is also possible, however, that they, like all of the supernatural elements of the Ancient Mariner's story, are merely figments of his imagination. That Coleridge leaves their identity somewhat open-ended harkens back to Burnet's musings on "invisible Natures"; humans cannot classify spirits, and therefore cannot really know them. Likewise, the Ancient Mariner - and the reader - cannot define what kind of spirits are speaking, or if they are indeed spirits at all. Burnet's statements are applicable to all humans. Furthermore, the reader is as subject to Coleridge's whims as his protagonist, and therefore cannot know any more than him. As humans - and therefore sinners - we can all identify with the Ancient Mariner, and are thus equally implicated in his crime.

Summary and Analysis of Part 6

Part 6 opens with a dialogue between the two voices: the first voice, the Ancient Mariner says, asked the second voice to remind it what moved the Ancient Mariner's ship along so fast, and the second voice postulated that the moon must be controlling the ocean. The first voice asked again what could be driving the ship, and the second voice replied that the air was pushing the ship from behind in lieu of wind. After this declaration, the voices disappeared. The Ancient Mariner awoke at night to find the dead sailors clustered on the deck, again cursing him with their eyes. They mesmerized him, until suddenly the spell broke and they too disappeared.

The Ancient Mariner, however, was not relieved; he knew that the dead men would come back to haunt him over and over again. Just then, a wind began to blow and the ship sailed quickly and smoothly until the Ancient Mariner could see the shore of his own country. As moonlight illuminated the glassy harbor, lighthouse, and church he sobbed and prayed, happy to be either alive or in heaven. Suddenly, crimson shapes began to rise from the water in front of the ship. When the Ancient Mariner looked down at the deck, he saw an angel standing over each dead man's corpse. The angels waved their hands silently, serving as beacons to guide the ship into port. The Ancient Máriner heard voices: a Pilot, the Pilot's boy, and a Hermit were approaching the ship in a boat. The Ancient Mariner was overjoyed to see other living human beings and wanted the Hermit to wipe him clean of his sin, to "wash away the Albatross's blood."

Analysis

In Part 6, the two voices offer a narrative and stylistic break in the poem. Whereas before the text was unbroken, their speech is structured much as in the script of a play. The voices are also omniscient in that they know everything that has happened up until now, and are able to offer the Ancient Mariner a more complete explanation of his situation. The manner in which the voices are presented lends a didactic, narratorial feel to their words. The voices leave because, like the Wedding Guest, they have somewhere to be; the second voice urges the first: "Fly, brother, fly! More high, more high! / Or we shall be belated." Yet unlike the Wedding Guest, the voices are not riveted by the Ancient Mariner's tale and can continue on to their destination after briefly stopping to consider him. They are like the two other guests walking with the Wedding Guest when the Ancient Mariner stops him; while his tale may interest them, they are not compelled to hear it.

When the Ancient Mariner is out in the open ocean, Coleridge's imagery is heavily visual and tactile, but also focuses on sound: the noises of the wedding merriment interrupt the Ancient Mariner's tale, "voices in a swound" fill the "rime", there is a terrible silence that abounds when the men are unable to speak, and the glorious music created by the ship and the sailors implies that fortune has once again smiled on the Ancient Mariner. Indeed, in Part 6 sounds are especially important. We know of the two voices only because they speak; they have no visible presence. If they are indeed spirits, then they are discernable to humans only because of the sounds that they make. Furthermore, the Ancient Mariner hears his rescuers before he sees them, although he does not cry out to them. Coleridge's focus on sound connects us to the fact that the Ancient Mariner is telling a story to the Wedding Guest. While readers must view the story on the page, the tale is being told aloud, and is meant to be passed on in this manner, much like a sermon.

As the ship enters the harbor, we once again get the sense that the Ancient Mariner will be redeemed, although we know that he is doomed to be haunted by the dead men indefinitely: The ship is now in the safety of the harbor, and home is in sight; two hundred angels, one for each dead man, silently guide the ship into shore, acting as beacons that attract the Ancient Mariner's rescuers. Not only are the Pilot and Pilot's Boy coming to rescue the Ancient Mariner, but a Hermit has come out of the woods to help them. By definition, a hermit is someone who lives in seclusion in a natural setting, making the natural world his shrine and living place. He does not venture out into society, and certainly not on the ocean. The Hermit that the Ancient Mariner meets is joyous and social, urging the Pilot and Pilot's Boy on even though they are afraid of the tattered ship. Although at the end of Part 6 the Ancient Mariner knows that he will soon be home and believes that the Hermit can absolve him of his sin, the reader can't help but suspect that more horror is in store.

Summary and Analysis of Part 7

The Ancient Mariner was cheered by the Hermit's singing. He admired the way the Hermit lived and prayed alone in the woods, but also "love[d] to talk with mariners." As they neared the ship, the Pilot and the Hermit wondered where the angels - which they had thought were merely beacon lights - had gone. The Hermit remarked on how strange the ship looked with its misshapen boards and flimsy sails. The Pilot was afraid, but the Hermit encouraged him to steer the boat closer. Just as the boat reached the ship, a terrible noise came from under the water, and the ship sank straightaway. The men saved the Ancient Mariner even though they thought he was dead; after all, he appeared "like one that hath been seven days drowned."

The boat spun in the whirlpool created by the ship's sinking, and all was quiet save the loud sound echoing off of a hill. The Ancient Mariner moved his lips and began to row the boat, terrifying the other men; the Pilot had a conniption, the Hermit began to pray, and the Pilot's Boy laughed crazily, thinking the Ancient Mariner was the devil. When they reached the shore, the Ancient Mariner begged the Hermit to absolve him of his sins. The Hermit crossed himself and asked the Ancient Mariner what sort of man he was. The Ancient Mariner was instantly compelled to share his story with the Hermit. His need to share it was so strong that it wracked his body with pain. Once he shared it, however, he felt restored.

The Ancient Mariner tells the Wedding Guest that ever since then, the urge to tell his tale has returned at unpredictable times, and he is in agony until he tells it to someone. He wanders from place to place, and has the strange power to single out the person in each location who must hear his tale. As he puts it: "I have strange power of speech; / That moment that his face I see, / I know the man that must hear me: / To him my tale I teach." The Ancient Mariner explains that while the wedding celebration sounds uproariously entertaining, he prefers to spend his time with others in prayer. After all, he was so lonely on the ocean that he doubted even God's companionship. He bids the Wedding Guest farewell with one final piece of advice: "He prayeth well, who loveth well / Both man and bird and beast." In other words, one becomes closer to God by respecting all living things, because God loves all of his creations "both great and small." Then the Ancient Mariner vanishes. Instead of entering the wedding reception, the Wedding Guest walks away mesmerized. We are told that he learned something from the Ancient Mariner's tale, and was also saddened by it: "A sadder and a wiser man, / He rose the morrow morn."

Analysis

As expected, things again go awry for the Ancient Mariner despite his momentary relief. Though safely in the harbor, the ship is pulled under by a forceful undertow, but the Ancient Mariner cannot drown since he is doomed to a living death. Just as he is compelled to tell the Wedding Guest his story, he is compelled to tell it to the Hermit. The Hermit does not ask him where he came from or how he got to the harbor, but rather asks, "What manner of man art thou?" as if to discern whether or not he is human. After all, the Ancient Mariner appears dead when the rescuers pull him into the boat, and suddenly comes to life to row the boat to shore. Instead of answering the Hermit's question directly, the Ancient Mariner is forced for the first time to tell his tale, or be consumed by agony. As he tells the Wedding Guest, he does not seek out certain people to whom to relate his tale, but rather knows them when he sees them. Since both the Hermit and the Wedding Guest are forced to listen to the tale, it is implied that there must be some similarity between the two men even though they appear to come from entirely opposite worlds.

The Hermit, a type of character often valorized by the Romantics, is pious and keeps to himself except to converse with transient sailors. He has divorced himself from worldly pleasures, preferring to live in harmony with nature. Meanwhile the Wedding Guest yearns to join his friends in a social and merry setting, full of decadent pleasures such as fine food, wine, song, and dance. The Ancient Mariner's final message is that by respecting all creatures, one can become closer to God.

This advice is certainly not new to the Hermit, who devotes his whole life to living in unity with nature and praying three times a day. If the Wedding Guest must be reminded of this because he is on his way to indulge in earthly pleasures separated from nature, why doesn't the Ancient Mariner stop either of the Wedding Guest's two companions? As in the rest of the poem, we cannot know more than the Ancient Mariner himself; by maintaining this device, Coleridge reminds us that we are subject to the same moral laws and consequences as his characters. He also maintains a position of authorial power, as though to remind us that while we inhabit his story, we are in his hands. Just as the Ancient Mariner can compel men to listen to his tale, Coleridge can compel us to read "The Rime of the Ancient Mariner" from first line to last, and communicate his message to us so that we become "sadder and...wiser."

Coleridge famously claimed that he did not intend for "The Rime of the Ancient Mariner" to have a moral, although he seems to phrase one neatly in the lines: "He prayeth best, who loveth best / All things both great and small; / For the dear God who loveth us, / He made and loveth all." Put differently, one becomes closer to God by respecting all his creations. Coleridge uses the word "teach" to describe the Ancient Mariner's storytelling technique, and says that he has "strange power of speech." In this way, he compares the protagonist to himself; both are gifted storytellers who impart their wisdom unto others. By associating himself with the Ancient Mariner, Coleridge implies that he - and by extension all writers - are tormented by their gift for storytelling; it is in fact a curse. Just as the Ancient Mariner is forced to balance in a painful limbo, the writer is compelled to balance in the liminal space of the imagination "until [his] tale is told." Both are like addicts, and storytelling is their drug; it provides only momentary relief until the urge returns. Coleridge paints an equally powerful and pathetic image of the writer. He is able to hold an audience's attention so completely that he can force a man to miss his next of kin's wedding reception. He is capable of forever changing his listeners, but is also the constant victim of his own talent - a skill that torments, but never destroys.

Chapter 8

Study Questions

Q1. Comment on Coleridge's Use of Precise Observations of the Natural World to Convey Wider Thematic Ideas in His Poetry.

Or

Q. Coleridge's poem revolves around eighteenth century philosophy of a dislocation between man and nature. Discuss

Or

Q. Coleridge's poetry relies entirely on a detailed analysis of nature.Discuss

Coleridge, in common with other romantic artists such as Wordsworth and Keats revolted against the artificial eighteenth century philosophy of a dislocation between man and nature. Coleridge developed an extremely analytical, passionate and spiritual interest in nature and the idea of 'the one life'. His belief that nature is "the eternal language which... God utters" fuels a vast, and unquestionably, eclectic collection of precisely observed images and themes which almost always focus on the natural world and are used to explore wider issues in his poetry.

The hypnotic rhythm of the Circassian Love-Chaunt created by a mixture of two regular rhyme schemes used intermittently throughout the poem helps to capture the sense of equilibrium, tranquillity and beauty Coleridge believed could be found in nature. Equally the repetition of the word "Lewti" five times in the opening two stanza's as well as the repetition of natural imagery such as the "rock" and the "stream" adds a sense of a natural monotonous charm to the poem suggesting an air of peacefulness and restfulness. The muted colours in the poem suggested by clouds of the "palest hue" as well as the "grey" and "flushed" landscape surrounding the clouds heighten the sense of tranquillity. Conversely, these muted images are directly contrasted with bolder images such as the "rich and amber light" of the moon shining through the cloud. There are almost an identical number of references to both the muted and the vibrant images in Lewti which creates a feeling of equilibrium in the poem further emphasising the natural balance and beauty of nature. In Sonnet to a River Otter the persona remembers in a rather paradoxical way "what happy and what mournful hours" he had by a brook.

Once again there is a feeling of equilibrium and balance created by contrasting images. However, the suggestion of beauty in something much more mundane, such as the "native brook" as opposed to Lewti who is an Arabian princess gives the impression that we are not just looking at the subjects but a more universal idea of a unifying beauty throughout the entire natural world. It is precisely this underlying interest in the beauty and natural equilibrium (which many eighteenth century industrialists threatened to ruin) that lies at the heart of poems such as Lewti. The paradoxical statement by the "ancient mariner" that there is "water, water every where, / nor any drop to drink" adds to the sense of a paradoxical natural world and the "beauty and the happiness" of the "slimy things" the mariner notices whilst at sea creates a similar paradoxical image. The inclusion of the word agony to describe the soul of the mariner is once again paradoxical as the word can mean both mental anguish and pleasure. This double meaning in describing the "soul" of the mariner symbolises the fact that the balance in nature is at the heart of the natural world as the soul is an important part of the mariner. Coleridge chooses to focus in a precise and detailed way on one subject, which becomes symbolic of a wider natural world. Through his use of equally balanced contrasts, both in terms of imagery and style, he is able to suggest a natural world that although often conflicting is always in perfect equilibrium.

Equally, through his precise observations of the natural world, Coleridge was able to explore the Eternity of nature. Kubla Khan's language hints at this timelessness with quasi-superlative language that describes the caverns as "measureless" and the forests as "ancient". The importance of these images is heightened by the fact they are mentioned within the first stanza. Furthermore, by mentioning specific antiquated names such as Xanadu and Kubla Khan, which are fairly obscure, Coleridge is able to suggest that human creation is not like the infinity of nature. By keeping the natural subjects in the poem unspecified and stereotypical, "green hill", "caves of ice" we feel a sense of timelessness in nature.

Furthermore, there is a hypnotic regularity in the entire poem and in particular the first stanza. Coleridge alliterates the last two words of each of the first five lines, "Kubla Khan", "dome decree", "sunless sea" giving the poem a bombastic, yet regular rhythm. Short exclamations such as "but oh!" and "a savage place!" coupled with excessively long exclamations created through enjambment "as holy and enchanted as e'er beneath a waning moon was haunted by a woman wailing for her demon lover!" Consolidate this feeling of 'ebbing and flowing' which is reminiscent of time ticking irregularly away and creates a sense of the infinite. Similarly, the Ancient Mariner reflects this timelessness through the regularity of the way in which he tells his story. He speaks within a rhyme scheme that becomes an almost comical 'nursery rhyme' in places due to the regularity and inexorable rhythm of the couplets. The use of the word "ancient" consolidates this idea of eternity as it is a word usually used for inanimate and often only natural subjects as does the vastness of the ocean he is marooned on. Furthermore his attention to detail in his story suggests he has told it many times and detailed observation such as his description of the albatross, "at first it seemed a little speck, /And then it seemed to mist" helps us realise this isn't just one story about the nemesis of the natural world being told at one precise moment in time but a timeless story of nature and the natural world.

Furthermore, the Mariner's unkempt yet charismatic appearance suggested to the reader through a repeated focus on his "glittering", "bright" eyes and his appearance as a "greybeard loon" and particularly his "long grey beard", suggests subtly that he has become a 'spokesman for nature.' The Mariner's timelessness in direct contrast to the deaths of all the other crew members helps suggest the eternity of nature he has become symbolic of.

The eternity of nature is actually looked at in a rather paradoxical way because by focusing briefly on events or single images that are symbolic of a wider natural world Coleridge creates a sense of the infinite shown through specific examples. This is perhaps also another example of Coleridge suggesting the paradoxes within the natural world by suggesting something infinite with a specific event or image.

Once again, in a slightly paradoxical sense, the poetry focuses on an idea of 'religion in nature', a view held by many romantic poets, notably Wordsworth. The Rime of the Ancient Mariner takes many religious images and 'naturalises' them. In part the third the mariner says "I beheld/ A something in the sky", which has subtle connotations of the star the three wise men followed. However, the "something" is in fact an albatross and like the star in the bible story the albatross is a key symbol in the Rime of the Ancient Mariner. "Life-in-Death" and "Death" "were casting dice" for the souls of the crew and once again this mirrors with a natural (or arguably supernatural) twist the soldiers who diced for Jesus' clothes after his death on the cross.

Ultimately the ancient mariner becomes less arrogant and shifts his perspectives, having repented for his sins and this has echoes of the Christian message except through his killing of the albatross the mariner's crime is directly against nature rather than a perceived 'God'. However, the suggestion of religion in nature becomes slightly less attractive when we see that ultimately the mariner is not forgiven for his sins unlike the Christian message of a forgiving God.

In the examination of religion in nature, the poems also focus closely on the power and nemesis of the natural world. The Mariner and his entire crew are tortured by the mistake of the mariner to kill the albatross. The poem hinges around the line "I shot the Albatross" which is made to seem significant by the fact the line is shorter than the other lines in the stanza, ends "part the first" and contains the word "albatross" in capital letters. Similarly the "pleasure dome" in Kubla Khan, which through its description as "stately" appears very grandiose, is dwarfed by the biblical, apocalyptic language that describes the natural world the dome is surrounded by, "romantic chasm", "ancestral voices". Furthermore, the description in the poem is extremely sensual and covers all the senses. The sensuous description of the natural images gives them an all-consuming and extremely powerful presence echoing the suggestion by Coleridge of the power in nature. The "sunless sea" and the "gardens bright" are both striking visual images, our ears are filled by the sound of the "woman wailing and the "damsel" who is "singing of mount Abora". "The incense-bearing tree" awakens our sense of smell. Equally the suggestion of the "earth breathing" and the fact the persona has "drunk the milk of paradise" ensures that our we both feel and taste the powerful language used to describe the natural world where Kubla Khan built "a stately pleasure dome."

Coleridge's poetry relies entirely on a detailed analysis of nature in order to present and further examine his bigger ideas such as 'religion in nature'. More specifically however, Coleridge relies on a 'zoom effect' to scan the general scenery and then focus in on one small natural subject at a time, which in turn becomes symbolic of nature as a whole

Q2. Analyse Coleridge's Christabel
Or
Q. Evaluate Christabel as a poem of nature
Or
Q. It has been said that "the thing attempted in Christabel is the most difficult in the whole field of romance: witchery by daylight." Comment

The first part of Christabel was written almost immediately after The Ancient Mariner, and shortly before the little band of Stowey was broken up, never again to meet under such "indulgent skies." The theme is of the same nature as in the preceding poem. It is handled with more artifice; but, just for that reason, perhaps with less of inspiration; certainly, with less of buoyant and exultant freedom. The "spring of love" that had gushed from the poet's heart, as, for the first time, he saw and felt how "excellently fair" were the "outward shows of sky and earth" and how deep the meaning that lay hidden within, could never again gush "unaware." And, when he speaks once more of the vision that had come in the first instant of his awakening, it is only to lament that it had been withdrawn almost as soon as it was given and had left nothing but yearning and self-reproach behind. In any case, the personal note, which is very strong in The Ancient Mariner and which some have thought has found its way too loudly into its closing verses, is deliberately banished from Christabel; or finds an echo only in the poignant passage about broken friendship, which he himself considered "the best and sweetest lines he ever wrote," and in the epilogue to the second part, which is partly an obvious suggestion from the "breeze-borne" elfish nature of his son, Hartley, partly a lament over the difficulty—the impossibility, as it proved—of the task which he had set himself: the solution of which, unlike the hopes and longings of the child, was always to seek and never, alas, to find.

The same elaboration is manifest, also, in the metre. Never before had the four-foot couplet been used with such variety and subtlety of effect. As the author himself points out, that effect is largely produced by a frequent use of the anapæstic movement, which had already found its way into the ballad measure of The Ancient Mariner; as in the lines—

For the sky and the sea,
and the sea and the sky
Lay like a load on my weary eye,
And the dead were at my feet.

But it is here invoked still more persistently; as, indeed, in general, there is a subtlety, not to say a finesse, about the rhythmical movement of this poem, which would have been quite out of place in the rushing narrative and more homely metre of the other. It is one more proof of the wide gulf by which, in spirit and in total effect, the two poems are divided. Of the subtlety which went to the creation of the metre in Christabel there could be no clearer illustration than the failure both of Scott and Byron—the one in the opening lines of The Lay of the Last Minstrel, the other in a cancelled introduction of The Siege of Corinth—to catch anything like the cadence of the rhythm which, avowedly, served for their model.

It has been said that "the thing attempted in Christabel is the most difficult in the whole field of romance: witchery by daylight." And nothing could come nearer the mark. The miraculous element, which lies of the face of The Ancient Mariner, is here driven beneath the surface. The incidents themselves are hardly outside the natural order. It is only by a running fire of hints and suggestions—which the unimaginative reader has been known to overlook—that we are made aware of the supernatural forces which lie in wait on every side. The lifting of the lady across the threshold, the moan of the mastiff bitch, the darting of the flame as the enchantress passes—to the heedful, all these things are full of meaning; but, to the unwary, they say nothing; they say nothing to Christabel. Yet, the whole significance of the poem is bound up with these subtle suggestions; though it is equally true that, if they were more than suggestions, its whole significance would be altered or destroyed. It would no longer be "witchery by daylight," but by moonlight; which is a very different thing.

To take a world not markedly different from that given to us in nature, and fill it with the presence, unseen but felt, of the supernatural; to tell a tale of human joys and sorrows, and make it seem "a story from the world of spirits"—this, indeed, was the aim of Coleridge. But no one was more keenly aware than he what were the obstacles to its achievement. "I have, as I always had," he said about a year before his death, "the whole plan entire from beginning to end in my mind"—it may be suspected that this is one of many similar delusions—"but I fear I could not [now] carry on with equal success the execution of the idea, an extremely subtle and delicate one." So subtle and delicate, in truth, that it is doubtful whether even a man of stronger will and more mastery of self could ever have ended the poem in the same tone in which it was begun. Even of the fragment, as it now stands, it can hardly be said that the second part carries out the design so perfectly as the first. The localisation of the scene in a familiar country may, as has sometimes been said, have something to do with this comparative failure. But it is due much more to other causes: to an almost inevitable inability on the poet's part to maintain himself indefinitely in the doubly distilled imaginings which were the essence of his undertaking. Even in the earlier part, it would seem that the right note had not always come to him at the first effort. For, if we are to believe a contemporary reviewer—it may have been Hazlitt—in The Examiner, the original version of

> A sight to dream of, not to tell!
> Was Hideous, deformed, and pale of hue;

and there are other instances of the same kind. The reviewer scornfully remarks that the rejected reading was "the keystone to the whole poem," and that it was rejected by the author for that very reason. In his heart, he must have known better. It is of the essence of the poem not to feed the mind with facts—still less, with gruesome facts—but to spur the imagination by a sense of mystery. It is manifest that the original reading renounces the latter purpose for the former. And, if this be the case, it is clear that Coleridge would have ruined his poem by retaining it.

The sketch of the projected continuation, which Gillman gives on the authority of the poet, reads poorly enough. But it is impossible to say what it, or any other raw material, might have become under the transforming breath of inspiration. Still, temperament and opium between them had so clouded the sense of fact in Coleridge that it would be rash to pronounce whether this was really the plan which he had in his mind from the beginning, or nothing more than the improvisation of the moment.

Q3. Comment on the major themes in the Rime of Ancient Mariner

Or

Q. The natural world's power in "The Rime of the Ancient Mariner" is unquestionable. Comment.

Or

Q. Rime of Ancient Mariner as a Metaphysical poem. Describe.

Or

Q. How does Coleridge incorporate style of story telling in the Rime of Ancient Marine.

The Natural World: The Physical:

While it can be beautiful and frightening (often simultaneously), the natural world's power in "The Rime of the Ancient Mariner" is unquestionable. In a move typical of Romantic poets both preceding and following Coleridge, and especially typical of his colleague, William Wordsworth, Coleridge emphasizes the way in which the natural world dwarfs and asserts its awesome power over man. Especially in the 1817 text, in which Coleridge includes marginal glosses, it is clear that the spiritual world controls and utilizes the natural world. At times the natural world seems to be a character itself, based on the way it interacts with the Ancient Mariner. From the moment the Ancient Mariner offends the spirit of the "rime," retribution comes in the form of natural phenomena.

The wind dies, the sun intensifies, and it will not rain. The ocean becomes revolting, "rotting" and thrashing with "slimy" creatures and sizzling with strange fires. Only when the Ancient Mariner expresses love for the natural world-the water-snakes-does his punishment abate even slightly. It rains, but the storm is unusually awesome, with a thick stream of fire pouring from one huge cloud. A spirit, whether God or a pagan one, dominates the physical world in order to punish and inspire reverence in the Ancient Mariner. At the poem's end, the Ancient Mariner preaches respect for the natural world as a way to remain in good standing with the spiritual world, because in order to respect God, one must respect all of his creations. This is why he valorizes the Hermit, who sets the example of both prayer and living in harmony with nature. In his final advice to the Wedding Guest, the Ancient Mariner affirms that one can access the sublime, "the image of a greater and better world," only by seeing the value of the mundane, "the petty things of daily life."

The Spiritual World: The Metaphysical:

"The Rime of the Ancient Mariner" occurs in the natural, physical world-the land and ocean. However, the work has popularly been interpreted as an allegory of man's connection to the spiritual, metaphysical world. In the epigraph, Burnet speaks of man's urge to "classify" things since Adam named the animals. The Ancient Mariner shoots the Albatross as if to prove that it is not an airy spirit, but rather a mortal creature; in a symbolic way, he tries to "classify" the Albatross. Like all natural things, the Albatross is intimately tied to the spiritual world, and thus begins the Ancient Mariner's punishment by the spiritual world by means of the natural world. Rather than address him directly; the supernatural communicates through the natural. The ocean, sun, and lack of wind and rain punish the Ancient Mariner and his shipmates. When the dead men come alive to curse the Ancient Mariner with their eyes, things that are natural-their corpses-are inhabited by a powerful spirit. Men (like Adam) feel the urge to define things, and the Ancient Mariner seems to feel this urge when he suddenly and inexplicably kills the Albatross, shooting it from the sky as though he needs to bring it into the physical, definable realm. It is mortal, but closely tied to the metaphysical, spiritual world-it even flies like a spirit because it is a bird.

The Ancient Mariner detects spirits in their pure form several times in the poem. Even then, they talk only about him, and not to him. When the ghost ship carrying Death and Life-in-Death sails by, the Ancient Mariner overhears them gambling. Then when he lies unconscious on the deck, he hears the First Voice and Second Voice discussing his fate. When angels appear over the sailors' corpses near the shore, they do not talk to the Ancient Mariner, but only guide his ship. In all these instances, it is unclear whether the spirits are real or figments of his imagination. The Ancient Mariner-and we the reader-being mortal beings, require physical affirmation of the spiritual. Coleridge's spiritual world in the poem balances between the religious and the purely fantastical. The Ancient Mariner's prayers do have an effect, as when he blesses the water-snakes and is relieved of his thirst. At the poem's end, he valorizes the holy Hermit and the act of praying with others. However, the spirit that follows the sailors from the "rime", Death, Life-in-Death, the voices, and the angels, are not necessarily Christian archetypes. In a move typical of both Romantic writers and painters, Coleridge locates the spiritual and/or holy in the natural world in order to emphasize man's connection to it. Society can distance man from the sublime by championing worldly pleasures and abandoning reverence for the otherworld. In this way, the wedding reception represents man's alienation from the holy - even in a religious tradition like marriage. However, society can also bring man closer to the sublime, such as when people gather together in prayer.

Liminality

"The Rime of the Ancient Mariner" typifies the Romantic fascination with liminal spaces. A liminal space is defined as a place on the edge of a realm or between two realms, whether a forest and a field, or reason and imagination. A liminal space often signifies a liminal state of mind, such as the threshold of the imagination's wonders. Romantics such as Coleridge, Wordsworth, and Keats valorize the liminal space and state as places where one can experience the sublime. For this reason they are often - and especially in the case of Coleridge's poems - associated with drug-induced euphoria. Following from this, liminal spaces and states are those in which pain and pleasure are inextricable. Romantic poets frequently had their protagonists enter liminal spaces and become irreversibly changed. Starting in the epigraph to "The Rime of the Ancient Mariner", Coleridge expresses a fascination with the liminal state between the spiritual and natural, or the mundane and the divine. Recall that this is what Burnet calls the "certain [and] uncertain" and "day [and] night."

In the Ancient Mariner's story, liminal spaces are bewildering and cause pain. The first liminal space the sailors encounter is the equator, which is in a sense about as liminal a location as exists; after all, it is the threshold between the Earth's hemispheres. No sooner has the ship crossed the equator than a terrible storm ensues and drives it into the poem's ultimate symbolic liminal space, the icy world of the "rime." It is liminal by its very physical makeup; there, water exists not in one a single, definitive state, but in all three forms: liquid (water), solid (ice), and gas (mist). They are still most definitely in the ocean, but surrounding them are mountainous icebergs reminiscent of the land. The "rime" fits the archetype of the Romantic liminal space in that it is simultaneously terrifying and beautiful, and in that the sailors do not navigate there purposely, but are rather transported there by some other force. Whereas the open ocean is a wild territory representing the mysteries of the mind and the sublime, the "rime" exists just on its edge. As a liminal space it holds great power, and indeed a powerful spirit inhabits the "rime."

As punishment for his crime of killing the Albatross, the Ancient Mariner is sentenced to Life-in-Death, condemned to be trapped in a limbo-like state where his "glittering eye" tells of both powerful genius and pain. He can compel others to listen to his story from beginning to end, but is forced to do so to relieve his pain. The Ancient Mariner is caught in a liminal state that, as in much of Romantic poetry, is comparable to addiction. He can relieve his suffering temporarily by sharing his story, but must do so continually. The Ancient Mariner suffers because of his experience in the "rime" and afterwards, but has also been extremely close to the divine and sublime because of it. Therefore his curse is somewhat of a blessing; great and unusual knowledge accompanies his pain. The Wedding Guest, the Hermit, and all others to whom he relates his tale enter into a momentary liminal state themselves where they have a distinct sensation of being stunned or mesmerized.

Religion

Although Christian and pagan themes are confounded at times in "The Rime of the Ancient Mariner", many readers and critics have insisted on a Christian interpretation. Coleridge claimed that he did not intend for the poem to have a moral, but it is difficult not to find one in Part 7. The Ancient Mariner essentially preaches closeness to God through prayer and the willingness to show respect to all of God's creatures. He also says that he finds no greater joy than in joining others in prayer: "To walk together to the kirk, / And all together pray, / While each to his great Father bends, / Old men, and babes, and loving friends, / And youths and maidens gay!" He also champions the Hermit, who does nothing but pray, practice humility before God, and openly revere God's creatures. The Ancient Mariner's shooting of the Albatross can be compared to several Judeo-Christian stories of betrayal, including the original sin of Adam and Eve, and Cain's betrayal of Abel. Like Adam and Eve, the Ancient Mariner fails to respect God's rules and is tempted to try to understand things that should remain out of his reach.

Like them, he is forbidden from being truly close to the sublime, existing in a limbo-like rather than an Eden-like state. However, as a son of Adam and Eve, the Ancient Mariner is already a sinner and cast out of the divine realm. Like Cain, the Ancient Mariner angers God by killing another creature. Most obviously, the Ancient Mariner can be seen as the archetypal Judas or the universal sinner who betrays Christ by sinning. Like Judas, he murders the "Christian soul" who could lead to his salvation and greater understanding of the divine. Many readers have interpreted the Albatross as Christ, since it is the "rime" spirit's favourite creature, and the Ancient Mariner pays dearly for killing it. The Albatross is even hung around the Ancient Mariner's neck to mark him for his sin. Though the rain baptizes him after he is finally able to pray, like a real baptism, it does not ensure his salvation. In the end, the Ancient Mariner is like a strange prophet, kept alive to pass word of God's greatness onto others.

Imprisonment

"The Rime of the Ancient Mariner" is in many ways a portrait of imprisonment and its inherent loneliness and torment. The first instance of imprisonment occurs when the sailors are swept by a storm into the "rime." The ice is "mast-high", and the captain cannot steer the ship through it. The sailors' confinement in the disorienting "rime" foreshadows the Ancient Mariner's later imprisonment within a bewildered limbo-like existence. In the beginning of the poem, the ship is a vehicle of adventure, and the sailors set out in one another's happy company. However, once the Ancient Mariner shoots the Albatross, it quickly becomes a prison. Without wind to sail the ship, the sailors lose all control over their fate. They are cut off from civilization, even though they have each other's company. They are imprisoned further by thirst, which silences them and effectively puts them in isolation; they are denied the basic human ability to communicate. When the other sailors drop dead, the ship becomes a private prison for the Ancient Mariner.

Even more dramatically, the ghost ship seems to imprison the sun: "And straight the sun was flecked with bars, / (Heaven's Mother send us grace!) / As if through a dungeon-grate he peered / With broad and burning face." The ghost ship has such power that it can imprison even the epitome of the natural world's power, the sun. These lines symbolize the spiritual world's power over the natural and physical; spirits can control not only mortals, but the very planets themselves. After he is rescued from the prison that is the ship, the Ancient Mariner is subject to the indefinite imprisonment of his soul within his physical body. His "glittering" eye represents his frenzied soul, eager to escape from his ravaged body. He is imprisoned by the addiction to his own story, as though trapped in the "rime" forever. In a sense, the Ancient Mariner imprisons others by compelling them to listen to his story; they are physically compelled to join him in his torment until he releases them.

Retribution

"The Rime of the Ancient Mariner" is a tale of retribution, since the Ancient Mariner spends most of the poem paying for his one, impulsive error of killing the Albatross. The spiritual world avenges the Albatross's death by wreaking physical and psychological havoc on the Ancient Mariner and his shipmates. Even before the sailors die, their punishment is extensive; they become delirious from a debilitating state of thirst, their lips bake black in the sun, and they must endure the torment of seeing water all around them while being unable to drink it for its saltiness. Eventually the sailors all die, their souls flying either to heaven or hell. There are at least two ways to interpret the fact that the sailors suffer with the Ancient Mariner although they themselves have not erred. The first is that retribution is blind; inspired by anger and the desire to punish others, even a spirit may hurt the wrong people.

The second is that the sailors are implicated in the Ancient Mariner's crime. If the Ancient Mariner represents the universal sinner, then each sailor, as a human, is guilty of having at some point disrespected one of God's creatures-or if not, he would have in the future. But the eternal punishment called Life-in-Death is reserved for the Ancient Mariner. Presumably the spirit, being immortal, must endure eternal grief over the murder of its beloved Albatross. In retribution, it forces the Ancient Mariner to endure eternal torment as well, in the form of his curse. Though he never dies - and may never, in a sense - the Ancient Mariner speaks from beyond the grave to warn others about the harsh, permanent consequences of momentary foolishness, selfishness, and disrespect of the natural world.

The Act of Storytelling

In "The Rime of the Ancient Mariner," Coleridge draws our attention not only to the Ancient Mariner's story, but to the act of storytelling itself. The Ancient Mariner's tale comprises so much of the poem that moments that occur outside of it often seem like interruptions. We are not only Coleridge's audience, but the Ancient Mariner's. Therefore, the messages that the protagonist delivers to his audience apply to us, as well. Storytelling is a preventative measure in the poem, used to dissuade those who favour the pleasures of society (like the Wedding Guest and, presumably, ourselves) from disregarding the natural and spiritual worlds. The poem can also be seen as an allegory for the writer's task. Coleridge uses the word "teach" to describe the Ancient Mariner's storytelling, and says that he has "strange power of speech." In this way, he compares the protagonist to himself: both are gifted storytellers who impart their wisdom unto others. By associating himself with the Ancient Mariner, Coleridge implies that he, and by extension all writers, are not only inspired but compelled to write. Their gift is equally a curse; the pleasure of writing is marred with torment.

According to this interpretation, the writer writes not to please himself or others, but to sate a painful urge. Inherent in the writer's task is communication with others, whom he must warn lest they suffer a similar fate. Just as the Ancient Mariner is forced to balance in a painful limbo between life and death, the writer is compelled and even condemned to balance in the liminal space of the imagination "until [his] tale is told." Like a writer, he is equally enthralled and pained by his imagination. Both are addicts, and storytelling is their drug; it provides only momentary relief until the urge to tell returns. In modern psychological terms, the Ancient Mariner as well as the writer relies on "the talking cure" to relieve himself of his psychological burden. But for the Ancient Mariner, the cure - reliving the experience that started with the "rime" by repeating his "rhyme" - is part of the torture. Coleridge paints an equally powerful and pathetic image of the writer. The Ancient Mariner is able to inspire the Wedding Guest so that he awakes the next day a new man, yet he is also the constant victim of his own talent - a curse that torments, but never destroys.

Q4. Write a close critical analysis of Coleridge's 'Frost at Midnight' in order to examine the extent to which the poem explores and embodies some of the key concerns of Romanticism.'

Or

Q Frost at Midnight' is a poem written without calculated adherence to established poetic conventions. Comment.

'Frost at Midnight' is generally regarded as the greatest of Samuel Taylor Coleridge's 'Conversation Poems' and is said to have influenced Wordsworth's pivotal work, 'Lines Composed a Few Miles above Tintern Abbey'. It is therefore apposite to analyse 'Frost at Midnight' with a view to revealing how the key concerns of Romanticism were communicated through the poem.

The Romantic period in English literature ran from around 1785, following the death of the eminent neo-classical writer Samuel Johnson, to the ascension of Queen Victoria to the throne in 1837. However, in the years spanning this period writers were not identified as exponents of a recognized literary movement. It was only later that literary historians created and applied the term 'Romanticism'. Since then, a further distinction has been made between first and second generation Romantic writers. But even within these sub-divisions there exist points of divergence.

As first generation Romantics, Coleridge and Wordsworth enjoyed an intimate friendship and collaborated to produce the seminal Romantic work, Lyrical Ballads (1798). But in his Biographia Literaria (1817) Coleridge cast a critical eye over the 'Preface to the Lyrical Ballads' (1800) and took issue with much of Wordsworth's poetical theory. Such discrepancies frustrate attempts to classify Romanticism as a monolithic movement and make establishing a workable set of key concerns problematic.

In his introduction to the Norton Anthology of English Literature M. H. Abrams attempts to overcome these difficulties by identifying the 'five cardinal elements' of Romantic poetry. According to Abrams, Romantic poetry is distinguished by the belief that poetry is not an "imitation of nature" but a "representation of the poet's internal emotions". Secondly, that the writing of poetry should be "an effortless expression" and not an "arduous exercise". The prevalence of nature in Romantic poetry and what Abrams calls "the glorification of the ordinary and the outcast" are identified as two further common elements, as is the sense of a "supernatural" or "satanic presence". It is with regard to this elemental understanding of Romantic poetry that I will conduct my close critical analysis of 'Frost at Midnight' to examine the extent to which the poem embodies and explores the key concerns of Romanticism.

'Frost at Midnight' is a poem written without calculated adherence to established poetic conventions. Comprising four stanzas of varying length, it is written in blank verse and adopts a conversational tone. The flexibility of the meter complements the spontaneous, impulsive nature of a poem containing both personal reflection and joyous visions, and further illustrates Abrams's claim that Romantic poetry should be an 'effortless expression' rather than an 'arduous exercise'. As an account of the speaker's present, past, and future circumstances, George Dekker has argued that the poem utilises a typically Romantic structure:

> The persona digresses from a carefully established scene to a former time and contrasting situation, then back to the present before moving into the future vision of prayer.

By its use of such a structure 'Frost at Midnight' also illustrates Abrams's observation that Romantic poetry should be less an 'imitation of nature' than a 'representation of the poet's internal emotions'. Contrary to the neo-classical emphasis on observation and objective knowledge, the speaker of 'Frost at Midnight' uses nature as the stimulus to turn inward. His perceptions transport him on a journey through memory and imagination and ultimately to a moment of personal insight. In 'Frost at Midnight', Coleridge highlights the Romantic conviction that the poet's role is not to hold a mirror up to nature but to use the fountains of memories and feelings which nature evokes to create something valuable and uniquely individual.

The personification of natural phenomena is pervasive throughout Romantic poetry. In the opening line of the poem the speaker personifies the frost by imbuing it with intention: "The Frost performs its secret ministry". Later in the poem, he personifies a film of soot flapping on the grate of the fire:

> Methinks, its motion in the hush of nature
> Gives it dim sympathies with me who lives,
> Making it a companionable form (lines 17-19).

Such instances are effective in illustrating the Romantic precept that the seemingly familiar or innocuous aspects of nature can still fill the viewer with awe – an example of the 'glorification of the normal' as described by Abrams. Coleridge is informed by a distinctly Romantic sensibility, one which takes issue with Samuel Johnson's assertion that "all wonder is the effect of novelty upon ignorance". Instead, Coleridge's speaker meditates with wonder upon such an ordinary thing as soot. As he does so he transforms the film into a friend and liberates the focus of the poem from the immediate confines of the cottage to the more promising realm of memory and imagination.

The speaker of 'Frost at Midnight' displays a characteristic reverence for nature – possibly the essential concern of Romanticism. In pious tones, he describes the "far other scenes" where his son will pass his boyhood "By lakes and sandy shores, beneath the crags/ Of ancient mountain" (lines 55-56). But it is not simply by the use of such grandiose language describing the topography of nature that nature is represented in the poem. By recalling his own upbringing in the city, the speaker further juxtaposes this reverent portrait of nature with the desolate urbanity of the city:

For I was reared
In the great city, pent 'mid cloisters dim,
And saw naught lovely but the sky and stars,
But thou, my babe! shalt wander like a breeze
By lakes and sandy shores (lines 51-55)

Coleridge's word choice here is significant. By juxtaposing the confines of the 'dim cloisters' of the city with a description of his son 'wandering like a breeze' the sense of freedom and light which nature brings to human experience is brought into sharper contrast.

The speaker's vision of his son's upbringing is further significant in highlighting the Romantic preference for intellectual stimulation and development through a study of nature rather than a 'conventional' education. The child will learn "far other lore" in these "far other scenes" (lines 50-51); he will see and hear

The lovely shapes and sounds intelligible
Of that eternal language, which thy God
Utters, who from all eternity doth teach
Himself in all, and all things in himself.
Great universal Teacher! he shall mould
Thy spirit, and by giving make it ask. (lines 59 - 64)

Coleridge believed that both nature and human beings partook of a divine element and that a reverent appreciation of nature would nourish an intelligent and inquisitive mind. The belief that an open appreciation for the divine in nature is the greatest of educations is also one of the main themes of Wordsworth's 'The Tables Turned':

Come forth into the light of things,
Let Nature be your teacher...
One impulse from vernal wood
May teach you more of man,
Of moral evil and of good,
Than all the sages can.

This concern with nature as a divine education finds some correspondence in Abrams's claim that Romantic poetry is distinguished by a 'sense of the supernatural'. However, it has been more clearly described by Aidan Day in his book Romanticism:

> The mind possesses a faculty which enables it to see through the forms of the material world to a greater, spiritual reality behind it.

Day's explanation highlights the way in which 'Frost at Midnight' embodies and explores not just the literary principles of Romanticism but also its wider philosophy. J. P. Mileur writes in his study Coleridge's Art of Immanence that one of the key characteristics of Coleridge's philosophy is the idea "that we receive from Nature what be bestow". Although nature is the teacher, it is important to acknowledge that the conclusion to the poem describes a process of education in which the mind plays an active role. The 'Great Universal teacher' moulds the human spirit by giving it the ability to ask its own questions. By celebrating the potential of the human mind, 'Frost at Midnight' embodies a distinctly Romantic epistemology. It takes issue with the Enlightenment belief that reliable knowledge can only be accumulated through a process of passive observation and reflection upon the sensory world. By the end of the poem the speaker has emerged from his reveries a 'happier and wiser man'. Having imaginatively transformed his world the speaker takes comfort from the confident belief that his son too will be able to teach himself by actively interrogating the natural world.

In conclusion, 'Frost at Midnight' may be said to embody and explore the key concerns of Romanticism insofar as it displays those cardinal elements provided by Abrams. As a series of meditations written in blank verse with varying stanza length the poem creates the impression of being an 'effortless expression of the poet's emotions'. The multiple instances of personification serve to 'glorify the ordinary'. As Wordsworth declared in the 'Preface to the Lyrical Ballads', the new poetry should "throw over" familiar objects "a certain colouring of the imagination, whereby ordinary things are presented to the mind in an unusual way". Finally, in the course of contrasting his own childhood with the upbringing he imagines for his child, the speaker makes a typically Romantic connection between the natural and the supernatural worlds. This is perhaps the key concern of the poem as it is explored and related to the Romantic belief that nature is the best teacher. On this point Abrams's elemental understanding of Romantic poetry seems insufficient. However, this is perhaps significant in highlighting the difficulties involved in defining Romanticism as a coherent literary movement

Q5. Comment on the transforming creative self and the hermeneutics Of becoming in Samuel Taylor Coleridge's 'Kubla Khan' and 'Dejection: an Ode.'

the question of the transforming creative self and the aesthetics of becoming in Samuel Taylor Coleridge's 'Kubla Khan' and 'Dejection: An Ode', by reassessing certain strands of Romantic visionary criticism and Deconstruction, which are two major critical positions in the reading and interpreting of Romantic poetry. The poetics of becoming and the creative process place the self in Coleridge's aesthetic and spiritual idealism in what I have called a constructive deferral, since none of his poetic texts demonstrates the totality of experience or the impossibility of conceptual and theoretical discourse.

The aesthetic and spiritual advancement of the self delineates the self as conscious, anti-self-conscious, paradoxical, ironic and self-contradictory. These are the very states that necessitate and enhance change and dynamism rather than portray imaginative failure and impossibility. The two poems therefore display an intertextual relation with regard to the self's progress towards the attainment of its pursued ideals.

Introduction

The aim of this article is to discuss the issue of the transforming creative self as demonstrating a poetics of becoming in Coleridge's 'Kubla Khan' and 'Dejection: An Ode,' against the background of his aesthetic and spiritual idealism and postmodern criticism, especially Deconstruction. This presupposes an innovative intertextual treatment of the poems, intertextuality here not conceived as involving the relation between an author and a precursor expounded by Harold Bloom, but as a subtle elliptical psycho-aesthetic and spiritual mixture between the poems.

It will be important, first of all, to define certain key terms like the poetics of becoming and Deconstruction to situate the context in which the concept of the transforming creative self is discussed and analysed. Becoming is defined here as the self-conscious striving towards an aesthetic or transcendental ideal. Taking self-presence as a distinctive mark in Romantic discourse, becoming situates the self as engaged in a continuing process, which is characterised by irony, paradox, contradiction and anti-self-consciousness. It should be stressed here that the thrust of the argument does not wrestle with whether an ideal is attained or not. Rather, it is concerned with the enthusiasm and unceasing struggle for its attainment.

This definition therefore resists Anne Mellor's seminal discussion of the term. Mellor uses strands of Schlegelian philosophy of irony and becoming to formulate and substantiate her own notion of the term (that is, becoming) in the specific context of English Romanticism. Discussing Schlegel's notion that irony is characterised by permanent but non-progressive psychic tensions, and that understanding can be arrived at only through incomprehensibility, Mellor asserts that: "This chaos is abundantly fertile, always throwing up new forms, new creations. But insofar as these forms are static and finite, they are inevitably overwhelmed by and reabsorbed into the process of life."

Following Schlegelian terms, she stresses that thesis and anti-thesis remain in constant contradiction. Becoming to her is conceived as a never-ending ontological reality, and only an aesthetic mode, she contends, can sustain universal chaos, incomprehensibility and unpredictability. For any aesthetic mode to be appropriate as Romantic irony it must be a form that simultaneously creates and decreates itself. This form of creation and decreation, Mellor elaborates, makes works intrinsically antisystematic.

Mellor adopts an almost pro-deconstructnist attitude towards Coleridge. Her conviction is that, a guilt-ridden ambivalence deterred Coleridge's ironist enthusiasm; therefore she refuses his texts a treatment with regard to the philosophical and artistic implications of irony and becoming.

The contention here is that Coleridge philosophically and artistically manifests Romantic irony, which is more than Schlegelian enthusiasm. His texts are taken largely to be expressive of a systematic construction, whereby irony and anti-self-consciousness justify a deferral of a permanent structure. His texts are partial representations of his longings and as such not enclosed and finite entities. His philosophy of self shows it as dynamic, and his psycho-aesthetic treatment of this subject provides evidence for progress rather than stasis or fixity.

The term Deconstruction is a postmodern or post-structural coinage, which has broken new ground on the problems pertaining to theoretical and practical criticism in literature. It is quite a difficult and complex term to define, but there are a number of distinctive characteristics attributed to it. From the writings of its exponents like Jacques Derrida, Paul de Man and Hillis Miller, Deconstruction is seen as a radicalised form of postmodern or poststructuralist discourse on philosophy, linguistics and literature. Deconstruction is clearly at odds with Western idealism and logic; epistemologically, it is opposed to logocentric knowledge, and theologically, it is opposed to belief, faith, and spirituality. Yet, given that Deconstruction's basic premise is the subversion of or aversion to these, it is ironical that it is impossible to extricate itself completely from them.

The roots of Deconstruction can be traced in the German idealist philosophy and Romanticism. It is rhetorically oriented and contemplates knowledge and meaning as representations that are unavoidably enmeshed in the heterodox and contradictory nature of language and interpretation. In other words, Deconstruction points to the ability to uncover systematic incoherence in literary texts, strongly resisting any logically concluded concept or argument. It underscores the inherent fragmentations, ironies, ambivalences and the irreconcilable contradictions of texts. Literary texts are seen to have an authority that overpowers and destabilises the construing of theoretical concepts and construction of meaning. In this vein, Deconstruction emphasises non-conceptualisation, insisting that textuality ultimately subverts the attempt to master knowledge through language, and meaning through interpretation.

It will be important at this juncture to comment on the connection that Deconstruction has with Romantic idealism on which most of the poetics of Romantic visionary criticism is based. Deconstruction is primarily a critique of philosophy. Its heavy presence in literary and linguistic studies has to do with strands of philosophical discourse that have been used to formulate and expound literary theory and criticism. It is in this light that Romanticism has been associated logically with Deconstruction, given that deconstructive critique implicates the complexities of Kantian and post-Kantian philosophy, which greatly contributes to the theoretical formulations of visionary criticism. Important constructivist Romantic concepts like self-presence, self-textualisation, intentionality, subjectivity and individuation, aesthetic and spiritual enthusiasm are all dismissed in deconstructionist discourse of Romantic texts, with the claim that Romantics were the precursors of Deconstruction.

Coming back to the core of the argument, we want to assert the premise that Deconstruction's theoretical and textual discourse on Coleridge is an unfair dislocation of the philosophical, linguistic and literary context of his writings. We don't need to emphasise Coleridge's involvement with German idealist philosophy. Yet Coleridge's work nonetheless shows his constructivist struggles, and these struggles should be best understood by seeing the self in his psychology as progressive amidst the complexities of irony and contradiction.

'Kubla Khan' as a Constructive Deferral

The discourse on deferral here adopts a radically antithetical position to deconstructive deferral. Deconstruction addresses the issue of deferral in terms of continuous shifts in unclear meaning, stressing that all literature eludes theory and conceptualisation. Asserting that incomprehensibility, undecidability and irreconcilable contradictions abound in texts, Deconstruction claims that no constructivist attempt on a text is attainable. With regard to constructive deferral, the question is not centred on shifts in meaning, but the continual intention and process in the quest for an ideal. That is, the ideal is not deferred and texts, therefore, systematically construct the struggle towards the ideal.

Regina Hewitt has discussed 'Kubla Khan' on such deconstructive grounds, highlighting the conviction that both Kubla Khan and Coleridge exemplify poetic failure. She contends that:

> The tensions in 'Kubla Khan' may be seen as a tension between the extant themes of poetic creation . represented by the false poets . which Coleridge rejects and the new theory of imaginative creation that Coleridge embraces but cannot quite completely work out.

Hewitt's interpretation of the incomplete nature of the poem as poetic failure signals the problem of reading it as an independent structure that must show psycho-aesthetic totality. This problematises the poem as the end-product of the creative process rather than an integral part of the process, which presupposes further aesthetic production and idealistic speculation. But as we shall see Hewitt's statement works in favour of the formulation of the poetics of becoming and constructive deferral since the poem unquestionably interconnects with other poems rather than remains an isolated or an enclosed entity.

Hewitt's concern is not unrelated to Jean-Pierre Mileur's critical assessment of Coleridge's hermeneutics of the imagination: "Coleridge's definition [of the imagination] does not appear to describe any poem that he succeeded in writing." Mileur argues that Coleridge's description of the poetic imagination and ideal perfection implies something he does not necessarily claim for himself, and which is not available to any poet. Mileur in this instance simply falls short of understanding Romantic textuality. The fervent conviction in this essay is that no single poem of Coleridge can be interpreted phenomenologically as an independent self-contained enclosure, which should fully expresses his idealist philosophy of the imagination. He was obviously conscious of the dangers of claiming a totality of experience, which as his philosophy and aestheticism show was always positioned in the future.

That 'Kubla Khan' is a quintessential Romantic poem, concerned with the process of creating poetry, the role of the imagination and its affiliation with the mystical and spiritual, is tenable. Yet critics have strongly held opposing positions as to how this view ought to be judged. That Postmodernist discourse or more specifically Deconstruction discredits or even dismisses this ideal is very problematic, considering what the essential Romantic hermeneutics on irony and fragmentation were. From a technical perspective the poem is structurally incomplete, therefore, fragmentary, justified by the subtitle, 'A Vision in a Dream. A Fragment'. In fact, Coleridge's prefatory remarks situate the poem "rather as a psychological curiosity, than on the ground of any supposed poetic merits." This is not a statement to be taken (un)critically as an apologetic or self-subverting or self-undoing judgement of the poem.

Contrary to Coleridge's stance, the poem is one of the greatest Romantic statements on the complexity of the creative process. The poem does not demonstrate a closure, but points to the inconclusive and dynamic nature of aesthetic productivity. The intriguing issue is that, the poetic merit of the text lies not only in its content, since the content points to future aesthetic creations. So the philological and philosophical implications of the poem are an apt demonstration of the Romantic poetics of becoming.

As a constructive deferral, the poem is not concerned with linguistic or conceptual impasse from a deconstructionist point of view. It is not concerned with conflicting shifts in or dissolution of meaning as expounded by Jacques Derrida's notion of iterability and dissemination.

Not being expressive of aesthetic totality, the poem partly textualises and defers this enthusiasm as it contains allowance for subsequent inspiration and creativity. One can see here an exemplification of Coleridge's consciousness of the Socratic irony on which Schlegel modelled the Romantic or Philosophical irony that permeates the poem. Coleridge's disclaimer of the poem's aesthetic intensity, negatively describing it as a fragment and psychological curiosity, can be considered as a subtle performative strategy to credit the poem's strength. Contrary to accusations of guilt and creative inability, this prefatory statement saves him from the narcissistic traits of self-praise and self-inflation, or again, it saves him from being seen as seeking adulation from another.

The main question wrestles with why we posit this contention. The answer is fundamentally important, because it maps the context in which the persuasion on the poetics of becoming is endorsed and examined. It is irony that necessitates self-consciousness, anti-self-consciousness and progress, lending credence to the unacceptability of a fixed and unchanging self. 'Kubla Khan' aptly justifies this conceptualisation in terms of the self-constructive process that characterises its inspiration and contents. It, therefore, is a positive aesthetic and spiritual impasse.

From a hermeneutic and phenomenological standpoint this fragmentary and open-ended nature of the poem, strongly connected with irony and paradox, presupposes a complexity and subtlety of argument that goes beyond the rhetorical figures or literary devices in a deconstructionist perspective. An enormous energy infuses the poem, leading to what can be described as an ecstatic quality, not necessarily as an aroused experience by the critical reader, but detected from the poem and, therefore, a justification of Coleridge's self-textualisation. This means that natural and sublime imagery permeates the poem, and its overall contents relate to some of the pre- and post-conceptualisations Coleridge expounded on with regard to the creative and redemptive power of the imagination.

For a better analysis of this poem as concerns the poetics of becoming, we propose radical antithetical critical readings from Romantic visionary criticism and Deconstruction. These will then provide an antithetical or contrastive context for the new line of argument proposed here. Two insightful partitioning models come in handy when discussing the surface and deep structures of the poem. Rolf Breuer, an idealist critic, has noted in "Coleridge's Concept of Imagination - With an Interpretation of 'Kubla Khan'" (1980), that both the first and second stanzas of the poem (L. 1 - 11 and 12 - 36) can form a substratum for the poem's structural analysis since they thematically belong together. The third stanza constitutes the second part.

According to Breuer's scheme, part one describes the landscape, the first stanza containing the more static description of the garden and the second stanza being the more dynamic description of the river, while part two consists of the accompanying visions and reflections of the lyrical I. Breuer calls these two parts level and metalevel, stressing that they show the poem as having an extremely incomplete structural design, necessitating a kind of synthesis in a Hegelian sense.

The second structuring model is proposed by the Deconstructionist David Hogsette. In "Eclipsed by the Pleasure Dome: Poetic Failure in Coleridge's 'Kubla Khan'" (1997), he sees the poem as presenting scholars with chronic critical problems, pointing out that 'Kubla Khan's textual history remains unclear, its prefatory explanation suspicious, and the poem itself generally cloudy in meaning. In analysing the subtitle and preface as metalinguistic keys to the poem's interpretative and performative context, Hogsette poses the thesis that the poem will be discovered to have nothing to do with imaginative redemption or Romantic irony. On the contrary, he underscores, 'Kubla Khan' offers a series of false poetic figures, ultimately demonstrating that the ideal (pro)creative redemptive imagination lies beyond the grasp of the mortal poet, remaining an external and unobtainable Other.

Hogsette's concern with the creative realm, places emphasis on the figure of Khan, the sacred river Alph, and the fountain which to him prefigure and/or illustrate Coleridge's phenomenological model of fancy, the primary imagination and the secondary imagination. Hogsette argues that Khan produces an enchanting paradise, a pleasure dome which is clearly an Edenic realm infused with (masculine) virility ('walls and towers') and seething with sensuality (blossoming incense-bearing trees and soft hills enfolding spots of greenery) and sexual potency ('fertile ground' through which runs 'sinuous rills'). This, he stresses from his deconstructionist poetics, has mislead readers into thinking that the core content of the poem deals with the creative imagination and aesthetic enthusiasm. This is a typical critical situation which M. H. Abrams' strong anti-Deconstruction stance has referred to as construing and deconstructing. Hogsette can deconstruct Coleridge's Romantic idealism only through constructing and affirming it.

In what turns out to be a criticism of scepticism Hogsette asserts the poem's failure, refusing it the concept of Romantic irony and arguing that the imaginative and visionary potential that Coleridge seeks is an unobtainable Other from the poet's self. Thus the text is seen from the second reading strategy proposed in Derridean Deconstruction as non-communicative of any move towards an ideal, since it is self-deconstructive in its metaphysics of presence.

With regard to the question of the Hegelian dialectic that Breuer proposes above, he is of the conviction that it is the result of what he calls the paradoxical approach that best suits the interpretative context of the poem. His remarks as to whether the poem attains a deep structural unity are worth critically examining, because they throw light on the thrust of our argument. It must have occurred to Coleridge, Breuer holds, that the fragmentary nature of his abandoned 'Kubla Khan' would be the ideal symbol of its perfection. He further argues that the poem has two distinctive features:

On the surface a fragment, in its deep structure complete. In this contradiction, the poem is a symbol of the split of life into thinking and being. Its dialogic construction, its fragmentary nature, the lack of a keystone, all suggest the spirit from which it arose - the dialectical spirit of the interaction between part and whole.

It is obvious that Breuer adopts the Hegelian position he contends and advances, seeing the poem, therefore, as a unified totality. In this context, the text is interpreted as a permanent closure without any further possibility of opening. This cannot be convincing, because the poem's intertextual relations show that it strongly resist Hegel's idealist dialectics. Reuven Tsur's critical conclusion in The Road to 'Kubla Khan:' A Cognitive Approach (1987) also values the poem on similar lines to Breuer. He advances the view that the poem "deals with the irruption of the irrational and of chaos into our rational and ordered world, with a force that is unprecedented in lyric poetry". This kind of interpretation is very characteristic of visionary critics who see most poems as finished entities of self-portrayal or complete aesthetic fulfilment. Breuer's and Tsur's interpretative stance is too idealistic, leaving the impression of complete transcendence. Such idealist readings, which see texts as delineating a totality of self, greatly problematise visionary criticism and necessitate re-evaluation. The question of synthesis from a Hegelian perspective that Breuer proposes is rather puzzling and even enigmatic if we assert that Coleridge subsequently wrote several other poems and prose works, demonstrating his usual paradoxical and antithetical thinking or anti-self-consciousness. No text can demonstrate the totality of experience or knowledge as expounded by Hegel's transcendental dialectics.

The radical or extremist position advanced on deconstructive grounds only complicates a comprehensive reading and interpretation of Romantic aesthetics and spirituality. Even if 'Kubla Khan' demonstrates the complexity of critical insight in reading and interpretative processes, enacting deconstructive gestures, it sounds misapprehending to argue that it intentionally explicates Deconstruction or that Coleridge is a proto-Deconstructionist or a precursor of Deconstruction as Kathleen Wheeler and Joseph Swann assert respectively.

To summarise the argument, while Romantic visionary criticism has often uncritically treated the poem as a quintessential Romantic poem, Deconstruction's extremist position accepts this view only to demonstrate that it is an exemplary piece that delineates the poetics of Deconstruction and is therefore radically subversive to its premised idealism. We therefore, though still adopting a visionary stance, pursue a plausible middle path in the debate, the poetics of becoming.

'Kubla Khan' exemplifies the antithetical or polarised thinking that characterises Coleridge's notion of the imagination, and, therefore, throws light on the question of becoming - the constant self-transforming process, characteristic of irony, paradox and logical and constructive self-contradiction, that possibly leads to the attainment of aesthetic and/spiritual ideals. Breuer's paradoxical approach could be justifiable as long as the poem is not seen as structurally unified but open-ended. The poem's open-ending justifies the concept of process, therefore, becoming. It is not a demonstration of the limitations of the imagination; it is an expression of the fullness of imaginative experience however momentary or brief. 'Kubla Khan' is an instance of Coleridge's anti-self-consciousness. That is, he is aware not only of imaginative bliss but also the challenges posed to it.

The first two stanzas show Coleridge's exploration of his creative and artistic potential. The sacred river (depicting a continuing and transforming life process), the bright gardens with sinuous rills (delineating fertility), the measureless caverns, the sunless sea, the lifeless sea (suggesting conscious and unconscious processes), the fertile ground, the ceaseless turmoil seething, the pleasure dome, the fountain and caves (depicting a paradisal realm), and the prophesying of war by ancestral voices, all associate with and capture Coleridge's oceanic conception of life. They mark both the signs of chaos, incomprehensibility, but at the same time, order, possibility in transformation and transcendence to spirituality.

Stanza One places emphasis on Kubla Khan and gives the impression that the poet is merely recounting what he seems not to be part of. But, as we will realise, the subject matter of the poem is not the historical figure of Kubla Khan, but the poetic personae himself, engaged in a self-reflexive and self-investigative activity, the result being the written poem and the possibility of subsequently composing others.

The last stanza as famous as it is needs citing for convenience sake:

A damsel with a dulcimer
In a vision once I saw:
It was an Abyssinian maid,
And on her dulcimer she played,
Singing of Mount Abora.
Could I revive within me
Her symphony and song,
To such a deep delight t'would win me,
That with music loud and long,
I would build that dome in air,
That sunny dome! those caves of ice!
And all who heard should see them there,
And all should cry, Beware! Beware!
His flashing eyes, his floating hair!
Weave a circle round him thrice,
And close your eyes with holy dread,
For he on honey-dew hath fed,
And drunk the milk of Paradise
(L. 37 – 54)

This last stanza points to the question of self-referentiality, which necessitates our understanding of becoming as an intrinsic quality in Coleridge's poetics. Coleridge's sudden change of emphasis from Kubla Khan to the personal pronouns "I' and "me" shows the intensity of his self-involvement in the creative process.

This shift of emphasis validates his self-consciousness of imaginative energy that is deferred, but not at all pointed towards a lost ideal. Systematically, we have, "In a vision once I saw: .../Could I revive within me .../ I would build that dome in the air." "Vision" and Mount Abora represent the ideal that is sought for, and "revive within me" suggests a potential that he already possesses. The reawakening or reactivation of his aesthetic and spiritual potentials will place him in a like manner as Kubla Khan not only to create more poems but also to affirm these potentials for subsequent use. So we can conveniently talk of a deferral of creative inspiration and aesthetic enthusiasm and not of imaginative paucity. The seeming loss of imaginative strength is ironically a resolve to continue in the direction of aesthetic and spiritual achievement. 'Kubla Khan' is certainly not the last and greatest poem that Coleridge composed. It is better to describe it as a transitory poem.

Coleridge can hardly be said to be lamenting imaginative failure in the above lines. On the contrary, he is grappling with desire for further inspiration and imaginative exuberance. Denying him the ideal of becoming and the possibility of transcendence and eventual paradisal communion may sound misjudging and unfair. Seeing the poem as an expression of a psychically distorted personality obviously signals the wrong inspiration and intention behind the poem's composition. Refusing the poem any theoretical and conceptual bases only wrongly helps in distancing it from its aesthetic, linguistic and philosophical context. Using Breuer's partitioning model, the two parts of the poem undoubtedly suggest a missing/absent synthesising passage, justifying the open-endedness and, therefore, providing grounds for self-questioning, self-seeking for a final principle, a self-quest for certitude in the ongoing processes in experience. The poem is paradoxical because it succeeds when it seems to fail, because it is simultaneously itself and its mirror image. It marks a harvest and at the same time, provides fertility for further growth and fruition.

'Dejection: An Ode': Constructive Anti-self-consciousness

This poem, composed several years after 'Kubla Khan,' furthers and advances the preceding discussion on 'Kubla Khan,' highlighting once more the question of aesthetic intertextuality and the dynamics of constructive deferral. It underscores the issue of the creative self amidst antithetical psycho-aesthetic processes. The assertion that this poem is one of, if not the last great poem Coleridge composed, is a misconstrued apprehension of the poet's creative career. Anne Mellor's discussion of this poem stresses her conviction that the polarity of self does not move to reconciliation, but to an intensified awareness of the distance between contradictory human conditions. Therefore, Coleridge can only create images of separation, alienation, self-destruction and pain. The critical position that Brian Wilkie, in a like manner, asserts with regard to disunity in Coleridge's poetics, is highly illogical and not convincing. He attributes no visionary potentials to Coleridge. Wilkie's contention that there is no such thing as reconciliation between childhood and adulthood but contradictory intricate overlays or super-impositions, is a curious dismissal of the question of Romantic self-questing, which Coleridge's poem evinces.

'Dejection: An Ode' is a revised edition of the epistolary poem 'Dejection: A Letter.' Coleridge wrote this letter in connection with his overwhelming passion for Sara Hutchinson and did not intend to publish it, but he revised it later into a polished poem with the intention of publication. In this version Coleridge demonstrates a significant change of emphasis. He is more personal and self-referential.

'Dejection: An Ode' has been paralleled with 'Frost at Midnight' as poetic expressions of Coleridge's recuperative attempts to restore unity in his split self. It should be stressed that the centrality of the poem in the present argument does not lie on the psychological reliance on an Other but on the impacting context of the poet's self-investigation and self-mirroring. This implies that the allusion to an Other is not part of the psycho-dynamics of transference or projection, since it does not deter the poet's self-centred imaginative attitude.

Coleridge's speaker is lamenting the loss of imaginative potential, encapsulated in his expression of aesthetic and spiritual deprivation. This connects with his childhood yearnings and visionary gleam in nature rather than with the loss of or the impossibility of imaginative regeneration. Coleridge's paradoxical presentation of this state of despair and agony clearly represents his antithetical thinking, which connects with the phases of his psychological development since childhood:

> A grief without a pang, void, dark, and drear
> A stifled, drowsy, unimpassioned grief.
> Which finds no natural outlet, no relief,
> In word, or sigh, or tear –
> O Lady! In this wan and heartless mood,
> To other thoughts by yonder throstle woo'd,
> All this long eve, so balmy and serene,
> Have I been gazing on the western sky,
> And its peculiar tint of yellow green:
> And still I gaze – and with how blank an eye!
> And these thin clouds above, in flakes and bars,
> That give away their motion to the stars;
> Those stars, that glide behind them or between,
> Now sparkling, now bedimmed, but always seen:
> Yon crescent Moon, as fixed as if it grew
> In its own cloudless, starless lake of blue;
> I see them all so excellently fair,
> I see, not feel, how beautiful they are!
> (L. 21 – 38)

This excerpt expresses a strong grain of Coleridgean paradox and anti-self-consciousness. Coleridge characteristically uses aesthetic potential to talk about its very failure. In fact, this is where the strength of the poem interestingly lies; the psycho-aesthetic ability to express the inability to express the same potential, and as we shall see, the deferring of this ability to subsequent aesthetic exploration.

In the third stanza, Coleridge highlights this plight:

My genial spirits fail;
And what can these avail
To lift the smothering weight from far off my breast?
It were a vain endeavour,
Though should I gaze for ever
On that green light that lingers in the west:
I may not hope from outward forms to win
The passion and the life, whose fountains are within.
(L. 39 – 46)

Coleridge's expression of failure does not signal an incurable degenerate self, for his speaker is conscious of the fact that remedial measures lie not elsewhere but within his self. This means that the regenerative force is not dead even if it appears degenerate. It can still be revived, as was expressed in 'Kubla Khan'. The interesting question is why there exists this consciousness of the force from within? The dynamics of psychological retrospection and introspection best answers the question. The developing self is one, and the storehouse of memory can be activated through imaginative potential. So self-struggle cannot be cut off from the history of the self's past. The self relies on its past for its (re) construction. So even if Coleridge portrays a psychologically embattled life, it also positively depicts psycho-aesthetic therapy through self-mirroring and self-textualising.

The other central stanzas of the poem with relation to our discussion are the sixth and eighth stanzas. In the sixth stanza Coleridge's speaker takes the reader down memory lane:

There was a time when, though my path was rough,
This joy within me dallied with distress,
And all misfortunes were but as the stuff
Whence Fancy made me dreams of happiness:
For hope grew round me, like the twining vine,
And fruit and foliage, not my own, seemed mine.

> But now afflictions bow me down to earth:
> Nor care I that they rob me of my mirth;
> But oh! Each visitation
> Suspends what nature gave me at birth,
> My shaping spirit of Imagination.
> (L. 76 – 86)

These lines echo the failure of 'genial spirits' inscribed in the third stanza. Two important words capture our attention: failure and suspension. These words do not expressly state but imply that there is still possibility of regeneration rather than definite aesthetic, psychological and spiritual stasis. The 'shaping of Imagination' that nature gave the speaker at birth connects the present phase of his life to that of his childhood and youth, and points to the fact that he is not resigned to despair and frustration. Even if he expresses uncertainty, he is not destitute or entirely robbed of his visionary potentials.

William Wordsworth's philosophy in 'Ode: Intimation of Immortality From Recollections of Early Childhood' is important here, given that it was influential on Coleridge:

> And when
> Our trance had left us, oft have we, by aid
> Of the impression which it left behind,
> Looked inward on ourselves, and learned, perhaps,
> Something of what we are. Nor in those hours
> Did we destroy
> The original impression of delight,
> But by such high retrospect it was recalled
> To yet a second and a second life.
> While in this excitation of the mind
> A vivid pulse of sentiment and thought
> Beat palpably within us, all shades
> Of consciousness were ours.

Wordsworth clearly sees the self as progressively transforming and not self-deconstructing, or progressively regressing and deteriorating.

Through retrospection and introspection the history of the self does not designate two selves, but the same self that must undergo changes, and not without overwhelming difficulty and complexity. Arguing that Coleridge's speaker seeks to be a child again or be reborn, will sound too simplistic and naïve. The question of a second life, which Wordsworth mentions, is to be understood as a major phase in the self's developmental history. This necessitates a more philosophical re-adaptation of past visionary gleam into the complex realities of the present for continuity. The past provides a psychological context, which generates and assures self-continuity. In 'Dejection: An Ode' this hope for regenerative growth is captured in the last stanza, 'May this storm be but a mountain-birth.' This has a resonance with the poetics of becoming, discussed in the previous section with reference to 'Kubla Khan,' which explains the paradox of the limitations of creative and visionary enthusiasm and the possibility of renewed and more complex imaginative and aesthetic and spiritual strength. Associating this poem with paradoxical or antithetical thinking is justifiable, given that Coleridge laments a lost ideal but which in the very act of the creative process is averted, resulting to a poem of great and canonical significance.

The poem, we reiterate, is a great instance of aesthetic and spiritual possibility and continuity. One can say that it is through the act of envisioning that one understands the greatness of human consciousness. Regeneration here connects with the thread of childhood and points to the imaginative reworking of memory for the enhancement and engendering of self - understanding, harmony and redemption. So the poem is far from what the romantic visionary critic M. H Abrams styles as Coleridge's despairing farewell to health, happiness, and poetic creativity. It continues to resist the arguments of Anne Mellor and Brian Wilkie.

The poet's sense of remorse, his supposed awareness of poetic and imaginative inability are only a firm statement of the possibility of resolution and restoration, a reaffirmation of self-reflective and corrective will. The poems, therefore, become great utterances of the paradox and irony in the Romantic mind. The placing of the poems, especially 'Dejection: An Ode,' as part of canonical creative achievement cannot evade the fact that they are great poems whose subject matter curiously is about the inability to write good poetry because of reasons already stated.

Far from being instances of self-disillusion, self-disability, self-deconstruction, they are hermeneutically rooted expressions of self-confrontation, self-assurance and continuity towards a desired goal. To put it alternatively, the self-textualising aspect of poetry, therefore, far from being an ideal or a finite portrayal of the self, is a partial but constant self-seeking and questing for a certain ideal, in this case the life-long search for fusion with the One.

The irony, fragmentation and apparent contradiction inherent in Coleridge's works and life, place them as unfinished instances of self-portrayal and self-textualising processes, therefore justifying the hermeneutic and phenomenological interpretation that the paradoxical and antithetical understanding of the self does not delineate it as a fixed entity, but unfolding in the process of becoming which is not the ultimate reality in itself, but the necessary medium through which the greater reality of the One, I AM or Logos is attained.

We do not need to emphasise that Coleridge lived for thirty-two more years after the composition of 'Dejection: An Ode'. And during this period, he showed proof that the storm could always give room for further aesthetic creativity and spiritual reassurance. Judging Coleridge's greatness only from his poetic productivity is an incomplete view of his entire aesthetic and philosophical career. The writing of Biographia Literaria (1817) was obviously not an escape from poetic failure to philosophical speculation. He was still concerned with poetic composition. Besides, later poems like 'Youth and Age' (1823), 'The Pang More Sharp than All. An Allegory' (1825), and 'phantom or Fact' (1830) share similar concerns with 'Dejection: An Ode'.

These poems strongly delineate aesthetic and thematic intertextuality with 'Kubla Khan', and evince the argument that the dynamics of becoming best explains Coleridge's transforming creative self

Q6. These are some of the implications of the word "burst." At one point in The Prelude, Wordsworth describes the bust of Sir Isaac Newton, calling it, "The marble index of a mind forever voyaging through strange seas of thought alone." Certainly that is what Coleridge's poem is about as well. The Mariner is going to travel into strange seas of thought.

Or

Q. Go back to the word "burst." It does suggest birth, but what else? We're talking about going from point A to point β, so why does Coleridge use the word "burst"? It signifies breakage. Romantic poetry is often about boundary breaking.

Or

Q. What else does "burst" suggest? What's the nature of "bursting" into something? Energy . . . violent energy. Think about the structure of this work. The event that really launches the poem, and lies at the heart of the Mariner's journey, is the shooting of the Albatross. So it's not just breaking boundaries: it's an act of violent transgression. And yet this will somehow lead to knowledge and the growth of the poet's mind, to rebirth. That's very Romantic. It is a violation that cannot be undone. In that sense, it is like birth. Once we are born, we are cast out into the world; then the struggle is inevitable.

Down, Down, Down . . .

Many Romantic poems are about a journey, and often you'll find—alongside the literal, physical journey portrayed in the poem—some image that suggests descent. This implies that the real journey is psychological. Early in "The Rime of the Ancient Mariner," for instance, we have the lines,

Merrily did we drop
Below the kirk, below the hill,
Below the lighthouse top.

The boat sails over the horizon. That's literally what's happening in the imaginative fiction of the poem, but Coleridge uses this kind of imagery and language several times to suggest a psychological quest. There's going to be a descent into the underworld—the otherworld of deep, irrational consciousness.

The green world in Shakespeare is one in which the ordinary rules don't seem to apply or function properly. There's something similar in the Romantics. We get outside of the city, into the world of the imagination. Lord Byron talks about the Mediterranean world as "the greenest island of my imagination." In contrast, he calls England "tight," where "winter ends in July, only to recommence in August."

What we're talking about is a symbolic typography of the mind. All of these places of nature are literally the physical landscape, but the Romantic writer often uses the real-world, external typography to talk about internal states of mind. He or she talks about the mind in geographic terms. Blake makes it very clear that whenever he uses the image of a "cavern" or "abyss," he's referring symbolically the human mind. There's a famous passage in The Prelude where the Imagination rises from the mind's abyss. This is a typical Romantic use of the external to talk about states of mind, or the internal. It's what Eliot calls an "objective correlative," e.g., some kind of external object that correlates to an internal reality.

The imagery of descent in "The Rime" is not just psychological, though—it's also mythic. It's the mythic other world. In Native American culture, the way you enter paradise is to climb a tree and reach the sky gods. Another mythological path is through the omphalos, the Greek word for navel. It's a place where you pass from one world to another. And Shakespeare's green world suggests that as well, a place of "crossing over" and transformation.

In still other terms, the descent leads to the heightened world. It's life idealized—the life of the transcendent self.

Q7. Critically Analyze Coleridge's "The Rime of Ancient Mariner".

Or

Q. Discuss the various symbols in "The Rime of Ancient Mariner".

Or

Q. What are the various themes in the poem "The Rime of Ancient Mariner".

From the Known to the Unknown . . .

Think too about the phrase "silent sea." It's a form of personification. The Mariner's bursting disturbs the silence of the sea, and the sea, in effect, retaliates. In mythic terms, the sea is associated with the Otherworld, the Unknown. The Mariner begins in the known, the familiar, the natural. The silent sea symbolizes everything that is not those things. It is not known, it is not conventionally natural. It's not the familiar world of habit and custom.

Think back to the term "genius loci" .In "The Rime," we have the polar spirits. They start to control the world in which the Mariner finds himself. In the poem, then, there is a "spirit of place" in this Antarctic region. Notice that Antarctica is a descent into the unknown realm of the mind, too. So what we have then is a protagonist who violently intrudes, interlopes, blasphemes a world in which there is a "genius loci"—a collection of polar spirits.

And what happens? They strike back. Think about American Western movies of the fifties. You have the white settlers who discover gold. Where? On Indian burial grounds. What happens to them? The spirits rise and pursue them. Think of Lon Chaney in The Mummy. What happens? They break into the pyramid and rouse the mummy. In Greek tragedy, what happens to the classical protagonist when he violates the moral order? The Furies retaliate.

A Romantic Internalizing of the Myth of the Profane Man and a Rite of Passage . . .

On one hand, then, the poem taps into something ancient and mythic that goes far beyond Romanticism—a larger pattern. There is a protagonist, the Mariner. A scholar of comparative religion or myth would call him a "profane man." This protagonist is unaware that there is a spiritual dimension to reality. In The Prelude the is a section in which the boy Wordsworth sets out alone and is "a trouble to the peace." The cliffs start to chase him. He hears voices.

In Coleridge's poem, we've got the Mariner, the Everyman. He's unimaginative, profane, ignorant, and he's about to enter the Otherworld. On one level, the spirit of place is going to pursue him. But that is the way one discovers the spiritual dimension. You often have in Romantic literature (the boy in The Prelude and the Mariner) a figure whose imagination projects all this haunting and fearful pursuit. That's the way we discover. We project with our mind, and it seems to be out there, mirrored back to us in dramatic form. That is how we discover it.

Think of the beginning of "The Rime":
The ship was cheered, the harbour cleared,
Merrily did we drop
Below the kirk, below the hill,
Below the lighthouse top.

Selection is meaning. So why does Coleridge say to us that the Mariner is leaving the church and going down? It's a movement away from the conventional, ordinary, and safe religious world. The phrase that the Irish use for this is "sailing beyond the pale." You go outside the safety of the society and enter the sublime unknown of the Otherworld. Even while, on the level of the poem's plot, the Mariner sails outside the safe harbor of the known world, on a psychological level, the journey all takes place within himself.

A New View of Reality Based on a New View of the Self...

In the poem, there's "the Line." This is the equator—another boundary that he crosses. In mythic terms, this crossing of the line is called a "passage." When viewed as a literary archetype, the journey is called a "rite of initiation," or "rite of passage." In a rite of passage, what the protagonist originally thinks gets torn down, and something else gets built up in its place. And that thing is a new view of reality based on a new view of the self. There's a fundamental transformation of the initiate. He begins one person, and very often during the initiation he is given a new name.

Think of Roots. Kunta Kinte leaves the village, goes into the woods, and enters a tent. In mythic terms, the tent symbolizes a womb. They go into the womb and come out new people. It's like Jonah going into the belly of the whale. These are all archetypal images of descent into some womb-like structure that gives birth to a new person. Joseph Campbell once argued that at the heart of all myths—not just rites of initiation, but all myths—is the notion of metamorphosis. That's what we're talking about. You begin one person, and then there's a transformation and you become someone else.

But makes this poem distinctively Romantic?

How do these mythic structures signify particularly Romantic themes and concerns?

The aforementioned examples of mythic transformations and rites of passage are not distinctively Romantic at all. But remember, Romanticism is all about tradition and revolution, secularization and internalization. The Romantic writer works within tradition, within all of these ancient patterns, archetypes and rituals and myths. But the Romantic poet internalizes them. So the passage and the Otherworld are going to have to do with perception and imagination, rather than with sky gods, or whales, or a traditional religious perspective.

We can compare this poem to the medieval quest, too. Romanticism is often defined as "the internalization of quest romance." The general claim is this: the great hero is Imagination. This is an imaginative odyssey, a growth of the poet's mind and a rite of passage toward a heightened Imagination.

A Romantic Internalizing and Secularizing of Christian Myth . . .

You can interpret any work of art from a religious perspective—any religion can be a lens through which someone sees everything in the world, including works of art. "The Rime" encourages that kind of approach, as well as the approach of mythic rite of passage. What details suggest this?

- They hang the Albatross instead of the cross around his neck.
- They hail it in God's name as if it were a Christian soul.
- The penance of life falls upon the Mariner.
- The Virgin Mary.

The poem is filled with Christian references. So another way of looking at this is through an important literary genre in the 19th century—the pattern of religious conversion, with its four parts of sin, punishment, penance, and redemption. But again, the Romantic artist is not simply going to reproduce that established pattern. He or she will revise, internalizing and secularizing.

The Netherworld . . .

In the broadest terms, think about this poem as being about an imaginative journey into the Otherworld, especially the Netherworld. What does "Underworld" suggest that is different from "Otherworld"? Hell, Hades. Is there anything in the poem that supports this? The ship of the dead. The sun looks like blood. The water burns like witch's oil. But on the other hand, where was heaven in classical mythology? How did one get there? Where are the Elysian Fields? They are in the Underworld.

So there's ambiguity in every Underworld. And this of course should make us think of psychological depths. So this is a journey to Otherness. On the one hand, this Otherness is "out there" for Coleridge: it's the "sublime," an Otherworld that we are unaware of in our normal waking hours. But the Otherworld is also within, the world of our own psyche that we are not normally aware of either—the netherworld of the unconscious. In a particularly Romantic vein, Coleridge is going to explore elements of the unconscious. He's going to "map" the unconscious in this poem.

In many respects, that is what Romantic art is all about—that cusp between full waking consciousness and the world of dreams and images and sleep. Note that Coleridge subtitles this poem, "A Poet's Reverie." Reverie is a word you'll find again and again in English Romanticism. It's a twilight zone of the mind. Logic, prudence, reason—all of those things are relaxed. They're not gone, but they are subsided. We're not asleep, we're not fully dreaming. Instead, we're in a state of mind somewhere in between wakefulness and sleep, and that's where imagination resides. And so this poem is about that Otherworld as well.

The Mariner as Seer . . .

Like many Romantic poems, "The Rime" is circular in its poetic pattern. We begin at the end. The experience has already happened, and the Mariner is telling it to the Wedding Guest. But how is the Mariner described? For one example, he's got a "glittering" eye. He's a seer. In folk art, the eyes are the windows on the soul. He can be understood as a visionary. He has seen something remarkable that the Wedding Guest is unaware of. And from the perspective of Romantic poetic themes, that's true. But what does the Wedding Guest mean when he says that the Mariner has a "glittering" eye?

The Mariner hypnotizes the Wedding Guest. He can't move. So the Wedding Guest thinks that the eyes are those of an evil man. This is the evil eye to the Wedding Guest. He says,

God save thee, ancient Mariner!

From the fiends, that plague thee thus!

The Wedding Guest thinks that the Mariner is possessed by demons. So on the one hand, we have the "bright-eyed" mariner who has the enlarged vision that the Wedding Guest is incapable of having. And on the other hand, the Wedding

Guest thinks that the Mariner is evil incarnate. There's also the sense that the Mariner is crazy—the "grey-beard loon." So these are the conditions we have to confront. Is this a madman? Is this someone who is demonically possessed? Or is he someone who is a visionary seer?

Notice that what the Wedding Guest says may represent only the limited view of the typical bourgeois person, who is never going to leave that safe harbor and journey out, cross the line. This kind of sublime, supernatural figure is one, perhaps, that the Wedding Guest and his ilk can only dismiss as evil or mad.

But before we blithely condemn the Wedding Guest's judgment, we need to consider what the Mariner does. He shoots the Albatross. He's responsible for the death of his crew, including his own brother's son. So there is at least some justification for thinking of him as evil.

The Mariner as a Janus Figure . . .

Many Romantic figures like this symbolize both one thing and its opposite simultaneously. A way of describing this is to call them "Janus figures." Janus was a Roman God. He faces all new beginnings and all endings, and January is named for him. He looks both one way and the opposite at the same time. So this is a term to describe these extremely ambiguous figures who can be at the same time both heroic and evil. Think of Ahab and Dostoyevsky's heros.

Also, think of Keats's "negative capability"—"the ability of being in mysteries and uncertainties and doubts without an irritable reaching after fact or reason." Janus figures force us as readers to have negative capability if we are to understand them.

Coleridge made an important distinction between an allegory and a symbol. Spenser's Red-Cross Knight is an allegory. He is clearly representative of a certain fixed number of associations. This is not so with the highly ambiguous Mariner. We have a shifting, kaleidoscopic image where the Mariner is both heroic and crazed simultaneously.

Shooting the Albatross . . .

Why does the Mariner shoot the albatross?

Literally, what's going on before the Albatross comes?

They are stuck in the ice. The Albatross comes suddenly and the ice breaks. They attribute, at least initially, their sudden good fortune to the Albatross. Later, they retract there initial interpretation, claiming that in fact the albatross did not split the ice, and that the bird was responsible for the storm and the mist. But initially they regard him as a good omen.

Some readers might suggest—in trying to answer why the Mariner shoots the albatross—that the Mariner is the captain of the ship, and that he may be jealous of the bird, because the bird is suddenly controlling things and in power. These answers are plausible. But what we find is that the poem really doesn't give us an answer.

"In mist or cloud, on mast or shroud,
It perched for vespers nine;
Whiles all the night, through fog-smoke white,
Glimmered the white Moon-shine."
"God save thee, ancient Mariner!
From the fiends, that plague thee thus!—
Why look'st thou so?"—With my cross-bow
I shot the Albatross.

What literally happens? The Mariner is telling his story, and then the Wedding Guest interrupts and reacts with shock and horror because the Mariner's face is contorted and wrenched. He's thinking about killing the Albatross. He's haunted, convulsed. The Mariner is not just retelling the experience, he's reliving it. We are in the world of time, of logic and sequence. The story is taking place in that time. Suddenly, in the most important event in that narrative, there's a break. The Wedding Guest blurts out, "What's happening to you?" So we can imagine why the Mariner shot the Albatross, we can speculate about what makes sense. But notice that we are given no explanation before or after. And furthermore, there is a sudden break, with no preparation. We're given no explanation. That seems very purposeful on Coleridge's part. He wants to leave us in "mists." That's part of the intention.

So how are we to understand it if he simply picks up the crossbow and shoots the bird?

What conclusions can you draw about the significance of the act, which seems strikingly unmotivated?

The act is totally irrational, instinctive, unmotivated. In one sense that makes it all the more troubling. Often, this idea is very upsetting to those readers who come up with plausible explanations. They could be right. We can't say for certain whether they are right or wrong. Perhaps the Mariner was indeed jealous of the bird. But try to support it. Is there any language that can support a particular claim? There's no support in the text for any claims. And that's the most frightening thing of all.

This is the world of the modern mind. It's the mind of the Jeffrey Dahmers of the world. There may be an explanation. Often for these people, the cause is physiological—something about the chemicals in the brain. But for most of the 20th century, one of the most frightening things is this kind of act of violence has no explanation at all.

Now step back and think about the Christian myth of the Fall. It's everywhere in Romantic poetry. If this is the myth of the Fall, what explanation can we give for why he shot the Albatross? Original Sin. And remember that Original Sin is an imaginative construction to explain something that can't be explained in any other way.

There seems to be something radically wrong with the human will that causes us to act against our own self interests. This is the bird that—as far as they know—is responsible for rescuing them. And the Mariner kills the very thing that would save them. We're asked to think about that as a possibility. That's the true nightmare, because he doesn't know why he did it.

Darkness . . .

Another definition of Romanticism is "the rediscovery of the Dark Ages after the Enlightenment." Remember that the period before the Romantic Age is the so-called Age of Reason. The Middle Ages and the so-called "Dark Ages" can be used as a metaphor for everything that is not rational about the human being. These are nightmare visions of the imagination. That's the dark world the Mariner inhabits at that moment. It is the deepest level of our humanity. Coleridge's poem is not just about a journey to the Other World. It's also about a journey into the heart of darkness.

We're talking about darkness in two traditional senses: this is about sin, irrationality, violence, destruction and evil. But at the same time it's about the sublime, the mysterious, the non-rational imagination and what it can do for good and for ill.

Q8. On the one hand, the shooting of the Albatross may be read as a Romantic version of the myth of the Fall, the act as a symbol of Original Sin. But we can we go deeper.

Or

Q. What might the Albatross symbolize?

1. It can be interpreted as goodness or innocence, and this brings us back to an approach that emphasizes Coleridge's exploration of evil, of the heart of darkness. In that sense, this is the place where evil begins and the heart of darkness is entered—when the Mariner lashes out (without understanding why) against something that is good and wholesome. One of the patterns that Blake explicitly uses is that life is about a journey from innocence to experience. So we can think about the Mariner's journey in that way as well. The journey into the world of experience begins with the destruction of something innocent.
2. We can also see it as a thing of the earth. It seems to represent what in "The Aeolian Harp" Coleridge calls

"the one Life within us and abroad," and what Wordsworth calls "the wedding of man and nature." The Albatross clearly is associated on one level with nature. And so the Mariner's crime is that he doesn't understand (at this point in the poem, at least) "the one Life within us and abroad." He lacks that vision, lacks an understanding that there can be a fruitful wedding of man and nature. So we have what we found in Wordsworth's visionary "spots of time": that the wedding is not a given. It's a discovery. The visionary figure has to take an active part and half-create the spot of time. Initially the boy in The Prelude is alone and seems to be "a trouble to the peace." The Mariner is also ignorant, profane, and so he violates nature, but this eventually leads to discovery.

If the ideal in Coleridge is "the one Life," and the Mariner doesn't understand this, then what would be the appropriate poetic justice, the appropriate punishment for him? That he would be alone:

> Alone, alone, all, all alone,
> Alone on a wide wide sea!

It's poetic justice. Think of solitude leading to the ideal of relationship. Here we have the Mariner in solitude, and he turns that solitude into total isolation due to the violence of that crime. So one way to look at this is to see the Albatross as symbolizing nature—and not just nature in the literal sense, but Nature as an embodiment of some kind of divinity that gets violated.

3. But we know specific, literal things about the Albatross that go beyond the more general fact that it is a part of nature. The Albatross comes from another world. It's an emissary. There is a sense of freedom and something transcendent about the Albatross. And the Mariner isn't aware of the transcendent possibilities of life. Think about it this

> way: What does the Albatross do first, literally? It breaks the ice free, or at least they assume it does. Here's a ship stuck in the ice, then, the ice splits and the ship sails free. It rescues them when they are trapped. So the Albatross represents a kind of salvation, a kind of Christ-like symbol.

(Be sure, though, to make a distinction between saying the Albatross is a "symbol for Christ" and saying it's a "Christ-like symbol." There's a huge difference. The poem doesn't work in a mechanical way where the bird represents exact episodes or features of Christ's life. When you say that the Albatross is a symbol for Christ, then it starts to sound like allegory. Coleridge wasn't interested in allegory as much as he was in symbol. If you say, however, that the bird is a "Christ-like" symbol, there may be no one-to-one parallel to Christ. So it avoids that kind of explicit, overt, mechanical identification, but its general significance has parallels with the significance and doings in the life of Christ—salvation, for example.)

The bird comes suddenly. The sailors aren't expecting it. It rescues them. So Coleridge seems to be suggesting that there is a Christ-like, redeeming spirit at work in the universe, whether the Mariner and his crew are aware of it or not. It's Coleridge's intuition that the universe is divinely ordained, that there is something out there working on our behalf. The Albatross symbolizes that world, that genius loci. Or in mythic terms, it is the emissary of the gods, sent to take the initiate across the threshold into the new world.

In Christian terms, what do you call what the albatross symbolizes? It rescues them. It saves them. You don't ask for it. It suddenly comes. It's grace. Coleridge views the Albatross through the concept of grace. So it's something like grace, something freely given. And the Mariner rejects grace. Now ask yourself: what are the consequences of denying grace? Damnation. What does Red-Cross Knight suffer from in The Faerie Queene? He suffers from "wane hope," or despair. That's damnation. So that's another way of understanding this act in the middle of the poem. It's a state of damnation, a state of "wan hope," and a state of despair.

4. The Albatross can also symbolize the transcendental and imaginative possibly within the Mariner, which he rejects in himself. Sir Philip Sidney, in his famous Defence of Poesy, written during the Renaissance, describes what art does, and he says that art offers "a golden world." For the Romantics, paradise and heaven are our life heightened, composed, filled with meaning. And so that's what the Albatross symbolizes, and everything that happens is because of what the Mariner himself launches it. He has to assert himself eventually before that "golden world" can become the world around him.

The Over-reacher and the Theme of Evil . . .

We can also think of the Mariner in terms of the classical tragic hero, the over-reacher. The tragic flaw is called "harmartia," and the etymology of the term comes from archery. It means to miss the bull's eye in one way: by overshooting it. So the tragic hero is the Over-reacher. If you come back to the theme of evil, the Mariner as the over-reacher is guilty of hubris because he usurps the prerogatives of the gods. He acts as if his will were universal will. He doesn't consult the members of the crew, what they think about the bird. There's no democratic vote. He simply asserts his own will. In this, he's like Lucifer, who usurps the will of God.

But on the other hand, the word "Lucifer" means "light-bearer." The Mariner is also like Prometheus, who usurps the will of authority and brings light. Think in terms of Romantic mythology. The Romantics draw upon many great myths of the classical world, but use them in distinctly Romantic ways. So the Mariner is like Lucifer, in the sense that he would war with God, the albatross being the emissary of God. He would usurp the prerogatives of God. But he's also like Prometheus. His act is one of dynamic self-assertion.

Two Ways of Viewing Evil . . .

Think about the Mariner's punishment. Does it seem fair? Basically, the Mariner picks up a cross bow and shoots a bird, and for that he has to suffer damnation. Is that fair or not?

One way to define evil is a utilitarian way—that is, by considering its consequences. By this definition, Hitler is far more evil that the man who beats his wife. But there are non-utilitarian ways of viewing evil. A non-utilitarian view sees evil as having to do not with consequences, but with the impulses and motives that go into it. By those terms, the man who beats his wife is as evil as Hitler.

You can also think about some of the absolute statements that Christ makes in the New Testament, such as "In as much as you do to the least of these, so do you unto me." If you take the poem in this way, symbolically, then perhaps the Mariner's punishment is appropriate. He's like the man who beats his wife from the non-utilitarian viewpoint. He deserves an absolute punishment. But many readers are bothered by this. For them, the punishment seems too harsh. The death of all the crew?—is that fair?

A Poem that Resists Definitive Explanations . . .

Things don't always quite fit in this poem. In many ways it both works and doesn't work. In that way, it seems very modern. Particularly in modern art, the most interesting places in the work of art are the places where interpretation breaks down, where logical explanation somehow falls short. Modern art, with all its irony, complexity, ambiguity, often reveals that the writer's vision is more comprehensive than we thought. He or she sees not only what we think he or she sees, but something else as well. There is something else that contradicts the overall point of view of the poems. This is a telling example of that.

The Middle of the Poem . . .

In the beginning of the poem, the Mariner shoots the Albatross. The ending beings when he blesses the water snakes. In the middle he enters the state of "Life in Death."

In Christian terms, he's in torment and despair. This is hell. But in Romantic terms, this is a psychological understanding of the hell of the mind. The Mariner loathes himself. He's filled with self-disgust. Mystics call this "the dark night of the soul." It's something that goes beyond just a sense of sin. It's a sense of self-disgust. We get this in Gerard Manley Hopkins's "Terrible Sonnets." They try to describe a "terrible" state of mind. "I am heartburn," he writes. Hopkins was a Jesuit priest who also wrote poetry. There's one sonnet in which he uses the Biblical story of Jacob wrestling with God. The speaker of the poem has a nightmare experience in a dream, and then wakes up and tastes himself, his heartburn. The Mariner seems to experience something similar.

So the middle section of "The Rime" captures that kind of agony. It's not just someone who's been bad and is being punished. This is the extremity of desperate existence in which we loathe ourselves. It's that mental and emotional where nothing means anything.

It's fruitful to understand the Mariner's descent as an entrance into the mysterious recesses of consciousness, and a part of that is the depths of despair and self-loathing. In psychological terms, we can also describe this as insanity or madness. It's the nightmare of the mind. The mind works all of the time. It creates images all of the time. When we use the term "creative imagination," we use it as if it were always positive. But the mind can create images that are not at all positive. It's not that the Mariner is literally hallucinating. Dramatically, we are meant to take everything as having external reality. But in terms of significance in the poem, this is the world he creates.

What do you think Coleridge means by Life-in-Death?

Her lips were red, her looks were free,
Her locks were yellow as gold:
Her skin was as white as leprosy,
The Night-mare Life-in-death was she,
Who thicks man's blood with cold.

If you are interested in myth, she's the White Goddess. She's also a vampire after "blood." This is the Gothic influence of English Romanticism. These mythic figures suck life—emotional, spiritual, imaginative life. Again, this is very traditional. This is the femme fatale, the temptress, the vampire. Remember that the vampire makes us one of them. So the Mariner is physically and biologically alive, but dead in every other way: spiritually, emotionally, imaginatively. This is a kind of zombie existence.

The Will . . . Exerted and Lost

This is a work in which not much happens. Consider what the Mariner actually does in this poem:

1. He shoots the bird.
2. He tries to pray, but can't. Then he sucks the blood out of his arm.
3. He blesses the snakes.

Notice that this is another aspect of crime and punishment that Coleridge explores. The Mariner loses his will. He can't act. After he acts as if his will is universal will—by shooting the Albatross—then he's paralyzed. He can't act or move. The doldrums are entered. The ship is like: "a painted ship / Upon a painted ocean." It's a state of pure stasis.

The Possibility of Chance . . .

But there is something that happens in the middle part of the poem. They play dice. Why? The game captures the randomness and chance of existence. Here is a poem which we try to interpret logically, analytically. We talk about a world where there is some sense and meaning. If you do something like reject mercy and grace, then you are going to be damned. It's very causal. Everything is somehow knowable. But here, in one of the most crucial points in the whole work, it's a crap shoot. Coleridge seems to desperately wonder in this work if the world does contain "one Life within us and abroad," or whether it is sheer hit-or-miss.

Coleridge wonders: Is it a Christian world of sin and suffering, but ultimately redemption and love? Is it this world where the Mariner can say:

Farewell, farewell! but this I tell
To thee, thou Wedding-Guest!
He prayeth well, who loveth well

Both man and bird and beast.
He prayeth best, who loveth best
All things both great and small;
For the dear God who loveth us,
He made and loveth all.
Is it? On the one hand, yes.

Is it a work in which we journey into the heart of darkness and discover that we control our fate imaginatively? Yes.

Is it fair that he should suffer the tortures of the damned for Over-reaching? Yes.

But also no.

At this crucial event in the poem, all the logic and rationality of the world escapes. It is true that the dice are loaded, there's no question about that. If Death wins the Mariner, instead of Life-in Death, well, the poem's over. He dies and that's the end of it. So we know on some level that Life-in-Death is going to win the dice match. But Coleridge has to be responsible for the implications of his images. And he has it decided by a crap shoot. That's meaningful. It seems to contradict all the interpretations we've been talking about. The image of the crap game disrupts easy readings of the work and easy readings of Coleridge's vision. It's slippery on purpose.

We have the ending, of redemption and love. Everything in the universe at the end is linked in a chain of love. But there's one thing the Mariner says that destabilizes that:

O Wedding-Guest! this soul hath been
Alone on a wide wide sea:
So lonely 'twas, that God himself
Scarce seeméd there to be.

That is, maybe this is a universe that doesn't even have a God at all. And we're talking about a Christian interpretation of the poem? Do you see how self-deconstructive it is in this regard? The poem seems to contradict itself purposefully.

Blessing the Water Snakes . . .

Why is the blessing of the water snakes the turning point, or denouement, of the poem?

What literally happens, and what does it symbolize?

Coleridge writes,

Beyond the shadow of the ship,
I watched the water-snakes:
They moved in tracks of shining white,
And when they reared, the elfish light
Fell off in hoary flakes.
Within the shadow of the ship
I watched their rich attire:
Blue, glossy green, and velvet black,
They coiled and swam; and every track
Was a flash of golden fire.
O happy living things! no tongue
Their beauty might declare:
A spring of love gushed from my heart,
And I blessed them unaware:
Sure my kind saint took pity on me,
And I blessed them unaware.
The spell begins to break.
The self-same moment I could pray;
And from my neck so free
The Albatross fell off, and sank
Like lead into the sea.

Remember that he's seen these same water snakes earlier in the poem,

The very deep did rot: O Christ!
That ever this should be!
Yea, slimy things did crawl with legs
Upon the slimy sea.

and later, after the crew drops dead and he's left alone, he says,

The many men, so beautiful!
And they all dead did lie:
And a thousand thousand slimy things
Lived on; and so did I.

He's seen them before, but now what's changed? Literally, he sees them now in moonlight, and that symbolizes illumination, understanding, the lamp of imagination. It's his ability to see imaginatively. That's pretty clear. But push a little further. He's seen these water snakes a couple times on this journey, and probably before. So they are not something he doesn't understand, or hasn't seen before.

This is different from the Albatross. At the beginning of the poem, he doesn't understand that there is a genius loci, that there is a divine presence. But he knows these snakes. So why can he bless them now, but couldn't before? What does Coleridge tell us? Here he blesses them "unawares." That's the key word. Why does he emphasize that twice? Why does he initially reject grace, and now accept it?

It's a very unfair question. There is no explanation. The key idea is "unawares." It's not conscious. It just happens. Why? There's really no answer. We talked about Original Sin. It was irrational, unpremeditated, "unawares." Why do we sometimes lash out "unawares"? Why do we sometimes love and accept "unawares"? It's a mystery. It has to do with the unconscious. There are things that we know and understand, but that's not only the answer. He's understood the ramifications of his actions for some time. He's regretted being responsible for the deaths of the crew. He's tried to pray. But he couldn't do it. It was a mystery.

The Irrational World . . .

So this is a journey that begins in mystery, in which he irrationally launches himself into another world by killing the Albatross. And the turning point or resolution is equally mysterious. We can speculate about his blessing in rational terms, as we can his killing of the Albatross. But there is a mysterious parallelism here of sheer mystery and inexplicability. Coleridge writes "unawares" twice.

We can analyse it and explain it after the fact. But our analysis doesn't tell us why it happened. It's like a spring of well-water. In "Dejection: An Ode," Coleridge describes joy as a fountain. Sometimes is bursts forth, sometimes it doesn't. The point isn't that we are not responsible for those acts like killing the Albatross. It's not that we should simply give up, and that we have no free will. But not everything is explicable.

The sea becomes a desert, and this is someone crying out in the wilderness, when suddenly, without premeditation or rational intent, he blesses the water snakes. It's as if the "one Life" has come together inexplicably. He sees life suddenly in the world of death. He sees into the life of things "unawares."

Escaping the Curse of Narrow Selfhood . . .

He's tried to pray, but why isn't prayer enough? Coleridge simply tells us that the blessing happens "unawares." In Coleridge's terms, he suddenly escapes the curse of narrow selfhood. The ego is not longer completely dominating. He can see other things that are alive and are a part of the "one Life" inside and outside our beings. They have value and meaning that is transcendent of self.

But what's the Mariner like at the end? Is this what we'd expect after someone has experienced a radical conversion? Do we have an apostle filled with a beautific smile, standing up to the world to tell of the glory of Christ? Look at the language:

The ancient Mariner earnestly entreateth the Hermit to shrieve him;

and the penance of life falls on him.
'O shrieve me, shrieve me, holy man!'
The Hermit crossed his brow.
'Say quick,' quoth he, 'I bid thee say—
What manner of man art thou?'
Forthwith this frame of mine was wrenched
With a woeful agony,
Which forced me to begin my tale;
And then it left me free.

And ever and anon through out his future life an agony constraineth him

to travel from land to land;
Since then, at an uncertain hour,

That agony returns:
And till my ghastly tale is told,
This heart within me burns.

It's doubtful that Billy Graham will be using this as an emblem of the meaning of Christian redemption. So what's going on here?

Think about this psychologically. He can talk about the poem in terms of birth and creativity, but who wants the Mariner's life at the end? Remember that this is a journey, and we associate the journey with the accumulation of knowledge and discovery. That's all happened to the Mariner. And we've talked about that. But why is Coleridge describing him in this way? He's not sharing the Christian message of joy at the end. The Mariner is in agony. And again it's as if he has no free choice. It's as if this story were haunting and possessing him. He has no power over it: it has all the power over him. He's forced to tell it, and it's only after he's told it that there is any peace at all. And the suggestion is that his peace doesn't last very long. Why?

The Wandering Jew and the Burden of Full Consciousness ...

He's like The Wandering Jew, Ahasuerus. This legend is not from the Bible, although it's a Biblical story. It's from legend, going back at least to the Middle Ages. It was popular during the Renaissance, but is even more popular during the Romantic era. Ahasuerus meets Christ when Christ is on his way to Gologotha, the place of skulls. There are several versions. In one Christ asks Ahasuerus to help him carry the cross. He asks him in other versions for a drink of water. But the result is always the same. Ahasuerus not only refuses, but he curses Christ. In turn, he is cursed to wander forever alone and to be unable to die.

In Romantic poetry, the Wandering Jew is a recurring symbol. And he symbolizes for the Romantics the curse of the burden of full consciousness. Think back to the myth of the Fall. Adam and Eve fall because they eat of the tree of Knowledge of Good and Evil.

Think about what the Mariner has learned. He has learned that there is this universal love, the "one Life within us and abroad." But he's also learned that he is capable of evil and destructiveness. And he's responsible for the death of his entire crew, including his own nephew. Well how do you live with that? That's the burden of full consciousness. And that's what Romantic art is all about.

Again, just as we saw that moments of vision carry with them disturbing things like vertigo and the disappearance of the physical world, so does full consciousness. That's what it means to be the archetypal Romantic rebel, the over-reacher. It is positive. It leads to full consciousness. It leads to sympathy. It leads to imaginative revelation. It also leads—in those deep recesses of human consciousness—both to our imaginative gifts, but also to our burden as well. So Ahasuerus neither lives nor dies. He's the perpetually wandering Romantic figure.

Think also about the similarities between the Mariner and Prometheus. There are lots of differences. But here is someone who steals fire from the gods, in the sense that he too goes into uncharted waters. He violates something. The Wedding Guest, on the contrary, symbolizes Everyman. He's a safe, bourgeois person. The Mariner brings back the fruits of his Promethean knowledge, that glittering light. And the Wedding Guest has the benefit of that knowledge, without having to undergo the journey himself. But Prometheus was chained to a rock in the Caucasus Mountains with a vulture pecking at his liver for all of eternity. So he is the endlessly suffering god. Often times, the Romantic protagonist is this kind of endlessly suffering god, some half-man, half-god who brings back knowledge but eternally suffers for it.

It all has to do with what you think about knowledge and God. If you are conservative, people like the Mariner and Prometheus are evil villains. You think man has his proper place and shouldn't go beyond the pale. If, on the other hand, you believe in human aspiration, if that's what it means to be fully human, and if you seek after knowledge, even if some of the consequences will be negative as well as positive, Prometheus is a hero.

In his poem "The Tyger," Blake has his speaker—who represents the typical person of experience, like the Wedding Guest—say: "What the hand dare seize the fire?" In other words, "How dare you seize this fire?" There's moral outrage in his voice. But Blake, behind those lines, chants a celebration of the seizer. It's all a matter of value. When you get into Romanticism, you are talking about a value system, a very complex one.

On the primary level, then, this poem offers us Coleridge's vision of reality. It is a world that is divinely ordained. It is a world of cause and effect. That's what Coleridge thinks and hopes the world is like. But in those moments when interpretation breaks down, there seems to be a sense of a universe that Coleridge deeply fears, a universe perhaps run by a harsh Calvinist God, or the Jehovah of the Old Testament, where "Alone on a wide wide sea: / So lonely 'twas, that God himself / Scarce seemėd there to be."

Or it is a world of pure chance without design, the universe as a game of dice. That's the universe that Coleridge fears. This universe rears its image in Coleridge's dreams. And both are true. Because we half create the world in which we live. So there is the world that Coleridge desires it to be, and the world that Coleridge sometimes, in his darkest moments, dreads.

Q9. How far do you think Kubla Khan is a romantic poem.
Or
Q. How is Kubla Khan different from other poems of Coleridge?
Or
Q. Samuel Taylor Coleridge uses amazingly implicative imagery and allegory to show his romantic ideals of paganism over Christianity. Comment

This poem has very symmetrical and clear composition. We can divide this poem in two parts. The first part is narrative-descriptive part written in the third person, The second part is lyrical and written in the first person in short verse form. Despite the differences within the poem Kubla Khan possesses the unity of style and atmosphere.

The first part is description of dome and large garden which Kubla Khan arranged for his own pleasure. The dome is described as "stately" and "sunny". The garden is portrayed as earthly heaven. Although surrounded by ancient forests ,it is blooming and bright .The sacred river Alph flows through this garden. The second part is description of the poet's past experience. He depicts the Abyssinian maid playing on her dulcimer and singing of Mount Abora .The images of pleasurable dome and beautiful garden conjure up creativeness. Coleridge refers to pleasures of poetry. The poet is the one who arranges the luxuriance of nature and encloses it with walls and towers. But he is unable to control the sacred river Alph ,his own ability to create poetry. Therefore we can come to conclusion that the first part represents the dialectic of artistic creation. The poet creates with his skill ,but great and magnificent energy of nature gives life to his work.

The Abyssinian maid, in the second part, represents heavenly muse of poetry ,divine inspiration.

It seems like Coleridge wants to say that if he would have this gift(the gift of playing dulcimer and singing of Mount Abora) he would spontaneously create more beautiful and artistic work .But the public would see this art as a fruit of abnormality, as a gift of opium and not as a gift of God.

It also seems that the poet wants to say that there are two different categories of poetry-earthly and heavenly, human and divine poetry.

Kubla Khan is a magic poem about magic charms of poetry .It is one of the most successful, symbolic poems written in English language.

'Kubla Khan,' by Samuel Taylor Coleridge, is one of the most enigmatic and ambiguous pieces of literature ever written. Allegedly written after a laudanum (an opiate) induced dream, the author claims to have been planning a two hundred to three hundred line poem before he got interrupted by a 'man from Porlock,' after which he had forgotten nearly all of his dream. This may have been merely an excuse, and the poem was scorned at the time for having no poetic value, one critic even going so far as to call it 'more a musical composition than a poem.' This is partly true, as the language seems to strive for an aural beauty more than a literary beauty, although it accomplishes both.

Like many great artists, Coleridge has been most appreciated after his death, when his radically different works could be justified, as the ideas presented in his works hadn't been popular during his life. Coleridge's philosophy in life was very romantic, and so nearly all of his poems exemplify the romantic ideal, especially Kubla Khan. This romantic poem uses brilliant imagery and metaphors to contrast the ideals of romantic paganism with often ungracious Christianity.

The vision of paganism is the first idea introduced in the poem. The super-natural reference to 'Alph,' or Alpheus as it is historically known, 'the sacred river, [which] ran/ Through caverns measureless to man/ Down to a sunless sea,' begins this pagan theme by referring to an underground river that passed through dimensions that could not be understood by any man, and then emptying into an underground sea. This also introduces an idea of the lack of human understanding that recurs at the end of the poem, one of the common elements that tie the poem's seemingly two-part separate structure together. Xanadu's walls enclosed 'gardens bright with sinuous rills.' These gardens represent the Garden of Eden, or a natural paradise on Earth. The degree of nature in this paradise is such that, although it is a biblical reference, it is still connected to pagan and romantic ideals.

The 'sinuous rills' flowing through this garden can be taken as two different metaphors. The word 'rills' can mean either a stream or a valley on the moon. The moon is seen as the source of all creativity in romantic idealism, and so this first metaphor is significant in the poem. The lunar reference's antithesis comes at the end of the stanza, when it speaks of 'forests ancient as the hills,/ Enfolding sunny spots of greenery.' This reference to the sun contrasts with the valleys on the moon. The second metaphor is that of the snake in the Garden of Eden. The word sinuous implies snakelike, and the connection of these small tributaries to the river Alph shows that they are lustful, tempting, and bring about the destruction of those that offend paradise. These qualities are shared with the Snake from the Garden of Eden and the River Alph (as will soon be seen). The Garden of Eden idea is further shown with the description of the

> ...deep romantic chasm which slanted
> Down the green hill athwart a cedarn cover!
> A savage place! as holy and enchanted
> As e'er beneath a waning moon was haunted
> By woman wailing for her demon lover!
> (lines 12-16)

Coleridge uses syntax to exaggerate his emotion in the description of the 'chasm' with his use of an exclamation point in the middle of a sentence in line 14. The author is barely able to contain himself, so 'romantic' this chasm is, and so his sentence climaxes before it is even finished, then climaxes again at the end. This builds intensity until the eruption of the chasm that follows.

The woman here is Eve, and she is 'wailing' for the source of her desires, literally her demon lover, but figuratively the apple that got her kicked out of Eden. This connects her to the dome, which is also offending paradise, and this wailing is what seems to set off the chasm and become the dome's and (presumably) her demise. The idea of this material dome of pleasure floating above paradise is reminiscent of a sort of inverted Tower of Babylon, where, instead of building up to reach paradise, the dome, and therefore Kubla Khan, is attempting to reach it from above. Simultaneously, the dome is mocking Heaven, a synonym for paradise, as the dome is a common symbol representing the heavens. This angers nature, and it attacks the dome with the river and the fountain from the chasm.

The river Alph is directly related to the Greek god Alpheus, who was the river god. According to Greek mythology, a pagan belief, the god Alpheus had fallen in love with Arethusa, the daughter of Nereus and a Hesperides. The Hesperides' are a type of nymph whom tend to a beautiful garden, or paradise, of unknown location. Alpheus took the nymph to Sicily, where Artemis, the god of childbirth and chastity, turned Arethusa into a fountain, so that the two could make love by mingling their waters.

The mingling of their waters is occurring in this chasm, where the 'mighty fountain' of Arethusa is located. To further this image of sex in nature, which Coleridge loved so much and was a large part of the romantic and pagan idea, the chasm is very much likened to a vagina, with its 'cedarn cover' like pubic hair, and its 'romantic' nature, which could mean either relating to romanticism or romance, both of which could have sexual implications. With 'fast thick pants,' the fountain bursts up and the chasm spews out 'dancing rocks' like 'chaffy grain beneath the thresher's flail.' Coleridge uses syntax to emphasize the excitement of the climax by not using a comma between the words 'fast' and 'thick.'

This speeds up the narration and sends the reader into a state of heart-pounding excitement and elation, showing that the destruction of the dome is a good thing. The choice of diction with the 'dancing rocks' comes to the same effect. These rocks are described as 'chaffy grain,' relating the fragments to the figurative semen, or seed, that the river is spewing out. In this destructive orgy paradise's wrath is invoked upon the dome, which is knocked down into the river and swept into the caves at it's end to rest in the 'lifeless ocean' (line 28). Both the sex in the chasm and the dome entering the caverns before sinking into the sea present the idea of convex and concave.

This juxtaposition of a protruding object with a hole or depressed object adds to the two-part structure of the poem, and also lends to the ambiguity that creates complementary opposites in the work. The presence of a material dome and materialistic ruler in a romantic setting is one example of this juxtaposition, as well as the opposite juxtaposition of the immaterial dome and inspired poet with the ignorant Christians in the second half of the poem. Another example of concave and convex is line 36, 'A sunny pleasure-dome with caves of ice!' The juxtaposition here is further dramatized by the combination of the convex with heat and the concave with ice.

The materialism of this dome is proven and emphasized when the author writes: 'The shadow of the dome of pleasure/ Floated midway on the waves.' The description of the dome's shadow proves that the dome is material because only those things constructed of real material can cast a shadow. The romantic term 'suspension of disbelief' is shown when Coleridge describes the 'mingled measure/ From the fountain and the caves.' The suspension of disbelief is when an author writes something that is factually impossible, but must simply be read as it was written by the author for the effect of the writing. This ocean was described as being 'silent' at the beginning of the poem, and it was five miles away from the fountain that could be heard from it.

This term was originally coined by Coleridge, one year after the poem was published. The number five can be found twice in Kubla Khan, the first time when speaking of Khan's palace of Xanadu. Coleridge goes out of his way to use the number five here, saying 'twice five miles' instead of simply saying ten. The second use of the number five is after the pleasure dome has been subdued by nature's wrath. The significance of the number five is huge in paganism. The number five refers to the fifth element, spirit, which in pagan belief is the source of all magic and life on Earth.

The pentacle and pentagram are symbols of the number five, and the space within a pentagram is said to be separate from this plane of existence, much like the pleasure dome in the second part of the poem, and the paradise of Xanadu. This paganism ties in with romanticism, as they both can worship multiple gods and also see nature as living and animate.

After line 36, an abrupt change in subject, writing style, and tone occurs. This marks the shifting from paganism to Christianity in his studies. This is also an example of the idea of convex versus concave, as the first line of the first section is 'In Xanadu did Kubla Khan,' while the first line of the second section is 'A damsel with a dulcimer.' This sharp contrast between the convex Kubla Khan, a male, and the concave damsel, a female, both continues this theme of convex versus concave, emphasizing the change in sections and the difference between paganism and Christianity, as well as continuing Coleridge's obsession with sex in nature.

This portrayal of humans having sex in the same poem as the sex occurring in the chasm with the two paganistic gods show the author's desire to connect humanity with nature, a true romantic ideal. The damsel, an Abyssinian (Ethiopian), is the concave force in another relationship, that of her with the 'sunny dome.' The opposite forces of the maid with the dome are further dramatized by the dark and light relationship between them. This clashing of light with dark shows the romantic ideology of the sun versus the moon. In romanticism, sunlight is a harsh, evil force, while moon light is the source of all creativity, and thus good.

This is significant, as this maid is Coleridge's muse, his source of creativity. The maid is directly related to night, and the moon, in this poem, and so is pure good. Conversely, the pleasure dome is directly related to the sun, and thus to evil and the opponent to creativity. Much like the paradox of the material dome in the romantic garden, there is another dome in this section, although it is one made from the imagination and brought on by creativity (the maid). This dome represents the true paradise, one that can not be created from materials, and is strongly connected to the pagan pentacle. A pentacle was believed to mark a space that was separated from our plane of existence, much like the paradise created in this second romantic and pagan dome. The dome is juxtaposed with the ignorant christians, who ironically scorn this true paradise, and cry 'Beware! Beware!' Martin Priestman, in an analysis of this pagan romanticism, noted:

We may detect here some of the seeds of Coleridge's idea of a Kubla Khan.'

This lashing out at Christianity and Christians in general may have also been a reaction to his minister father, as the role of the father at the time of Coleridge's childhood was somewhat alienated from the family. The fact that the Christians don't accept this heaven that the speaker has created may also hint that Coleridge believes that the Christian idea of heaven is false. The repetition of the word 'Beware!' is an example of a common device in romantic writing. When an author wanted to stress an image or a feeling that a word was implying, the author would repeat the word, drilling it into the reader's mind.

The author desired to emphasize the rejection that the Christians had upon his heaven, and thus on him. This may have been an allegory for the isolation and rejection that he felt at the hands of his critics, who did not appreciate him during his time as much as he deserved. The three circles that they 'weave' around him are both an ancient, superstitious (and thus pagan) ritual to keep an evil spirit at bay, and a reference to the holy trinity (with the number three). This ironic juxtaposition of Christians cursing the speaker with a pagan ritual further displays the ignorance of these fools, and also provides a final connection between the pagan first section and the Christian second. The poem is closed with a description of the gustatory delights of paradise, making a final attempt to lure the probably biased reader into the fruits of this pagan and romantic paradise.

Coleridge did not live in a vacuum, and so he was affected by both past and present while writing this poem. Kubla Khan was inspired by the great Kublai Khan (this is an example of one of the author's numerous spelling errors in this poem). Historically, this thirteenth-century descendant of Genghis

Khan had built the palace of K'ai P'ing, which roughly translates to a homophone of Xanadu. Kublai Khan's greatest accomplishment was the conquering of China, and one can think of the 'pleasure dome' that he constructed as his reign over the lands of China, just as his dome floats above the land inside the boundary of his walls, or dominion. Khan's rule was ended in 1368 by the Ming dynasty, in a presumptuously bloody takeover.

This is the reason behind the 'ancestral voices prophesying war,' as they are speaking of the Ming that are soon to come. The choice of a military ruler in the poem may have been influenced by the period in which this poem was written: the Napoleonic era. Napoleon was deeply hated by the British, and so warmongering may have been a subject that he had hoped people could relate and thus connect to. It didn't seem to have worked, however, as his work was widely scorned.

Despite this scorning, however, Kubla Khan is a literary work that has stirred more interest than almost any other poem ever written, at least one of such short length. Samuel Taylor Coleridge uses amazingly implicative imagery and allegory to show his romantic ideals of paganism over Christianity. He does this with amazingly complex metaphors and imagery, such that are so ambiguous as to suggest not having a purpose at all. The ambiguousness he creates is a strong example of romanticism, something that is ambiguous in of itself, as one writer said:

Some scholars see romanticism as completely continuous with the present, some see it as the inaugural moment of modernity, some see it as the beginning of a tradition of resistance to the Enlightenment, and still others date it firmly to the direct aftermath of the French Revolution. The topic is complex enough that most characteristics taken as defining Romanticism have also been taken as its opposite by different scholars. This ambiguity creates a sort of literary mist, and one can not help but to feel that somewhere underneath this mist, perhaps in a chasm or a cave, is the meaning of life itself. This feeling is what draws so many to Kubla Khan, and it is this unexplainable feeling that keeps such fervid study buzzing about it. Such a feeling can only be created by a True Genius, and Coleridge proves himself to be one in Kubla Khan.

Q10. Evaluate the Symbolism in The Rime of the Ancient Mariner.

Or

Q. To what extent is The Rime of Ancient Mariner a symbolic poem.

A close reading of The Rime of the Ancient Mariner will reveal that the Ancient Mariner-who is at once himself, Coleridge and all humanity-having sinned, both incurs punishment and seeks redemption; or, in other words, becomes anxiously aware of his relation to the God of Law (as symbolized by the Sun), and in his sub-consciousness earnestly entreats the forgiveness of the God of Love (represented by the Moon-symbol).

...For Professor Lowes, while he has disclosed a Coleridge of amazing intellectual grasp ... stops short on the border line of purely imaginative experience. In his long study of The Ancient Mariner, he seems to miss the essential allegory.... when all is said, his unsparable book is content to be a review of Coleridge's intellectual and creative relation to his available sources in books, in conversations and in his life history, not (save on occasion as supplying a casual argument) to articulate part with part in the poetic intention as a whole ....

... There is nowhere here or elsewhere in the book [The Road to Xanadu] a hint of the history behind the Mariner's glittering eye, a suggestion of the poet's bold transfer of the glitter in the dead seamen's eyes (Death) to those of the Mariner (Life-in-Death). The poet introduces the Mariner abruptly and repetitively as one with a glittering eye. A similar emphasis is given to the epithet bright-eyed (as in the penultimate stanza of Part VII); and when the fearful question, "Why look'st thou so?", is asked, our thoughts revert to that sinister glitter. Now consider this stanza in Part III:

One after one, by the star-dogged Moon,
Too quick for groan or sigh,
Each turned his face with a ghastly pang,
And cursed me with his eye,

and these stanzas also from Part IV:

The cold sweat melted from their limbs,
Nor rot nor reek did they:
The look with which they looked on me
Had never passed away.
An orphan's curse would drag to hell
A spirit from on high;
But oh! more horrible than that
Is a curse in a dead man's eye!
Seven days, seven nights, I saw that curse,
And yet I could not die;

and these again from Part VI:

All stood together on the deck,
For a charnel-dungeon fitter:
All fixed on me their stony eyes,
That in the Moon did glitter.
The pang, the curse, with which they died,
Had never passed away:
I could not draw my eyes from theirs
Nor turn them up to pray.

All that Professor Lowes says about the glittering eye is true, but it inadequately vindicates Coleridge's unerring choice of the adjective as expressing that uncanny communication of quality between the dead and the quick.

But to return to my thesis-that the Sun (with the Polar Spirit and the First Voice) is conceived in Coleridge's imagination as suggesting the stern, just, masculine, punitive side of the nature of God; and that the Moon (with the Hermit and the Second Voice) normally symbolizes the gentle, feminine, redemptive side. The whole ballad presents a tale of sin and salvation, of crime and compassion, of the operation of inflexible Law and the intervention of inexhaustible Love.

The passages quoted above from Coleridge's own works, considered cumulatively, seem to reinforce this interpretation of the symbols we are considering. In the poem itself it will be noticed that there are eleven references to the Sun and fourteen to the Moon, and that these are the chief recurrent symbols. In the first edition there are ten references to the Sun and fifteen to the Moon. The total number of references to Sun and Moon in the editions of 1798 and 1817 is, however, the same-namely, twenty-five. None of these appears in Part VII in either version, and this, as we shall see, for a reason.

In the pictures of the Sun he appears first as the ship drives southward across the Equator-the Sun coming up upon the left, shining bright, and setting on the right. "The vertical sun," as Professor Lowes explains, "stands over the mast for an instant at noon, to mark the crossing of the Line." After the vessel rounds Cape Horn the positions of sunrise and sunset are reversed. Both passages are temporal and positional in content, Saxon and almost monosyllabic in diction. God is present and omnipresent.

The third reference is more significant. After the wanton slaughter of the Albatross,

Nor dim nor red, like God's own head,
The glorious Sun uprist.

The majesty of the Divine slowly and steadily reveals itself until the Sun has climbed to the meridian. Then there appears one of the most impressively symbolic stanzas in the poem:

All in a hot and copper sky,
The bloody Sun, at noon,
Right up above the mast did stand,
No bigger than the Moon.

The avenging process has begun; the ship is suddenly becalmed; the Polar Spirit plagues the sailors; the dead Albatross is hung about the Mariner's neck; weary and menacing days dawn and die; the crew are suffering from drought and fear; when at last the phantom vessel is descried:

See! See! (I cried) she tacks no more!
Hither to work us weal,-
Without a breeze, without a tide,
She steadies with upright keel!
The western wave was all aflame,
The day was well nigh done!
Almost upon the western wave
Rested the broad bright sun;
When that strange shape drove suddenly
Betwixt us and the Sun.
And straight the Sun was flecked with bars,
(Heaven's Mother send us grace!)
As if through a dungeon-grate he peered
With broad and burning face.
Alas! (thought I, and my heart beat loud)
How fast she nears and nears!
Are those her sails that glance in the Sun,
Like restless gossameres?
Are those her ribs through which the Sun
Did peer, as through a grate?
And is that Woman all her crew?
Is that a Death? and are there two?
Is Death that woman's mate?

Guilt and Fear have interposed themselves between God and the sinful Mariner and his mates, who find themselves now wholly in the power of Death and of Life-in-Death. The crew become the prey of Death, while the Mariner falls to the lot of Life-in-Death. She whistles thrice, and a that sinister signal the sense of the Divine presence is wholly lost:

The Sun's rim dips; the stars rush out:
At one stride comes the dark;
With far-heard whisper o'er the sea,
Off shot the spectre-bark.

One after one, under "the star-dogged Moon" (distorted symbol, for the moment, of an alienated Love), the sailors perish, and the Mariner is abandoned to the horror of utter separation from his Creator. By his own act he has become a castaway. No saint takes pity on his soul in agony. Like Claudius and Macbeth, he seeks to pray and fails to pray. Divorced altogether from hope or help, for seven days and seven nights he watches the curse in the dead men's eyes, and yet, like the Wandering Jew, he himself cannot die. As he declares to the Wedding- Guest in Part VII:

O Wedding-Guest! this soul hath been
Alone on a wide, wide sea:
So, lonely 'twas, that God himself
Scarce seemed there to be.

All is foul and fixed, as though for ever. Suddenly in this static horror pair something moves,-the only moving, hope-renewing object w t n that wilderness of sea and sky. It is the normal, familiar Moon -symbol, as we have seen, of the inexhaustible loving-kindness of God. No contrast could be greater than that between the misery of the Mariner in his ominous surroundings and gentle rising of the friendly Moon. Rossetti was always eloquent in his praise of the first stanza of Part V:

Oh sleep! it is a gentle thing,
Beloved from pole to pole!
To Mary Queen the praise be given!
She sent the gentle sleep from Heaven,
That slid into my soul.

But it is hard to find in The Rime of the Ancient Mariner more beautiful lines than the following, especially as related to their context:

The moving Moon went up the sky,
And nowhere did abide:
Softly she was going up,
And a star or two beside-

Note the word softly and note its reappearance when the poet describes the Second Voice:

The other was a softer voice,
As soft as honey-dew:
But tell me, tell me! speak again,
Thy soft response renewing-
The moonbeams, says Coleridge,
... bemocked the sultry main,
Like April hoar-frost spread!
But where the ship's huge shadow lay,
The charmed water burnt alway
A still and awful red.

That is, all is now bathed in moonlight save the shadow of the ship. The Mariner looks beyond the shadow, and for the first time sees from the Point of view of the God of Love those sea- creatures whom he had previously despised and condemned as "a thousand slimy things." Beheld in this moonlight aspect, they reveal unsuspected grace and charm:

O happy living things no tongue
Their beauty might declare:
A spring of love gushed from my heart,
And I blessed them unaware;
Sure my kind saint took pity on me,
And I blessed them unaware.

Seen thus from the higher point of view, the Mariner sees them thus thereafter, even within the shadow of the ship. "The spell," says the gloss, "begins to break."

Corresponding to the transfiguration of the water-snakes comes soon afterwards, in Part V, another change. The souls of the Mariner's companions "that fled in pain" are replaced by "a troop of spirits blest." The sounds of their singing are sustained with an exquisite sweetness, and they renew that sweetness by darting to their source in the Sun. But there is another spirit who does not sing. "The lonesome Spirit from the south-pole," says the gloss, "carries on the ship as far as the Line, in obedience to the angelic troop, but still requireth vengeance." The Polar Spirit and the Sun are at one in this, for, as the poet immediately declares:

The Sun, right up above the mast,
Had fixed her to the ocean:
But in a minute she 'gan stir,
With a short uneasy motion-
Backwards and forwards half her length
With a short uneasy motion.
Then like a pawing horse let go,
She made a sudden bound:
It flung the blood into my head,
And I fell down in a swound.
How long in that same fit I lay,
I have not to declare;
But ere my living life returned,
I heard, and in my soul discerned,
Two voices in the air.

The two voices, let it be repeated, simply vary the symbols of Law and of Love, of Retribution and of Redemption. The First Voice relates the story of the crime, and knows full kinship and stern sympathy with the wrongs of the Polar Spirit. The Second Voice pleads gently that the Mariner

hath penance done,
And penance more will do.

The Second Voice also reveals the power of the prime corresponding symbol, the Moon:

Still as a slave before his lord,
The ocean hath no blast;
His great bright eye most silently
Up to the Moon is cast-
If he may know which way to go;
For she guides him smooth or grim.
See, brother, seel how graciously
She looketh down on him.

The voices fade away; the Mariner awakens; the Moon is high; the dead men stand on deck with that eerie punitive glitter in their eyes, the spell of which the Mariner, even when redeemed, can never wholly forget. But for the moment the spell is snapped, and the Mariner views the ocean, no longer as slimy, or rotting, or painted, but as fresh and clear and green. "The curse," says the gloss, "is finally expiated." The two motives of Retribution and Redemption are drawing together and a great wind bears the ship towards her haven.

It raised my hair, it fanned my cheek
Like a meadow-gale of spring
Dread expresses itself in the next line:
It mingled strangely with my fears,
and hope in the fourth line:
Yet it felt like a welcoming.

The almost magical manner in which the poet combines these opposing motives here and in the next stanza deserves especial attention. Dread appears in Swiftly, swiftly flew the ship, and hope in the reappearance of the familiar reassuring word softly

Yet she sailed softly too.
Hope is augmented in the line:
Sweetly, sweetly blew the breeze-

But lingering dread lifts itself again in the melancholy reflection:

On me alone it blew.

The Mariner prays (for he has learned long since to pray) that his incredible homecoming may not be as the vision of a dream. "He beholdeth," says the gloss, "his native country." And he loves it as never before, not only for the welcoming that its familiar landmarks offer his heart, but also because the Moon still accompanies him, steeping in calm and silentness the bay, the rock, the kirk, the steady weathercock. He had not heeded the white moonshine that glimmered through night and fog when he slew the Albatross; but now he knows the meaning of the Moon-the eternal Love of God-and he turns to the Hermit for confession and absolution. Confession made, he is duly shriven, but, says Coleridge in the gloss, with penetrating intention: " - Th penance of life falls on him. And ever and anon throughout his future life an agony constraineth him to travel from land to land. And to teach by his own example love and reverence to all things that God made and loveth.

It should be added, in conclusion, that the resolved dualism of Part VII does not require the final presence of either Sun or Moon, since both of the Divine functions which these two respectively rep. resent have been harmonized as necessary and interdependent. This persistent dualism, monastically resolved, is of the very bones and blood of the ballad as a whole. The major symbols, Sun and Moon, First Voice and Second Voice, Polar Spirit and Hermit, and the chief supporting symbols (not considered here)-the unselected Wedding Guests and the one of three, the Albatross and the skylark, the ship and the home country, the corpses and the seraphs, and the reluctantly listening Wedding-Guest of Part I as against the sadder and wiser man of Part VII who "turned from the bridegroom's door"-these constitute an imaginative harmony, a parabolic wholeness that we dare not ignore, for the poet does for all humanity what the Mariner does for the Wedding- Guest. He speaks to the idealist in each of us, and makes us poets too.

Q11. Can we say that Coleridge's writing are Explosive in nature?

Coleridge is so often described in terms which are akin to the word, "explosive," and by all accounts he was at times an unusually dynamic, charismatic and unpredictable person. His writings themselves could also be termed "explosive" merely from their physical form; a fragmented mass, some pieces finished but most not, much of his writing subject to procrastination or eventual change of mind. Today I want to address a moment in his life which produced, as Richard Holmes has characterized it, an explosion of his poetic talent—Autumn 1799, when he first met Sara Hutchinson, and wrote, amongst other poems, the ballad, "Love." In addressing this moment, I want to suggest that the voice of Coleridge at this time was explosive, vital and new, but only when set against the "ancient" balladic tradition with which he engaged. Whilst accepting the dynamism and the unpredictability of Coleridge, I want to show that his acceptance of a formal mode allowed him to find his own particular, romantic voice; for, as Stephen Parrish has pointed out, "for Coleridge, the passion was obscured unless the poet spoke in his own voice." The ballad revival of the eighteenth century supplied Romantic writers with an archive of voices from the past, a past which many seemed to idealize as a time of true feeling, when Nature not only had its place but was also imbued with a raw power. Particularly in the late 1790s, Coleridge worked within such a tradition, and in so doing, found his own voice from the minstrelsy of the past.

I want to begin by illustrating the literary environment in which Coleridge found himself at the end of the eighteenth century. Ancient ballad and song culture was being revived throughout Europe from the early eighteenth century onwards, possibly beginning with the "Ossian" fragments in Scotland. Although most British commentators were skeptical of the authenticity of Ossian, as Hugh Trevor-Roper reports, they were feted in other parts of Europe; and Germany in particular. The title of this conference is "The National Graduate Romanticism Conference"; the proximity of "Romantic" and "National" in this tag is fortuitous, since it is important to realise the close relationship between the ballad revival and a sense of nationhood.

In Johann Herder's famous essay on Ossian, the place of the song or ballad as a kind of national cultural archive is made plain. He refers to the ballads as "the gnomic song of the nation," and continues, in letter form, to his "friend":

> What I wanted to do was remind you that Ossian's poems are songs, songs of the people, folk-songs, the songs of an unsophisticated people living close to the senses, songs which have been long handed down by oral tradition.

Herder locks into the fashionable Rousseauian notion of the "Noble Savage." He goes on:

> Know then, that the more barbarous a people is - that is, the more alive, the more freely acting (for that is what the word

means) - the more barbarous, that is, the more alive, the more free, the closer to the senses, the more lyrically dynamic its songs will be, if songs it has. The more remote a people is from an artificial, scientific manner of thinking, speaking and writing, the less its verses are written for the dead letter.

The attraction of this national voice is its proximity to nature; and thus, proximity to a kind of raw reality. Herder makes clear that this "ancient" verse is a superior form for it is from "Nature" and not from "Art." The present age, he observes, has made the mistake of foregrounding Art over Nature:

And if that is the way our time thinks, then of course we will admire Art rather than Nature in these ancients' poems; we will find too much or too little Art in them, according to our predisposition, and we will rarely have ears to hear the voice that sings in them: the voice of Nature.

Indeed the general thrust of this essay is to cry out for a natural poetic voice, the kind of voice that he found so evident in the Ossian fragments. He complains at the recent German translation of Ossian, by Michael Denis, because he used the polished hexameters of the German neo-classical idiom; a hated, artful masking of the Natural Voice.

At the end of the essay, Herder calls to his countrymen for a collection of German folk-songs. They are badly needed, he feels, to remind the nation of their own collective voice, a voice that has been suppressed. Herder holds up England's Bishop Percy as the great example. He says that, "the sturdy Englishmen were not ashamed of [their ballads], nor did they need to be." Whilst invoking the Elizabethan "Hearts of Oak" quality in the phrase "sturdy Englishmen," Herder reminds his public that they have theirs—and we should have ours. It is a national necessity. Eventually Herder fulfilled his own wish, and himself edited a two volume collection of folk-songs, entitled Volkslieder, which emerged in 1778-9. Herder was writing about Ossian around eight years after the first publication of Percy's Reliques of Ancient English Poetry, which came out in 1765. Although Percy was later to be hailed by many Romantics as a precursor to that movement, he underplays his contribution to any development in aesthetics, calling his collection "the barbarous productions of unpolished ages," and worrying that these poetic fragments are unworthy of patronage. However under this veneer of care and worry is a sly advancement of Herder's division between natural spontaneity and superfluous decoration. Percy immediately continues:

> But this impropriety, it is presumed, will disappear, when it is declared that these poems are presented to your ladyship, not as labours of art, but as effusions of nature, showing the first efforts of ancient genius, and exhibiting the customs and opinions of remote ages.

Percy, in his famous phrase, "effusions of nature," anticipates the explosion of Romantic voices. But in a similar vein to Herder, he points to the collective importance of the ancient fragments. Voices are not singled out in these minstrels' lays; partly because they are anonymous, but partly also, I think, because Herder and Percy saw the fragments as in fact a kind of corpus, which in some way represented the collective ancient whole of a nation. Thus Percy refers to the works as the efforts of "genius," not "genii." For the generations who grew up with Percy's Reliques, this collection of songs would prove extremely influential.

By the end of the century, publication of songs had become even more popular and profitable. One of the most influential of these, as well as one of the most comprehensive, was Sir Walter Scott's Minstrelsy of the Scottish Border, of 1802. Here was the historical archive of ancient Scotland; the second chapter of Ossian, perhaps. Scott emphasized the link between poetry and national history, thus:

> The historian of an individual nation is equally or more deeply interested in the researches into popular poetry, since he must not disdain to gather from the tradition conveyed in ancient ditties and ballads, the information necessary to confirm or correct intelligence collected from more certain sources.

Hugh Trevor-Roper states that, "Before he had ever written a novel, Scott had eclipsed the two founding fathers of the romantic revival. He was at once the new Percy of his country, the new Ossian of his time." Trevor-Roper's thesis in this 1969 Coffin Lecture is that Scott changed the writing of history, by peopling it. Enlightenment historians—Hume, Gibbon and Robertson, for example—"saw history as a process, and a process, moreover, of improvement, of "progress." "But", as he goes on to say, if they thus penetrated to the inner meaning of history, they did so, too often, by overlooking the human content. The men of the past entered their story only indirectly, as the agents or victims of 'progress': they seldom appeared directly, in their own right, in their own social context, as the legitimate owners of their own autonomous centuries. The romantic writers changed all that.

Appearing "directly," in one's "own right," becomes of crucial importance when considering the emergence of an individual voice in Coleridge's early ballads.

Thus Britain at the end of the eighteenth century, according to Dianne Dugaw, "was being swept, bottom to top, by a spirit of antiquarianism, a sentimental and revivalist love for old ballads and histories." Wordsworth and Coleridge were caught up in this surge of sentimental interest and, whilst walking on the Quantock Hills in the late nineties, would conceive the idea of the Lyrical Ballads. In the later Supplementary to the Preface (1815), Wordsworth makes clear his, or their, debt to Percy:

I have already stated how much Germany is indebted to this . . . work; and for our own country, its poetry has been absolutely redeemed by it. I do not think that there is an able writer in verse of the present day who would not be proud to acknowledge his obligations to the Reliques; I know that it is so with my friends; and, for myself, I am happy in this occasion to make a public avowal of my own.

Wordsworth and Coleridge were undoubtedly influenced by Percy. But, as Mary Jacobus points out, the English romantics were equally stimulated by a descendent of Herder, the German balladeer, Gottfried Bürger.[In the nineties, ballad imitations—rather than the ancient originals so praised by Herder and Scott—were becoming increasingly sensational and poorly written. Bürger was a welcome relief. Jacobus comments: "As no-one in England had done, Bürger transformed the traditional ballad into something both novel and contemporaneous." Bürger's ballad, "Leonore," had been in circulation in England from the early nineties, and it thrilled the English writers. Charles Lamb wrote to Coleridge in 1796, "Have you read the Ballad called 'Leonora', in the second Number of the 'Monthly Magazine'? If you have !!!!!!!!!!!!!!"

Coleridge found himself at a time of intense interest and debate over the ballad form. His closest friends were writing to him about the Bürger ballads; he talked about the ballad form with Wordsworth, in particular; and he was deeply interested in German aesthetics. He had taught himself German in the mid-nineties, because, as Richard Holmes puts it, "he considered [it] to be far more advanced, both scientifically and philosophically, than French and English." During the Lyrical Ballads months, he composed many experimental ballad poems: between September 1797 and April 1798 he began The Rime of the Ancient Mariner, Christabel, "The Three Graves," and "The Ballad of the Dark Ladie." Soon after, he traveled to Germany with the Wordsworths; he spent virtually a year there, reading German philosophy and aesthetics voraciously, particularly Kant, Schelling, and the Schlegels. It was during this visit that he bought Herder's Volkslieder.

He returned to England in July, 1799. And in the autumn of that year, amid his failing marriage, he traveled to Durham and met Sara Hutchinson whilst with the Wordsworths. He fell in love with her. Holmes comments: "This love affair underlay, and to some degree undermined, almost everything he did and wrote in the next ten years. It broke his marriage, it helped to break his health, and it very nearly broke his will to go on with his work." But at this time, Coleridge was ignited, regenerated in a passion for life and for writing. "His notebooks, previously used largely for memoranda of his reading, lists, addresses and accounts, suddenly explode into life with descriptions of the rivers and mountains, and the subtle effects of light and weather." From this regeneration, came immediately the poem "Love"—another experimental Gothic ballad. It was the only other ballad apart from the Mariner which he actually completed.

Coleridge's personal explosion here, although important, is somehow not unexpected. His life seemed to be a series of violent outbursts and then of silences, of tremendous energy, and then of procrastination. Dorothy Wordsworth, impressed by Coleridge in at least the early years of their friendship, describes the energy of his arrival at Racedown in June 1797: "he did not keep to the high road, but leapt over a gate and bounded down the pathless field by which he cut off an angle." One of the more famous, early, descriptions of Coleridge is from William Hazlitt. Hazlitt describes the scene, when Coleridge arrived at his local town to preach in 1798:

> He did not come till late on the Saturday afternoon before he was to preach; and Mr Rowe, who himself went down to the coach in a state of anxiety and expectation, to look for the arrival of his successor, could find no one at all answering to the description but a round-faced man in a short black coat (like a shooting jacket) which hardly seemed to have been made for him, but who seemed to be talking at a great rate to his fellow-passengers. Mr Rowe had scarce returned to give an account of his disappointment, when the round-faced man in black entered, and dissipated all doubts on the subject, by beginning to talk. He did not cease while he staid; nor has he since, that I know of. He held the good town of Shrewsbury in delightful suspense for three weeks that he remained there.

Coleridge himself, in describing his habit of procrastination, says, castigating, "it is a deep & wide disease in my moral Nature . . . Love of Liberty, Pleasure of Spontaneity, these all express, not explain, the fact."

Such "Pleasure of Spontaneity" is, as Thomas McFarland notes, most fully felt in Coleridge's notebooks and marginalia. These fragmentary effusions of the poet's mind work well with McFarland's thesis, which to simplify, sees expressions of ruin and fragmentation as a core or bedrock of Romanticism. He says, "It is my judgment, and I believe of many and perhaps most scholars actively engaged in Coleridge studies, that Coleridge's most pregnant, vital and idiosyncratic work is to be found in his pure fragments: in the haphazard entries of his notebooks, and in the immediacies of marginal notations in books he was reading." Many of Coleridge's poems are fragmented, too; Christabel was written in a series of pieces, over a period of time; and Kubla Khan's form, actually described by the poet as "A Fragment," is a result of interruption and forgetfulness. Friedrich Schlegel, in one of his own "Fragments," responds to this modern habit, and relates it to the ancient tradition: "the works of the ancients have become fragments; the works of the moderns are fragments at their inception."

But the poem "Love" is a completed ballad. If there is fragmentation here, it seems to be of a more subtle kind. I suggest that the "ruin," to use McFarland's word, is that of the ancient national tradition. In this balladic experiment, Coleridge works within the by now predictable voices of the tradition, and from their ruins builds a personal emergent voice. The poem "Love" reminds us that you cannot have ruins without having a castle in the first place; Coleridge's own voice is new, but it is the product of a knowledge and love of the historical voice which Herder and Scott refer to in their own ways. Stephen Parrish, in his article, "The Wordsworth - Coleridge Controversy," simplifies nicely the difference in approach for Wordsworth and Coleridge in writing songs and ballads: the crucial difference lay in Wordsworth's adoption of the dramatic method in his ballads. and Coleridge's rejection of it. To put it in the simplest way, the passion that Wordsworth expressed in poetry was likely to be that of his characters, the passion that Coleridge looked for was mainly that of the poet. For Wordsworth, the passion could appear only if the poet maintained strict dramatic propriety; for Coleridge, the passion was obscured unless the poet spoke in his own voice.

Coleridge approaches the balladic tradition and takes what he needs in order to experiment with his own voice. The voice speaks out of generations of voices.

At the time when he met Sara, Coleridge's notebooks teem with jagged shards of life, to use a McFarland turn of phrase. Not only are the entries for November 1799 about as long as all the entries for the preceding six months, but the mental leaps of imagination, excitement and wonder as revealed in the entries is disorienting:

Less than a month after these entries, "Love" was published in the Morning Post, on 21 December 1799, as "Introduction to the Tale of the Dark Ladie." It was considerably edited and newly titled "Love" for the 1800 edition of the Lyrical Ballads. It appears on the page as a controlled, completed, twenty-five stanza poem; evidence of romantic fragmentation here will certainly not come from the format of the verse. The ballad structure is rigid; every stanza is four lines long, the first three of eight syllables, and the last of six syllables. Coleridge dots the poem with the obligatory archaisms of the "ancient tradition": for instance, "ladie," "lay," and "minstrel."

The story within the poem is recognizably of the antiquarian tradition, too: the wooing of a Lady by a Knight, "that wore / Upon his shield a burning brand." This story is told by a minstrel, who himself is wooing a woman. When it first appeared, the poem was prefaced by a letter which Coleridge wrote to the editor of the newspaper, and the letter makes a case for his modern balladeering. Coleridge's list of excuses makes interesting reading in the light of our discussion today:

As it is professedly a tale of ancient times, I trust that 'the affectionate lovers of venerable antiquity' (as Camden says) will grant me their pardon, and perhaps may be induced to admit a force and propriety in it. A heavier objection may be adduced against the Author, that in these times of fear and expectation, when novelties explode [Coleridge's emphasis] around us in all directions, he should presume to offer to the public a silly tale of old fashioned love; and, five years ago, I own, I should have allowed and felt the force of this objection. But, alas! explosion has succeeded explosion so rapidly, that novelty itself ceases to appear new; and it is possible that now, even a simple story, wholly unspired [sic] with politics and personality, may find some attention amid the hubbub of Revolutions, as to those who have resided a long time by the falls of Niagara, the lowest whispering becomes distinctly audible.

Coleridge is coy in this letter. We should not believe that he, of anyone, has not been affected by the explosion of "novelties" in "these times of fear and expectations." "Personality," or the individual person, is actually deeply involved in this poem; we do not need, in this case, the benefit of Holmes' and other modern biographical scholarship, for E.H. Coleridge glosses the history of this poem in the Poetical Works, and he points out a clear connection between this pseudo-medieval fable and Coleridge's personal life. He details the visit to Sockburn, and goes on to show direct links between the poem and this visit; for instance, he says that lines 13-16 describe scenes from Sockburn church and the "field near the farm-house."

More than plain biographical and topographical links, an individual personality or voice emerges from the story of the minstrel singing to his princess, the story which frames the Knight's tale. Because the minstrel/poet is the real subject of the poem, the ballad form is taken from historical fragment to personal, romantic song. The poem becomes less of an ancient imitation, less of a "simple song," than an expression of love, and at the same time, a statement of personal poetic ambition. The poet's love for Genevieve seems more concrete, more real, than the Knight's story, which is transparent by comparison. The Knight's story is constantly interrupted by the poet observing Genevieve react to him; her blushing, and finally, their embrace. "Love" does not end with the Knight, but with the minstrel: "And so I won my Genevieve, / My bright and beauteous bride." The poem foregrounds the minstrel's vocation as a poet, a singer and a teller, by repeating verbs which emphasize such a role: "I told her of the Knight" . . . "I told her how he pined" . . . "I sang an old and moving story." From this, the reader is encouraged, I think, to realise the triple relationship occurring; at the same time, three sets of voices compete for love's sake; Knight and Ladie, Minstrel and Genevieve; Coleridge and Sara. The ninth stanza in particular seems to indicate the importance of finding your way through a poem's voices:

> I told her how he pined: and ah!
> The deep, the low, the pleading tone
> With which I sang another's love,
> Interpreted my own.

At the same time as the minstrel is interpreting his love from the Knight's, so too do we interpret Coleridge's love for Sara from the minstrel; Sara seems very close to the text here. But there are other issues of interpretation going on, too. In this poem, Coleridge has moved the balladic voice from an impersonal story-teller to a doubly personal voice: the minstrel/narrator and Coleridge behind the scenes. Layers of interpretation unfold in this poem: from historical legend to ancient minstrel to romantic poet. Coleridge, in the letter to the editor, complains at "novelty," but in fact what he is doing here seems new and characteristically Romantic. He delves into the historical, cultural archive of songs and ballads - the univocal, raw, voice of a nation as described by Herder - and works within such a frame to produce his own voice. It is a voice both of love and of individual poetic vocation. Parrish reminds us that, for Coleridge, "passion was obscured unless the poet spoke in his own voice." In his ballads, as shown in this example, Coleridge's is not the only voice; but in competing with other, older voices his emerges as dominant and individual. Coleridge, the explosive romantic, becomes one of the writers, according to Hugh Trevor-Roper, who would influence the way people thought and wrote about history. He did this by creating his own voice from the old voice of the nation; by writing "directly," and in his "own right."

Q12. Critics say that there is poetic failure in Coleridge's 'Kubla Khan'. Do you agree?
Or
Q. The poem celebrates the creative imagination. Do you agree?

'Kubla Khan' is now one of Coleridge's best known and most widely read poems, yet it still presents twentieth-century scholars and readers with many of the same critical problems that confounded its contemporary reviewers. It's textual history remains unclear, Coleridge's prefatory explanation of the poem's production is often considered dubious, and scholars just can't agree on what it 'means' or if it means anything at all. Most readers interpret 'Kubla Khan' as an allegory for the creative process, relying heavily upon a perpetuated Romantic formulation of the redemptive imagination as described separately by M. H. Abrams and Geoffrey Hartman. Such critics as Humphry House, Harold Bloom, and Kathleen Wheeler ignore the melancholia of the preface and the last stanza, and decide that the poem celebrates the creative imagination.Other readers like R. H. Fogle and Peter Huhn argue that Coleridge achieves thematic and structural unity by reconciling the celebratory and melancholic opposites evident in the poem. Finally, readers such as Kenneth Burke, Paul Magnuson, and Anne Mellor suggest that Coleridge sustains a contradictory duality in which he bemoans the poet's creative limitations while simultaneously hailing the power of the imagination and celebrating the process of life, thus expressing what Mellor calls Romantic irony.

While seemingly different in their final readings of the poem, these various critical stances locate the redemptive power of the creative imagination within the poet. Further, these readings do not explore in any great detail the rhetorical relationship between the preface and the poem proper and the ways in which this relationship informs Coleridge's complex representation of the creative imagination and the poet figure. If we analyse the subtitle and preface as metalinguistic keys to the poem's interpretive and performative context, we will discover that the poem is not about imaginative redemption or Romantic irony. Rather, 'Kubla Khan' offers its readers a series of false poetic figures, ultimately demonstrating that the ideal (pro)creative and redemptive imagination lies beyond the grasp of the mortal poet, remaining an external and unobtainable other.

The subtitle and preface to 'Kubla Khan' are indeed curious aesthetic and thematic elements that elicit numerous interpretive responses, editorial practices, and critical perspectives. One of the most common readings views the subtitle and the preface as rhetorical apologies added by Coleridge in an attempt to assuage his guilt and/or to avoid harsh criticism. Such a reading ascribes a biographical legitimacy to the introductory note, assuming that the speaker is indeed Coleridge. As a result, the preface is elevated to the literal and misconstrued as an expository addition to the imaginative poem, a supplement that should be distinguished from the aesthetic experience of the poem itself. But what if we denature this (artificial) separation between the prose preface and the imaginative poem and thus include it in the reading experience or, more accurately, in the performance context of the poem? Indeed, critics such as David Perkins, Fred Milne, Marjorie Levinson, and Paul Magnuson have considered this question, analyzing the rhetorical dimensions of the preface and noting the ways in which it informs the reader's interpretive horizon.

I am much indebted to these critical perspectives, for they indeed begin to answer my question concerning the relationship between the prose preface and the imaginative poem. However, they limit their discussions to textual considerations. On the one hand, the preface and the poem are obviously (printed) texts, and it makes sense to address the interpretive relationship between these texts in terms of rhetorical theory. On the other, however, the reading experience—that dialectic between the text and the reader which produces the aesthetic work—is also characterized by a performance context. In other words, the dialectic constituting the reading experience is itself a (cognitive) performance space, and as such presupposes a performance context. Understanding the poem more fully, then, involves a textual analysis that is coupled with a study of the poems performance contexts. I argue that the preface serves as a rhetorical monocle that allows us to glimpse the poem's performance context and thus better to understand Coleridge's ambiguous poetic metaphysics.

'Kubla Khan' exhibits meta communicative devices that remind its audience they are reading a fabricated narrative (the preface) and verse (the poem proper) tale and that reveal a specific understanding of this tale. The very existence or, more properly, the coming into being of the preface suggests that it is itself a rhetorical device that foregrounds the poem's performance context. Critics and literary historians have extensively debated the date of the poem's composition, suggesting dates that range from as early as 1797 to as late as 1800. The most convincing date of composition is Autumn (October or November) of 1797, for this is the date given in the Crew Manuscript endnote in which Coleridge writes, 'This fragment with a good deal more, not recoverable, composed in a sort of Reverie brought on by two grains of Opium, taken to check a dysentery, at a Farm House between Porlock and Linton, a quarter of a mile from Culbone Church, in the fall of the year, 1797.' Furthermore, in a letter to John Thelwall dated 14 October 1797 Coleridge mentions a brief absence that probably corresponds to his stay at Porlock where the poem was composed, and Coleridge goes on to say, 'My mind feels as if it ached to behold & know something great —something one & indivisible—and it is only in the faith of this that rocks or waterfalls, mountains or caverns give me the sense of sublimity or majesty!'.

Here, Coleridge seems preoccupied with the sublime and very specific natural imagery that appear in 'Kubla Khan', helping to confirm further that the poem or some version of it was most likely composed in the fall of 1797. We cannot know if the poem initially had textual supplements; but the 1810 autographed Crew Manuscript contains a short explanatory endnote, and the published 1816 manuscript begins with an elaborate preface. Why did Coleridge feel it necessary to supplement his later manuscripts with such addenda? One explanation concerns Coleridge's role as orator and his ability to affect audiences deeply through verbal performance.

Coleridge was indeed a powerful speaker, drawing crowds for his sermons and lectures. William Hazlitt remembered being awe-struck by Coleridge's preaching in January of 1798:

> As he gave out this text, his voice 'rose like a steam of rich distilled perfumes', and when he came to the two last words, which he pronounced loud, deep, and distinct, it seemed to me, who was then young, as if the sounds had echoed from the bottom of the human heart, and as if that prayer might have floated in solemn silence through the universe.

Coleridge also captivated his audiences with his poetic recitations, and 'Kubla Khan' left a significant impression on many of its listeners. For example, Sir Thomas Noon Talfourd noted a particular occasion sometime between 1815 and 1817:

> But more peculiar in its beauty than this [Coleridge's recitation of 'Christabel'], was his recitation of Kubla Khan . As he repeated the passage—
>
> A damsel with a dulcimer
> In a vision once I saw:
> It was an Abyssinian maid,
> And on her dulcimer she played,
> Singing of Mount Abora!
>
> His voice seemed to mount, and melt into air, as the images grew more visionary, and the suggested associations more remote.

And Leigh Hunt recalled the time Coleridge recited this poem to Byron, an event instigating the poems eventual publication: 'He recited his Kubla Khan one morning to Lord Byron, in his lordship's house in Piccadilly, when I happened to be in another room. I remember the other's coming away from him, highly struck with his poem, and saying how wonderfully he talked. This was the impression of everybody who heard him'.

These accounts suggest that Coleridge had a commanding presence and elicited intense reactions in his audiences. He was a master orator who performed his poetry effectively, and a portion of this poetic performance involved some kind of performative contextualization. For example, in 1811 John Payne Collier remembered engaging in a literary discussion of dreams with Coleridge and Charles Lamb, a discussion 'having been introduced by a recitation by Coleridge of some lines he had written many years ago upon the building of a Dream-palace by Kubla-Khan: he had founded it on a passage he had met with in an old book of travels'.

Even though Collier did not specifically mention a preface or endnote, he did note that Coleridge contextualized the poem for this audience by locating (as far as Collier remembers) its impetus in 'an old book of travels', a performative strategy anticipating the 1816 preface.

The endnote of the Crew Manuscript, the information concerning the possible source of the poem that Coleridge shared with Collier, and the later more developed preface to the 1816 published text suggest that Coleridge felt it necessary to contextualize this poem. However, Coleridge is not apologizing for this poem; rather, his contextualization provides an intellectual and epistemological performance context through which Coleridge attempts to assert his poetic authority (yet, as we will later see, he ironically fails in this effort) and with which Coleridge's audience (auditors of his recitations or readers of his printed text) can better understand the poem.

The first sentence of the preface is significantly set off from the rest as its own paragraph, implying that it holds a singular importance for our understanding of the preface and for the way we position ourselves in relation to the poem. On the surface, this first statement is simply an authorial disclaimer, whereby the speaker discounts his own poem as a 'fragment', a 'psychological curiosity' that caught the interest of some other poet (Lord Byron). One could read this disclaimer quite literally, as do many critics, and thus conclude that indeed Coleridge is dismissing his own work as a mere triviality or curiosity in an attempt to avoid charges of blasphemy or poetic and artistic ineptitude contrasting his attempt to argue for creative individuality in the preface to 'Christabel'. However, if we read the preface to 'Kubla Khan' as a key to performance, then an other reading presents itself, resulting in a more rich and complex understanding of the poem and Coleridge's poetic project.

Kathleen Wheeler provides one possible alternative reading, suggesting that the opening sentence of the preface is an advertisement for the poem that encourages the reader to approach the poem specifically as a 'psychological curiosity' and as a fragment. However, this reading focuses on the interaction between printed text and reader without sufficiently exploring the poem's performative dimensions. Many storytelling performances are initiated by the teller disclaiming his or her tale, attributing the source to some other storyteller or discrediting his or her storytelling ability. Such a strategy conditions listeners to the storytelling act and implies that what they are about to hear will indeed be an interesting and well-told story. The disclaimer is a sign of a good storyteller. Therefore, by subtitling his poem 'A Vision in a Dream. A Fragment' and classifying it as a 'psychological curiosity', Coleridge actually encourages his audience to consider the poem as more than a meaningless dream. Also, by deferring his own poetic authority to that of the celebrated Byron, Coleridge provides more authority to his poem than if he were to assert himself—as if boasting—that he has produced a poetic masterpiece.

Interestingly, this performative disclaimer differs from the traditional storytelling disclaimer in that Coleridge creates a speaker who presents himself as an editor of the printed text (or the orator of a poem he did not necessarily write) who is clearly separate from the Author figure. That is, this speaker is not reciting his own poem but that of some other poetic agent, and this rhetorical move identifies a poetic context in which the performance itself pertains specifically to poets and poetry. Furthermore, by imposing an artificial tension between psychological curiosity and aesthetic poetry, Coleridge effects the opposite: he conflates psychology with aesthetics, ultimately demonstrating that the workings of the (poetic) mind is indeed proper material to constitute a poetics. In effect, readers are not to dismiss the poem as a 'psychological curiosity' but to look for ways in which Coleridge creates a poetics concerning the faculty of poetic imagination. Coleridge's disclaiming the poem as a mere vision or reverie makes the psychology of poetic creation the subject of his poem.

The rest of the preface narrative outlines and foreshadows the ways in which the poet's mind becomes the subject of the poem, thus rhetorically schematizing the reader's horizon of interpretive expectation. By developing a narrative of failed poetic activity, the second section of the preface establishes the poem proper as an allegory of imaginative failure. In the preface narrative, readers encounter a clearly mortal and ill poet figure who possesses limited creative abilities. This figure is not the image of a divine creative entity; on the contrary, he is a frustrated poet who is contrasted later to the supremely powerful Kubla Khan and the demonic poet/seer in the last section of the poem proper. This contrast is foreshadowed and, simultaneously, concretized at the moment in his dream when the poet figure encounters his own subconscious double. He sees the imaginative other who he himself is not (and can never be). The Khan figure of the poet's dream whom the poet tries to render (and, thus, poetically and imaginatively resurrect) in his poem is the mirror image of the poet's creative desire (a mirroring that is thematically reinforced by the reflection image in the quotation from 'The Picture') a desire that can never be satisfied but, instead, can only remain as an eternal process of becoming. As the poet tries to obtain his desire in the form of the poem, as he tries to contain this personal objet petite a , it becomes a Lacanian gift of merde—a fragmented, lost vision. And it is this very narration of desire—coming to terms with poetic failure and coping with the longing to become a supremely powerful decreer of divine grandeur and splendor—that becomes the thematic context of the poem proper.

In other words, the preface provides a context through which to interpret the poem proper as an imaginative representation of failed poetic figures. It can be argued that the headnote (a fragment itself) abstracted from 'The Picture' posits a hopefulness that the vision may return. However, because this moment of re-vision, as the preface notes, 'is yet to come' this hopefulness is indeed ironic, thus suggesting that 'Kubla Khan' is not about poetic rediscovery but, instead, poetic failure. Xanadu—the fantastic realm where the Khan decrees his stately pleasure dome, where the sacred river Alph meanders down to depthless caverns, and where a constructive/destructive fountain breaks through the rocky surface—represents the creative cognition and the phenomenal mind. In this creative realm there are three key agents: the Khan, the sacred river Alph, and the fountain. In terms of the Coleridgean ideal imagination, these three agents correspond to the three faculties constituting Coleridge's phenomenological model—the fancy, the primary imagination, and the secondary imagination respectively. Coleridge had not yet outlined his phenomenological model when he first composed 'Kubla Khan' in 1797, and readers like Paul Magnuson find it too reductive to suggest that the poems exemplify Coleridge's later metaphysics. Wheeler answers this charge by deciding that in the very least, this phenomenal model is implicit in the poem.

But we can safely say that Coleridge's metaphysics is more than just implicit in his poetry; for while his poetry may not have been written to exemplify his prose metaphysics, his studies in philosophy and metaphysics indeed informs his poetic musing. We know that Coleridge was versed in German and familiar with German philosophy as early as 1796-97 (before and during the creative process generating 'Kubla Khan') because in May of 1796 Coleridge wrote Thomas Poole that he was already studying German and planning to study German metaphysics. By December 1796 he had already begun to read Kant, referring to the German metaphysician as 'the most unintelligible Emanuel Kant' in a letter to John Thelwall dated December 17, 1796. Furthermore, by 1796 Coleridge had become disillusioned by 'Mechanic Philosophy' and converted to 'Constructive Philosophy' which conceives the mind as a more active (as opposed to passive) player in the creation of knowledge and the structuring of perception. Even though Coleridge's specific position on the creative imagination is not formally published until 1817 in Biographia Literaria , he had been struggling with these various formulations of the imagination, and his continual work with theories of the mind, passive versus active imagination, and conceptions of the will (dating back as early as 1796) informs the thematics and aesthetics of his early poetry.

In relation to the poem proper, these philosophic theories and models of the creative imagination take the form of multiple poetic figures or creative agents. The first creative figure or agent in this phenomenal realm of Xanadu that we encounter is the Khan, a figure identified immediately with the creative process: 'In Xanadu did Kubla Khan/ A stately pleasure dome decree'. The Khan appears to be the ultimate poet/creator, for his utterances shape his material reality. His active will shapes not merely a poetic text but an aesthetic masterpiece of staggering proportions. The Khan produces an enchanting paradise:

> So twice five miles of fertile ground
> With walls and towers were girdled round:
> And there were gardens bright with sinuous rills,
> Where blossomed many an incense-bearing tree;
> And here were forests ancient as the hills,
> Enfolding sunny spots of greenery. (ll. 6-11)

This pleasure dome is clearly an Edenic realm infused with (masculine) virility ('walls and towers') and seething with sensuality (blossoming incense-bearing trees and soft hills enfolding spots of greenery) and sexual potency ('fertile ground' through which run 'sinuous rills'). It is therefore understandable that so many readers associate the Khan with the creative imagination. However, if we examine this Khan figure more closely, we will see that he is not an agent of the pure imagination but, instead, of what Coleridge called the fancy. While the Khan, as the object of the Author's desire, appears to be the reflection of what the poet cannot be, he ultimately embodies the same poetic failure represented by the Author figure in the preface. That is, in terms of creative ability these figures are opposites, but in terms of Coleridge's model of the imagination they are the same—failed poets of the fancy who do not achieve the Coleridgean ideal.

In Chapter XIII of Biographia Literaria , Coleridge describes the fancy as a non-creative faculty that is more empirical than the imagination. It is a lower cognitive faculty related to and influenced by the will, but not dependent upon the will for its operation: 'Fancy . . . has no other counters to play with, but fixities and definites. The fancy is indeed no other than a mode of memory emancipated from the order of time and space; and blended with, and modified by that empirical phenomenon of the will . . . It may appear as though the fertile gardens of the Khan's creation conforms to Coleridge's organic aestheticism; however, the Khan's kingdom—with its symmetric dome and rigid towers and confining walls—is more akin to a material, ordered realm of 'fixities and definites' that is controlled and mastered by the Khan. It is not an imaginative, ideal realm in which the individual can unite with the infinite. The Khan, rather than being associated with the powers of the pure imagination, is portrayed as a poet of the fancy.

As a poet of the fancy, the Khan is thus a failed poet who is unable to achieve the Coleridgean ideal. Khan's kingdom, with its caves of ice and sunny domes, is an oxymoronic realm inhabited only by the Khan himself. There is no mention of any other human being (the woman wailing for her demon lover is not a literal inhabitant of the pleasure dome, but a metaphor reinforcing the heterosexist perspective of the [pro-]creative process). Instead of establishing self-unity through community, the Khan's creative act effectively isolates him from outside human contact, like the Ancient Mariner who becomes lost on the cold, wide sea and like Christabel who is separated from her dead mother and becomes estranged not only from her lover Geraldine but also her father.

This communal estrangement is paralleled in the final section of the preface, where the Author, just on the brink of poetic genius, is interrupted by a member of his surrounding community and ironically loses the imaginative image. This loss is ironic because imaginative creation, in German and Romantic Idealism, represents an attempt to restore a fractured, disunified self. Because the community is an icon for social unity, it is ironic that an agent from the poet's community—an agent who attempts to conduct business and, thus, to include the poet in the (commercial) workings of that community—effects disunity of the poet's consciousness, resulting in further isolation from the community.

In addition to isolating him from human contact, the Khan's creative acts do not elevate him to prophetic heights as is expected by the Coleridgean ideal. Instead of actually prophesying the coming of war (a war that signifies further the destruction of the Khan's realm and a denial of imaginative creation) the Khan only hears it amid the tumult of the surging and plunging river Alph. Much like the Author figure of the preface (and the crazed poet in the last stanza) the Khan receives the prophecy, via inspiration, instead of originating it as would the true prophetic poet of the pure imagination. It is also important to note that the Khan never becomes united with these eternal ancestral voices: he remains finitely separate from the infinite. The Khan's eternal separation from the infinite is reinforced by his oppositional relationship to nature. His stately pleasure dome is interrupted and shaken—much like the vision that fades from the Author figure's mind in the preface after being interrupted by the business man from Porlock—by the upheaval that the seething fountain and the tumultuous river Alph initiate. As Regina Hewitt notes, 'the Khan's creative method results in an illusory order, a shaky structure on the brink of overthrow by the elements it could momentarily ignore but not permanently exclude'.

The Khan, as a false poet, creates a phantasmagoric realm that ultimately drifts away from him and fades into the prophetic ancestral voices, thus signifying and sealing his eternal isolation and separation from Coleridge's ideal 'infinite I Am'.

If the first stanza represents the Khan as the failed poet of the fancy, then the second stanza—clearly marked as a contrast to the preceding stanza (of the fancy) by the textual break and the dramatic 'But oh!' —allegorizes the pure imagination. For Coleridge, the pure imagination exists as a procreative duality consisting of the primary and secondary imagination. These two faculties are not individually distinct; rather, they are dialectically distinguishable. In other words, they are separate only insofar as they serve vaguely different functions. Yet at the same time these faculties are interrelated and dependent upon each other for their individual functioning and for the operation of the imagination. Again in Chapter XIII of Biographia Literaria , Coleridge describes the primary imagination as that creative power which links the individual with the eternal creative force of the 'infinite I Am' or the transcendental whole .

In 'Kubla Khan', this faculty is best represented by the sacred river Alph(a)—the beginning, the signifier of original and eternal creativity, 'the unifying first principle of all mental activity'—that produces and releases the prophetic ancestral voices. The river Alph is the source of the poet's prophetic powers that are achievable only by the primary imagination which unites the finite poet with the 'infinite I Am'. If the river Alph is the primary imagination, then the fountain, as the 'echo' of the river, represents the secondary imagination.

According to Coleridge, the secondary imagination is a reflection of the primary creative force, a preliminary sensory processor that attempts to unify apparent perceptual disunities into understandable perceptions before presenting them to the primary imagination. Arden Reed explains that 'the secondary imagination is obliged to 'dissolve, diffuse, dissipate' original perceptions before 'recreating' them, in a way that 'idealizes and unifies'. The fountain, with its heaving rocks and seething pants clearly represents this preliminary faculty that dissolves, diffuses, and dissipates phenomenal impressions, unifying them with the primary imagination or, in the context of the poem, the river Alph:

> And from this chasm, with ceaseless turmoil seething,
> As if this earth in fast thick pants were breathing,
> A mighty fountain momently was forced:
> Amid whose swift half-intermitted burst
> Huge fragments vaulted like rebounding hail,
> Or chaffy grain beneath the thresher's flail:
> And 'mid these dancing rocks at once and ever
> It flung up momently the sacred river. (ll. 17-24)

The fountain and the river are dynamically related, for out of the sexually destructive/constructive fountain bursts the prophetic, eternal river Alph, thus allegorizing the way in which the primary and secondary imaginations are dialectically interrelated.

Finally, Coleridge describes the primary and secondary imaginations as dynamic and vital, contrasting them to the fixed and dead nature of objects as objects. In other words, objects in themselves are fixed, dead, indeterminate material, but the powers of the imagination are life-giving in the sense that they transform the indeterminacy of objects in themselves into discernible meaning. We know objects only as phenomena, and it is the dialectic of the imagination that intuits (in the Kantian sense) or gives meaning to or represents the object in our minds and assigns an idea or image to that object. Of the elements in 'Kubla Khan', the river Alph and the fountain clearly represent vital agents, always in sensual motion and disruptive (yet constructive) turmoil. The Khan's pleasure dome is but a fixed structure enclosing the pulsing fountain and the meandering river, two agents that destroy in order to construct and to unify. This unifying process is of a sublime order that provides access to the 'infinite I Am' as signified by the ancestral voices. It is clear that the Khan is a failed poet of the fancy who attempts to contain the primary and secondary imaginative faculties, as his walls attempt to enclose the river, only to be left eternally isolated from his ancestral spirits and human community and from the imagination that makes such connections possible.

This middle stanza representing the integrated workings of the primary and secondary imaginations is interrupted by a final stanza that completes the frame of the preface: the Author figure is abruptly reintroduced, effectively jolting the reader back into the consciousness of the failed poet. The primary and secondary imaginations, in the context of this poem, are purely fanciful (that is, products of the Author's fancy) and remain eternally illusive. As the Author breaks from his vision and bemoans its loss, he fixates not on the river Alph or the fountain but on the aesthetically tangible caves of ice and pleasure dome: 'It was a miracle of rare device,/ A sunny pleasure dome with caves of ice!' (ll. 35-36). Instead of recalling the sublime river Alph or the fountain (images that would be more attractive to the poet of the imagination) the speaker attempts to revive the image of the Khan, to become a poetic agent akin not to the imaginative river Alph but to the fanciful Khan. He wishes to be inspired by the Abyssinian maid and to build his own dome and caves of ice, oxymoronic structures that would separate him from imaginative redemption; for to build this dome and caves of ice would necessitate a poetic possession, a succumbing to an external inspirational force.

This prostrate position relative to an external force is rhetorically paralleled by the Author in the preface who is overtaken by an opium trip and thus receives (instead of creating) the image of the Khan. A poetic process based upon inspiration, as Ken Frieden explains, is an unconscious process and, as such, a passive cognitive mechanism.

As early as 1796 Coleridge had rejected 'Mechanic Philosophy' that casts the mind in a passive role, and by the time he publishes Biographia Literaria , the mind to Coleridge is a dynamic and willful agent, divided into the more active primary and secondary imaginations and the more passive fancy. The Author figure clearly rejects the faculties of the active primary and secondary imaginations in favour of an unconscious, passive process that is antithetical to Coleridge's ideal poetic process. Furthermore, this inspiration invokes fear in his community:

> And all who heard should see them there,
> And all should cry, Beware! Beware!
> His flashing eyes, his floating hair!
> Weave a circle round him thrice,
> And close your eyes with holy dread,
> For he on honeydew had fed,
> And drunk the milk of Paradise. (ll. 48-54)

The poet given in to inspiration becomes an ostracized individual, akin to the Khan figure who is isolated in his pleasure dome and caves of ice and possessing a hypnotic gaze not unlike that of the Ancient Mariner or Geraldine in 'Christabel'. This crazed poet is a demonic figure who becomes inscribed and (textually) enclosed within a mystical circle marking him as an oddity. This poet/seer whom the Author holds as an exemplary creative figure is actually a contained failed poet like the Khan who is girdled with walls and towers. In the end, this Author is doubly failed: first, he does not situate himself with the proper imaginative faculty represented in the poem, choosing instead to identify with the Khan figure and thus missing the real vision in his dream—the nature of the pure imagination; and second, his desire to be a (false) poet secures his eternal isolation from human community. At first glance the Khan and poet/seer figures that the Author longs to emulate appear to represent the poetic ideal—an ideal the speaker fears he may never be able to achieve. Actually, they reflect the Author's own poetic failure. That is, as he attempts to internalize the various poet figures into a unified vision of himself as poet, he ultimately denies himself true identification with the (Coleridgean) poetic ideal, for what he desires is nothing but a projection of his own imaginative inadequacies.

'Kubla Khan' is indeed a 'psychological curiosity' in the sense that it establishes and foregrounds an aesthetics of the imagination. More specifically, the poem aesthetically represents Coleridge's formulation of the imaginative process that he began formulating as early as 1796 and that becomes most clearly articulated in his Biographia Literaria . However, in this poetic representation, the imagination is elevated to a naturalistic realm forever out of reach of the human poet, thus disillusioning all Romantic hope of imaginative redemption through artistic creativity. This Romantic disillusionment is contextualized by Coleridge's preface, for without the preface to the poem, it would be impossible not to identify Khan and the poet/seer at the end of the poem as ideal agents of the imagination.

However, when read from the context of disillusionment, we see that Coleridge actually represents these poetic figures as failed poets. Instead of simply apologizing for his poem via the preface and the subtitle, Coleridge was trying to establish a performance context (as he did when he recited this poem in person) in an attempt to foreground his aesthetic and philosophic insecurities and skepticism. As Hewitt concludes, 'the tensions in 'Kubla Khan' may be seen as a tension between the extant theories of poetic creation—represented by the false poets—which Coleridge rejects and the new theory of imaginative creation that Coleridge embraces but cannot quite completely work out'. And H. R. Rookmaaker suggests that, in the context of Coleridge's writings, 'Kubla Khan' allegorizes the metaphysical and aesthetic struggles through which Coleridge was attempting to work. While I agree for the most part with these conclusions concerning imaginative failure, I am suggesting that the poem foregrounds not a tension so much as a melancholic recognition and subsequent re-vision or relocation of vision.

That is, poetic vision is located not within the individual poet but, rather, in an external other. The poem depicts not what poetic creativity is but, instead, what it is not and cannot be. In this sense, the poem is negatively purposive, for it does not effect a celebration of the poet's divine ability to create sublime aesthetic moments that link the poet to the universal whole (the 'Infinite I Am') thus achieving imaginative redemption. On the contrary, 'Kubla Khan' underscores a disillusionment resulting from the recognition of the poet's imaginative lack, namely the inability to achieve redemption and unity of self through divine acts of poetic creation.

This lack or failure on the part of the various poet figures directs the audience to the moment in the vision that the Author misses, namely that the river Alph and the fountain signify the ideal imaginative faculty or, at least, the nature of the creative process and the rewards it brings in terms of a reunification with the community of the past and the future. 'Kubla Khan', then, is a poem about poetic failure, where agents of the pure imagination are represented not by human personae who are to be emulated but, rather, elements of a sublime natural realm that remain external to the individual and, thus, an always already unobtainable other. Any attempt to colonize this other, to girdle it with walls and towers—to fulfill the desire to become an ideal poet of the imagination—is effectively to destroy this other, to nullify the desire. Becoming the poet of the imagination for Coleridge is a desire always in process that cannot be obtained. For to obtain (and, thus, contain) this other is to render it as the self and, thus, to disable or destroy it. The imagination as aesthetically represented in 'Kubla Khan' is a natural other that cannot be obtained, contained, or harnessed by the poet.

Furthermore, 'Kubla Khan' underscores more specifically Coleridge's personal poetic disillusionment resulting from the recognition of his own imaginative lack, namely his inability to achieve redemption and unity of self through divine acts of poetic creation. As David Riede points out, Coleridge lost faith in his own poetic faculties, viewing himself as 'diseased in will almost to the point of madness'. Ironically, even though Coleridge bemoans his imaginative lack in this and other of his poems ('The Eolian Harp', 'Dejection: An Ode', and, to some extent, The Rime of the Ancient Mariner) his performance abilities suggest that he was a poet of great imagination and authorial command. Yet the literary reviews of 'Kubla Khan' demonstrate that he failed in the eyes of most of his contemporaries, many of whom ignored this poem, cast it in the critical shadow of 'Christabel', or simply dismissed it as a confused and disappointing effort, a fragment generated from his opium-induced sleep that should never have been printed. In the end, the poem not only depicts and explores poetic failure, but its nineteenth-century reception mirrors and reinforces this failure in Coleridge's self-imaging. The goal of becoming the sublime imaginative poet for Coleridge was a desire he could not fulfill; for even as many of the reviews of his earlier poetic works praised his genius and poetic promise, his later poems often confounded and frustrated most reviewers who felt his Germanic aesthetics to be childish, ineffective, and/or overdone. Thus he focused his attentions on proclaiming the imaginative authority of such poets as Milton, Shakespeare, and Wordsworth and establishing his own intellectual authority as literary critic, metaphysician, and theologian

Q13. Asses Coleridge as a poet.

Or

Q. Comment on Rosseti's statement "the leading point about Coleridge's work is its human love."

We may remember Coleridge's own words:

"To be beloved is all I need, And whom I love, I love indeed."

Yet love, though it is the word which he uses of himself, is not really what he himself meant when using it, but rather an affectionate sympathy, in which there seems to have been little element of passion. Writing to his wife, during that first absence in Germany, whose solitude tried him so much, he laments that there is "no one to love." "Love is the vital air of my genius," he tells her, and adds: "I am deeply convinced that if I were to remain a few years among objects for whom I had no affection, I should wholly lose the powers of intellect."

With this incessant, passionless sensibility, it was not unnatural that his thirst for friendship was stronger than his need of love; that to him friendship was hardly distinguishable from love. Throughout all his letters there is a series of causeless explosions of emotion, which it is hardly possible to take seriously, but which, far from being insincere, is really, no doubt, the dribbling overflow of choked-up feelings, a sort of moral leakage. It might be said of Coleridge, in the phrase which he used of Nelson, that he was "heart-starved." Tied for life to a woman with whom he had not one essential sympathy, the whole of his nature was put out of focus; and perhaps nothing but "the joy of grief," and the terrible and fettering power of luxuriating over his own sorrows, and tracing them to first principles, outside himself or in the depths of his sub- consciousness, gave him the courage to support that long, everpresent divorce.

Both for his good and evil, he had never been able to endure emotion without either diluting or intensifying it with thought, and with always self-conscious thought. He uses identically the same words in writing his last, deeply moved letter to Mary Evans, and in relating the matter to Southey. He cannot get away from words; coming as near to sincerity as he can, words are always between him and his emotion. Hence his over-emphasis, his rhetoric of humility. In 1794 he writes to his brother George: "Mine eyes gush out with tears, my heart is sick and languid with the weight of unmerited kindness." Nine days later he writes to his brother James: "My conduct towards you, and towards my other brothers, has displayed a strange combination of madness, ingratitude, and dishonesty. But you forgive me. May my Maker forgive me! May the time arrive when I shall have forgiven myself!" Here we see both what he calls his "gangrened sensibility" and a complete abandonment to the feelings of the moment. It is always a self- conscious abandonment, during which he watches himself with approval, and seems to be saying: "Now that is truly 'feeling'!" He can never concentrate himself on any emotion; he swims about in floods of his own tears. With so little sense of reality in anything, he has no sense of the reality of direct emotion, but is preoccupied, from the moment of the first shock, in exploring it for its universal principle, and then nourishes it almost in triumph at what he has discovered. This is not insincerity; it is the metaphysical, analytical, and parenthetic mind in action. "I have endeavoured to feel what I ought to feel," he once significantly writes.

Coleridge had many friends, to some of whom, as to Lamb, his friendship was the most priceless thing in life; but the friendship which meant most to him, not only as a man, but as a poet, was the friendship with Wordsworth and with Dorothy Wordsworth. "There is a sense of the word Love," he wrote to Wordsworth in 1812, "in which I never felt it but to you and one of your household." After his quarrel in that year he has "an agony of weeping." "After fifteen years of such religious, almost superstitious idolatry and self-sacrifice!" he laments. Now it was during his first, daily companionship with the Wordsworths that he wrote almost all his greatest work. "The Ancient Mariner" and "Christabel" were both written in a kind of rivalry with Wordsworth; and the "Ode on Dejection" was written after four months' absence from him, in the first glow and encouragement of a return to that one inspiring comradeship. Wordsworth was the only poet among his friends whom he wholly admired, and Wordsworth was more exclusively a poet, more wholly absorbed in thinking poetry and thinking about poetry, and in a thoroughly practical way, than almost any poet who has ever lived. It was not only for his solace in life that Coleridge required sympathy; he needed the galvanizing of continual intercourse with a poet, and with one to whom poetry was the only thing of importance. Coleridge, when he was by himself, was never sure of this; there was his _magnum opus_, the revelation of all philosophy; and he sometimes has doubts of the worth of his own poetry. Had Coleridge been able to live uninterruptedly in the company of the Wordsworths, even with the unsympathetic wife at home, the opium in the cupboard, and the _magnum opus_ on the desk, I am convinced that we should have had for our reading to-day all those poems which went down with him into silence.

What Coleridge lacked was what theologians call a "saving belief" in Christianity, or else a strenuous intellectual immorality. He imagined himself to believe in Christianity, but his belief never realised itself in effective action, either in the mind or in conduct, while it frequently clogged his energies by weak scruples and restrictions which were but so many internal irritations. He calls upon the religion which he has never firmly apprehended to support him under some misfortune of his own making; it does not support him, but he finds excuses for his weakness in what seem to him its promises of help. Coleridge was not strong enough to be a Christian, and he was not strong enough to rely on the impulses of his own nature, and to turn his failings into a very actual kind of success. When Blake said, "If the fool would persist in his folly he would become wise," he expressed a profound truth which Nietzsche and others have done little more than amplify. There is nothing so hopeless as inert or inactive virtue: it is a form of life grown putrid, and it turns into poisonous, decaying matter in the soul. If Coleridge had been more callous towards what he felt to be his duties, if he had not merely neglected them, as he did, but justified himself for neglecting them, on any ground of intellectual or physical necessity, or if he had merely let them slide without thought or regret, he would have been more complete, more effectual, as a man, and he might have achieved more finished work as an artist.

To Coleridge there was as much difficulty in belief as in action, for belief is itself an action of the mind. He was always anxious to believe anything that would carry him beyond the limits of time and space, but it was not often that he could give more than a speculative assent to even the most improbable of creeds. Always seeking fixity, his mind was too fluid for any anchor to hold in it. He drifted from speculation to speculation, often seeming to forget his aim by the way, in almost the collector's delight over the curiosities he had found in passing. On one page of his letters he writes earnestly to the atheist Thelwall in defence of Christianity; on another page we find him saying, "My Spinosism (if Spinosism it be, and i' faith 'tis very like it)"; and then comes the solemn assurance: "I am a Berkleyan." Southey, in his rough, uncomprehending way, writes: "Hartley was ousted by Berkeley, Berkeley by Spinoza, and Spinoza by Plato; when last I saw him Jacob Behmen had some chance of coming in.

The truth is that he plays with systems"; so it seemed to Southey, who could see no better. To Coleridge all systems were of importance, because in every system there was its own measure of truth. He was always setting his mind to think about itself, and felt that he worked both hard and well if he had gained a clearer glimpse into that dark cavern. "Yet I have not been altogether idle," he writes in December, 18OO, "having in my own conceit gained great light into several parts of the human mind which have hitherto remained either wholly unexplained or most falsely explained." In March, 1801, he declares that he has "completely extricated the notions of time and space." "This," he says, "I have _done_; but I trust that I am about to do more—namely, that I shall be able to evolve all the five senses, and to state their growth and the causes of their difference, and in this evolvement to solve the process of life and consciousness." He hopes that before his thirtieth year he will "thoroughly understand the whole of Nature's works." "My opinion is this," he says, defining one part at least of his way of approach to truth, "that deep thinking is attainable only by a man of deep feeling, and that all truth is a species of revelation." On the other hand, he assures us, speaking of that _magnum opus_ which weighed upon him and supported him to the end of his life, "the very object throughout from the first page to the last [is] to reconcile the dictates of common sense with the conclusions of scientific reasoning."

This _magnum opus_, "a work which should contain all knowledge and proclaim all philosophy, had," says Mr. Ernest Coleridge, "been Coleridge's dream from the beginning." Only a few months before his death, we find him writing to John Sterling: "Many a fond dream have I amused myself with, of your residing near me, or in the same house, and of preparing, with your and Mr. Green's assistance, my whole system for the press, as far as it exists in any _systematic_ form; that is, beginning with the Propyleum, On the Power and Use of Words, comprising Logic, as the Canons of _Conclusion_, as the criterion of _Premises_, and lastly as the discipline and evolution of Ideas (and then the Methodus et Epochee, or the Disquisition on God, Nature, and Man), the two first grand divisions of which, from the Ens super Ens to the _Fall_, or from God to Hades, and then from Chaos to the commencement of living organization, containing the whole of the Dynamic Philosophy, and the deduction of the Powers and Forces, are complete." Twenty years earlier, he had written to Daniel Stuart that he was keeping his morning hours sacred to his "most important Work, which is printing at Bristol," as he imagined. It was then to be called "Christianity, the one true Philosophy, or Five Treatises on the Logos, or Communicative Intelligence, natural, human, and divine." Of this vast work only fragments remain, mostly unpublished: two large quarto volumes on logic, a volume intended as an introduction, a commentary on the Gospels and some of the Epistles, together with "innumerable fragments of metaphysical and theological speculation." But out of those fragments no system was ever to be constructed, though a fervent disciple, J. H. Green, devoted twenty-eight years to the attempt. "Christabel" unfinished, the _magnum opus_ unachieved: both were but parallel symptoms of a mind "thought-bewildered" to the end, and bewildered by excess of light and by crowding energies always in conflict, always in escape.

Coleridge's search, throughout his life, was after the absolute, an absolute not only in thought but in all human relations, in love, friendship, faith in man, faith in God, faith in beauty; and while it was this profound dissatisfaction with less than the perfect form of every art, passion, thought, or circumstance, that set him adrift in life, making him seem untrue to duty, conviction, and himself, it was this also that formed in him the double existence of the poet and the philosopher, each supplementing and interpenetrating the other. The poet and the philosopher are but two aspects of one reality; or rather, the poetic and the philosophic attitudes are but two ways of seeing. The poet who is not also a philosopher is like a flower without a root. Both seek the same infinitude; one apprehending the idea, the other the image. One seeks truth for its beauty; the other finds beauty, an abstract, intellectual beauty, in the innermost home of truth. Poetry and metaphysics are alike a disengaging, for different ends, of the absolute element in things.

In Coleridge, metaphysics joined with an unbounded imagination, in equal flight from reality, from the notions of time and space. Each was an equal denial of the reality of what we call real things; the one experimental, searching, reasoning; the other a "shaping spirit of imagination," an embodying force. His sight was always straining into the darkness; and he has himself noted that from earliest childhood his "mind was habituated to the Vast." "I never regarded my senses," he says, "as the criteria of my belief"; and "those who have been led to the same truths step by step, through the constant testimony of their senses, seem to want a sense which I possess." To Coleridge only mind existed, an eternal and an eternally active thought; and it was as a corollary to his philosophical conception of the universe that he set his mind to a conscious rebuilding of the world in space. His magic, that which makes his poetry, was but the final release in art of a winged thought fluttering helplessly among speculations and theories; it was the song of release.

De Quincey has said of Coleridge: "I believe it to be notorious that he first began the use of opium, not as a relief from any bodily pains or nervous irritations—for his constitution was strong and excellent—but as a source of luxurious sensations." Hartley Coleridge, in the biographical supplement to the "Biographia Literaria," replies with what we now know to be truth: "If my Father sought more from opium than the mere absence of pain, I feel assured that it was not luxurious sensations or the glowing phantasmagoria of passive dreams; but that the power of the medicine might keep down the agitations of his nervous system, like a strong hand grasping the strings of some shattered lyre." In 1795. that is, at the age of twenty-three, we find him taking laudanum; in 1796, he is taking it in large doses; by the late spring of 1801 he is under the "fearful slavery," as he was to call it, of opium. "My sole sensuality," he says of this time, "was not to be in pain." In a terrible letter addressed to Joseph Cottle in 1814 he declares that he was "seduced to the _accursed_ habit ignorantly"; and he describes "the direful moment, when my pulse began to fluctuate, my heart to palpitate, and such a dreadful falling abroad, as it were, of my whole frame, such intolerable restlessness, and incipient bewilderment ... for my case is a species of madness, only that it is a derangement, an utter impotence of the volition, and not of the intellectual faculties." And, throughout, it is always the pains, never the pleasures, of opium that he registers.

Opium took hold of him by what was inert in his animal nature, and not by any active sensuality. His imagination required no wings, but rather fetters; and it is evident that opium was more often a sedative than a spur to his senses.

The effect of opium on the normal man is to bring him into something like the state in which Coleridge habitually lived. The world was always a sufficiently unreal thing to him, facts more than remote enough, consequences unrelated to their causes; he lived in a mist, and opium thickened the mist to a dense yellow fog. Opium might have helped to make Southey a poet; it left Coleridge the prisoner of a cobweb-net of dreams. What he wanted was some astringent force in things, to tighten, not to loosen, the always expanding and uncontrollable limits of his mind. Opium did but confirm what the natural habits of his constitution had bred in him: an overwhelming indolence, out of which the energies that still arose intermittently were no longer flames, but the escaping ghosts of flame, mere black smoke.

At twenty-four, in a disinterested description of himself for the benefit of a friend whom he had not yet met, he declares, "the walk of the whole man indicates _indolence capable of energies_." It was that walk which Carlyle afterwards described, unable to keep to either side of the garden- path.

"The moral obligation is to me so very strong a stimulant," Coleridge writes to Crabb Robinson, "that in nine cases out of ten it acts as a narcotic. The blow that should rouse, _stuns_ me." He plays another variation on the ingenious theme in a letter to his brother: "Anxieties that stimulate others infuse an additional narcotic into my mind.... Like some poor labourer, whose night's sleep has but imperfectly refreshed his overwearied frame, I have sate in drowsy uneasiness, and doing nothing have thought what a deal I have to do." His ideal, which he expressed in 1797 in a letter to Thelwall, and, in 1813, almost word for word, in a poem called" The Night-Scene," was, "like the Indian Vishnu, to float about along an infinite ocean cradled in the flower of the Lotus, and wake once in a million years for a few minutes just to know that I was going to sleep a million years more." Observe the effect of the desire for the absolute, reinforced by constitutional indolence, and only waiting for the illuminating excuse of opium.

From these languors, and from their consequences, Coleridge found relief in conversation, for which he was always ready, while he was far from always ready for the more precise mental exertion of writing. "Oh, how I wish to be talking, not writing," he cries in a letter to Southey in 1803, "for my mind is so full, that my thoughts stifle and jam each other." And, in 1816, in his first letter to Gillman, he writes, more significantly, "The stimulus of conversation suspends the terror that haunts my mind; but when I am alone, the horrors that I have suffered from laudanum, the degradation, the blighted utility, almost overwhelm me." It was along one avenue of this continual escape from himself that Coleridge found himself driven (anywhere, away from action) towards what grew to be the main waste of his life. Hartley Coleridge, in the preface to "Table-Talk," has told us eloquently how, "throughout a long-drawn summer's day, would this man talk to you in low, equable, but clear and musical tones, concerning things human and divine"; we know that Carlyle found him "unprofitable, even tedious," and wished "to worship him, and toss him in a blanket"; and we have the vivid reporting of Keats, who tells us that, on his one meeting with Coleridge, "I walked with him, at his alderman-after-dinner pace, for near two miles, I suppose. In those two miles he broached a thousand things.

Let me see if I can give you a list—nightingales—poetry—on poetical sensation—metaphysics—different genera and species of dreams— nightmare—a dream accompanied with a sense of touch—single and double touch—a dream related—first and second consciousness—the difference explained between will and volition—so say metaphysicians from a want of smoking the second consciousness—monsters—the Kraken—mermaids—Southey believes in them—Southey's belief too much diluted—a ghost story—Good- morning—I heard his voice as he came towards me—I heard it as he moved away—I had heard it all the interval—if it may be called so." It may be that we have had no more wonderful talker, and, no doubt, the talk had its reverential listeners, its disciples; but to cultivate or permit disciples is itself a kind of waste, a kind of weakness; it requires a very fixed and energetic indolence to become, as Coleridge became, a vocal utterance, talking for talking's sake.

But beside talking, there was lecturing, with Coleridge a scarcely different form of talk; and it is to this consequence of a readiness to speak and a reluctance to write that we owe much of his finest criticism, in the imperfectly recorded "Lectures on Shakespeare." Coleridge as a critic is not easily to be summed up. What may first surprise us, when we begin to look into his critical opinions, is the uncertainty of his judgments in regard to his own work, and to the work of his friends; the curious bias which a feeling or an idea, affection or a philosophical theory, could give to his mind. His admiration for Southey, his consideration for Sotheby, perhaps in a less degree his unconquerable esteem for Bowles, together with something very like adulation of Wordsworth, are all instances of a certain loss of the sense of proportion. He has left us no penetrating criticisms of Byron, of Shelley, or of Keats; and in a very interesting letter about Blake, written in 1818, he is unable to take the poems merely as poems, and chooses among them with a scrupulous care "not for the want of innocence in the poem, but from the too probable want of it in many readers."

Lamb, concerned only with individual things, looks straight at them, not through them, seeing them implacably. His notes to the selections from the Elizabethan dramatists are the surest criticisms that we have in English; they go to the roots. Coleridge's critical power was wholly exercised upon elements and first principles; Lamb showed an infinitely keener sense of detail, of the parts of the whole. Lamb was unerring on definite points, and could lay his finger on flaws in Coleridge's work that were invisible to Coleridge; who, however, was unerring in his broad distinctions, in the philosophy of his art.

"The ultimate end of criticism," said Coleridge, "is much more to establish the principles of writing than to furnish rules how to pass judgment on what has been written by others." And for this task he had an incomparable foundation: imagination, insight, logic, learning, almost every critical quality united in one; and he was a poet who allowed himself to be a critic. Those pages of the "Biographia Literaria," in which he defines and distinguishes between imagination and fancy, the researches into the abstract entities of poetry in the course of an examination of Wordsworth's theories and of the popular objections to them, all that we have of the lectures on Shakespeare, into which he put an illuminating idolatry, together with notes and jottings preserved in the "Table-Talk," "Anima Poetae," the "Literary Remains," and on the margins of countless books, contain the most fundamental criticism of literature that has ever been attempted, fragmentary as the attempt remains. "There is not a man in England," said Coleridge, with truth, "whose thoughts, images, words, and erudition have been published in larger quantities than _mine_; though I must admit, not _by_, nor _for_, myself." He claimed, and rightly, as his invention, a "science of reasoning and judging concerning the productions of literature, the characters and measures of public men, and the events of nations, by a systematic subsumption of them, under principles deduced from the nature of man," which, as he says, was unknown before the year 1795. He is the one philosophical critic who is also a poet, and thus he is the one critic who instinctively knows his way through all the intricacies of the creative mind.

Most of his best criticism circles around Shakespeare; and he took Shakespeare almost frankly in the place of Nature, or of poetry. He affirms, "Shakespeare knew the human mind, and its most minute and intimate workings, and he never introduces a word, or a thought, in vain or out of place." This granted (and to Coleridge it is essential that it should be granted, for in less than the infinite he cannot find space in which to use his wings freely) he has only to choose and define, to discover and to illuminate. In the "myriad-minded man," in his "oceanic mind," he finds all the material that he needs for the making of a complete aesthetics. Nothing with Coleridge ever came to completion; but we have only to turn over the pages about Shakespeare, to come upon fragments worth more than anyone else's finished work.

I find the whole secret of Shakespeare's way of writing in these sentences: "Shakespeare's intellectual action is wholly unlike that of Ben Jonson or Beaumont and Fletcher. The latter see the totality of a sentence or passage, and then project it entire. Shakespeare goes on creating, and evolving B out of A, and C out of B, and so on, just as a serpent moves, which makes a fulcrum of its own body, and seems forever twisting and untwisting its own strength. "And here are a few axioms: 'The grandest efforts of poetry are where the imagination is called forth, not to produce a distinct form, but a strong working of the mind'; or, in other words, "The power of poetry is, by a single word perhaps, to instill that energy into the mind which compels the imagination to produce the picture," "Poetry is the identity of all other knowledges," "the blossom and fragrance of all human knowledge, human thoughts, human passions, emotions, language." "Verse is in itself a music, and the natural symbol of that union of passion with thought and pleasure, which constitutes the essence of all poetry "; "a more than usual state of emotion, with more than usual order," as he has elsewhere defined it. And, in one of his spoken counsels, he says: "I wish our clever young poets would remember my homely definitions of prose and poetry; that is, prose— words in their best order; poetry—the best words in the best order."

Unlike most creative critics, or most critics who were creative artists in another medium, Coleridge, when he was writing criticism, wrote it wholly for its own sake, almost as if it were a science. His prose is rarely of the finest quality as prose writing. Here and there he can strike out a phrase at red-heat, as when he christens Shakespeare "the one Proteus of the fire and flood"; or he can elaborate subtly, as when he notes the judgment of Shakespeare, observable in every scene of the "Tempest," "still preparing, still inviting, and still gratifying, like a finished piece of music"; or he can strike us with the wit of the pure intellect, as when he condemns certain work for being "as trivial in thought and yet enigmatic in expression, as if Echo and the Sphinx had laid their heads together to construct it." But for the most part it is a kind of thinking aloud, and the form is wholly lost in the pursuit of ideas. With his love for the absolute, why is it that he does not seek after an absolute in words considered as style, as well as in words considered as the expression of thought? In his finest verse Coleridge has the finest style perhaps in English; but his prose is never quite reduced to order from its tumultuous amplitude or its snake-like involution. Is it that he values it only as a medium, not as an art? His art is verse, and this he dreads, because of its too mortal closeness to his heart; the prose is a means to an end, not an end in itself.

The poetry of Coleridge, though it is closely interwoven with the circumstances of his life, is rarely made directly out of those circumstances. To some extent this is no doubt explained by a fact to which he often refers in his letters, and which, in his own opinion, hindered him not only from writing about himself in verse, but from writing verse at all. "As to myself," he writes in 1802, "all my poëtic genius ... is gone," and he attributes it "to my long and exceedingly severe metaphysical investigations, and these partly to ill-health, and partly to private afflictions which rendered any subjects, immediately connected with feeling, a source of pain and disquiet to me." In 1818 he writes: "Poetry is out of the question. The attempt would only hurry me into that sphere of acute feelings from which abstruse research, the mother of self-oblivion, presents an asylum." But theory worked with a natural tendency in keeping him for the most part away from any attempt to put his personal emotions into verse. "A sound promise of genius," he considered, "is the choice of subjects very remote from the private interests and circumstances of the writer himself." With only a few exceptions, the wholly personal poems, those actually written under a shock of emotion, are vague, generalized, turned into a kind of literature. The success of such a poem as the almost distressingly personal "Ode on Dejection" comes from the fact that Coleridge has been able to project his personal feeling into an outward image, which becomes to him the type of dejection; he can look at it as at one of his dreams which become things; he can sympathize with it as he could never sympathize with his own undeserving self. And thus one stanza, perhaps the finest as poetry, becomes the biography of his soul:

"There was a time when, though my path was rough, This joy within me dallied with distress, And all misfortunes were but as the stuff Whence Fancy made me dreams of happiness: For hope grew round me, like the twining vine, And fruits, and foliage, not my own, seemed mine But now afflictions bow me down to earth: Nor care I that they rob me of my mirth; But oh! each visitation Suspends what nature gave me at my birth, My shaping spirit of Imagination. For not to think of what I needs must feel, But to be still and patient all I can, And haply by abstruse research to steal From my own nature all the natural man— This was my sole resource, my only plan: Till that which suits a part infects the whole, And now is almost grown the habit of my soul."

Elsewhere, in personal poems like "Frost at Midnight," and "Fears in Solitude," all the value of the poem comes from the delicate sensations of natural things which mean so much more to us, whether or not they did to him, than the strictly personal part of the matter. You feel that there he is only using the quite awake part of himself, which is not the essential one. He requires, first of all, to be disinterested, or at least not overcome by emotion; to be without passion but that of abstract beauty, in Nature, or in idea; and then to sink into a quiet lucid sleep, in which his genius came to him like some attendant spirit.

In the life and art of Coleridge, the hours of sleep seem to have been almost more important than the waking hours. "My dreams became the substance of my life," he writes, just after the composition of that terrible poem on "The Pains of Sleep," which is at once an outcry of agony, and a yet more disturbing vision of the sufferer with his fingers on his own pulse, his eyes fixed on his own hardly awakened eyes in the mirror. In an earlier letter, written at a time when he is trying to solve the problem of the five senses, he notes: "The sleep which I have is made up of ideas so connected, and so little different from the operations of reason, that it does not afford me the due refreshment." To Coleridge, with the help of opium, hardly required, indeed, there was no conscious division between day and night, between not only dreams and intuitions, but dreams and pure reason. And we find him, in almost all his great poems, frankly taking not only his substance but his manner from dreams, as he dramatizes them after a logic and a passion of their own. His technique is the transposition into his waking hours of the unconscious technique of dreams. It is a kind of verified inspiration, something which came and went, and was as little to be relied upon as the inspiration itself. On one side it was an exact science, but on the other a heavenly visitation. Count and balance syllables, work out an addition of the feet in the verse by the foot-rule, and you will seem to have traced every miracle back to its root in a natural product. Only, something, that is, everything, will have escaped you.

As well dissect a corpse to find out the principle of life. That elusive something, that spirit, will be what distinguishes

Coleridge's finest verse from the vèrse of, well, perhaps of every conscious artist in our language. For it is not, as in Blake, literally unconscious, and wavering on every breath of that unseen wind on which it floats to us; it is faultless; it is itself the wind which directs it, it steers its way on the wind, like a seagull poised between sky and sea, and turning on its wings as upon shifted sails.

This inspiration comes upon Coleridge suddenly, without warning, in the first uncertain sketch of "Lewti," written at twenty-two; and then it leaves him, without warning, until the great year 1797, three years later, when "Christabel" and "The Ancient Mariner" are begun. Before and after, Coleridge is seen trying to write like Bowles, like Wordsworth, like Southey, perhaps, to attain "that impetuosity of transition and that precipitancy of fancy and feeling, which are the _essential_ qualities of the sublimer Ode," and which he fondly fancies that he has attained in the "Ode on the Departing Year," with its one good line, taken out of his note-book. But here, in "Lewti," he has his style, his lucid and liquid melody, his imagery of moving light and the faintly veiled transparency of air, his vague, wildly romantic subject matter, coming from no one knows where, meaning one hardly knows what; but already a magic, an incantation. "Lewti" is a sort of preliminary study for "Kubla Khan"; it, too, has all the imagery of a dream, with a breathlessness and awed hush, as of one not yet accustomed to be at home in dreams.

"Kubla Khan," which was literally composed in sleep, comes nearer than any other existing poem to that ideal of lyric poetry which has only lately been systematized by theorists like Mallarme. It has just enough meaning to give it bodily existence; otherwise it would be disembodied music. It seems to hover in the air, like one of the island enchantments of Prospero. It is music not made with hands, and the words seem, as they literally were, remembered. "All the images," said Coleridge, "rose up before me as _things_, with a parallel production of the correspondent expressions." Lamb, who tells us how Coleridge repeated it "so enchantingly that it irradiates and brings heaven and elysian bowers into my parlour when he says or sings it to me," doubted whether it would "bear daylight." It seemed to him that such witchcraft could hardly outlast the night. It has outlasted the century, and may still be used as a touchstone; it will determine the poetic value of any lyric poem which you place beside it. Take as many poems as you please, and let them have all the merits you please, their ultimate merit as poetry will lie in the degree of their approach to the exact, unconscious, inevitable balance of qualities in the poetic art of "Kubla Khan."

In "The Ancient Mariner," which it seems probable was composed before, and not after "Kubla Khan," as Coleridge's date would have us suppose, a new supernaturalism comes into poetry, which, for the first time, accepted the whole responsibility of dreams. The impossible, frankly accepted, with its own strict, inverted logic; the creation of a new atmosphere, outside the known world, which becomes as real as the air about us, and yet never loses its strangeness; the shiver that comes to us, as it came to the wedding- guest, from the simple good faith of the teller; here is a whole new creation, in subject, mood, and technique. Here, as in "Kubla Khan," Coleridge saw the images "as _things_"; only a mind so overshadowed by dreams, and so easily able to carry on his sleep awake, could have done so; and, with such a mind, "that willing suspension of disbelief for a moment, which constitutes poetic faith," was literally forced upon him. "The excellence aimed at," says Coleridge, "was to consist in the interesting of the affections by the dramatic truth of such emotions, as would naturally accompany such situations," those produced by supernatural agency, "supposing them real. And real in this sense they have been to every human being who, from whatever sense of delusion, has at any time believed himself under supernatural agency." To Coleridge, whatever appealed vitally to his imagination was real; and he defended his belief philosophically, disbelieving from conviction in that sharp marking off of real from imaginary which is part of the ordinary attitude of man in the presence of mystery.

It must not be forgotten that Coleridge is never fantastic. The fantastic is a playing with the imagination, and Coleridge respects it. His intellect goes always easily as far as his imagination will carry it, and does not stop by the way to play tricks upon its bearer. Hence the conviction which he brings with him when he tells us the impossible. And then his style, in its ardent and luminous simplicity, flexible to every bend of the spirit which it clothes with flesh, helps him in the idiomatic translation of dreams. The visions of Swedenborg are literal translations of the imagination, and need to be retranslated. Coleridge is equally faithful to the thing seen and to the laws of that new world into which he has transposed it.

"The Ancient Mariner" is the most sustained piece of imagination in the whole of English poetry; and it has almost every definable merit of imaginative narrative. It is the only poem I know which is all point and yet all poetry; because, I suppose, the point is really a point of mystery. It is full of simple, daily emotion, transported, by an awful power of sight, to which the limits of reality are no barrier, into an unknown sea and air; it is realised throughout the whole of its ghastly and marvellous happenings; and there is in the narrative an ease, a buoyancy almost, which I can only compare with the music of Mozart, extracting its sweetness from the stuff of tragedy; it presents to us the utmost physical and spiritual horror, not only without disgust, but with an alluring beauty. But in "Christabel," in the first part especially, we find a quality which goes almost beyond these definable merits. There is in it a literal spell, not acting along any logical lines, not attacking the nerves, not terrifying, not intoxicating, but like a slow, enveloping mist, which blots out the real world, and leaves us unchilled by any "airs from heaven or blasts from hell," but in the native air of some middle region. In these two or three brief hours of his power out of a lifetime, Coleridge is literally a wizard. People have wanted to know what "Christabel" means, and how it was to have ended, and whether Geraldine was a vampire (as I am inclined to think) or had eyes in her breasts (as Shelley thought). They have wondered that a poem so transparent in every line should be, as a whole, the most enigmatical in English. But does it matter very much whether "Christabel" means this or that, and whether Coleridge himself knew, as he said, how it was to end, or whether, as Wordsworth declared, he had never decided? It seems to me that Coleridge was fundamentally right when he said of the "Ancient Mariner," "It ought to have had no more moral than the Arabian Nights' tale of the merchant's sitting down to eat dates by the side of a well, and throwing the shells aside, and lo! a genie starts up, and says he _must_ kill the aforesaid merchant, because one of the date-shells had, it seems, put out the eye of the genie's son."

The "Ancient Mariner," if we take its moral meaning too seriously, comes near to being an allegory. "Christabel," as it stands, is a piece of pure witchcraft, needing no further explanation than the fact of its existence.

Rossetti called Coleridge the Turner of poets, and indeed there is in Coleridge an aerial glitter which we find in no other poet, and in Turner only among painters. With him colour is always melted in atmosphere, which it shines through like fire within a crystal. It is liquid colour, the dew on flowers, or a mist of rain in bright sunshine. His images are for the most part derived from water, sky, the changes of weather, shadows of things rather than things themselves, and usually mental reflections of them. "A poet ought not to pick Nature's pocket," he said, and it is for colour and sound, in their most delicate forms, that he goes to natural things. He hears "the merry nightingale That crowds and hurries and precipitates With fast thick warble his delicious notes;"

And an ecstasy comes to him out of that natural music which is almost like that of his own imagination. Only music or strange effects of light can carry him swiftly enough out of himself, in the presence of visible or audible things, for that really poetic ecstasy. Then all his languor drops off from him, like a clogging garment.

The first personal merit which appears in his almost wholly valueless early work is a sense of colour. In a poem written at twenty-one he sees Fancy "Bathed in rich amber-glowing floods of light,"

and next year the same colour reappears, more expressively, in a cloud,

"wholly bright, With a rich and amber light."

The two women in "The Two Graves," during a momentous pause, are found discussing whether the rays of the sun are green or amber; a valley is

"Tinged yellow with the rich departing light;"

seen through corn at evening,

"The level sunshine glimmers with green light;"

and there is the carefully observed

"western sky

And its peculiar tint of yellow green."

"The Ancient Mariner" is full of images of light and luminous colour in sky and sea; Glycine's song in "Zapolya" is the most glittering poem in our language, with a soft glitter like that of light seen through water. And he is continually endeavouring, as later poets have done on a more deliberate theory, to suffuse sound with colour or make colours literally a form of music; as in an early poem

"Where melodies round honey-dropping flowers, Footless and wild, like birds of Paradise, Nor pause, nor perch, hovering on untamed wing."

With him, as with some of them, there is something pathological in this sensitiveness, and in a letter written in 180O he says: "For the last month I have been trembling on through sands and swamps of evil and bodily grievance. My eyes have been inflamed to a degree that rendered reading scarcely possible; and, strange as it seems, the act of mere composition, as I lay in bed, perceptibly affected them, and my voluntary ideas were every minute passing, more or less transformed into vivid spectra."

Side by side with this sensitiveness to colour, or interfused with it, we find a similar, or perhaps a greater, sensitiveness to sound, Coleridge shows a greater sensitiveness to music than any English poet except Milton. The sonnet to Linley records his ecstatic responsiveness to music; Purcell's music, too, which he names with Palestrina's ("some madrigals which he heard at Rome") in the "Table-Talk." "I have the intensest delight in music," he says there, "and can detect good from bad"; a rare thing among poets. In one of his letters he notes: "I hear in my brain ... sensations ... of various degrees of pain, even to a strange sort of uneasy pleasure.... I hear in my brain, and still more in my stomach."

There we get the morbid physical basis of a sensitiveness to music which came to mean much to him. In a note referring to "Christabel," and to the reasons why it had never been finished, he says: "I could write as good verse now as ever I did, if I were perfectly free from vexations, and were in the _ad libitum_ hearing of fine music, which has a sensible effect in harmonizing my thoughts, and in animating and, as it were, lubricating my inventive faculty." "Christabel," more than anything of Coleridge, is composed like music; you might set at the side of each section, especially of the opening, _largo, vivacissimo_, and, as the general expression signature, _tempo rubato_. I know no other verse in which the effects of music are so precisely copied in metre. Shelley, you feel, sings like a bird; Blake, like a child or an angel; but Coleridge certainly writes music.

The metre of the "Ancient Mariner" is a re-reading of the familiar ballad- metre, in which nothing of the original force, swiftness or directness is lost, while a new subtlety, a wholly new music, has come into it. The metre of "Christabel" is even more of an invention, and it had more immediate consequences. The poem was begun in 1797, and not published till 1816; but in 1801 Scott heard it recited, and in 1805 reproduced what he could of it in "The Lay of the Last Minstrel" and the other metrical romances which, in their turn, led the way to Byron, who himself heard "Christabel" recited in 1811. But the secret of Coleridge's instinct of melody and science of harmony was not discovered. Such ecstasy and such collectedness, a way of writing which seems to aim at nothing but the most precisely expressive simplicity, and yet sets the whole brain dancing to its tune, can hardly be indicated more exactly than in Coleridge's own words in reference to the Italian lyrists of the fifteenth and sixteenth centuries.

They, attained their aim, he says, "by the avoidance of every word which a gentleman would not use in dignified conversation, and of every word and phrase which none but a learned man would use; by the studied position of words and phrases, so that not only each part should be melodious in itself, but contribute to the harmony of the whole, each note referring and conducing to the melody of all the foregoing and following words of the same period or stanza; and, lastly, with equal labour, the greater because unbetrayed, by the variation and various harmonies of their metrical movement." These qualities we may indeed find in many of Coleridge's songs, part Elizabethan, part eighteenth century, in some of his infantile jingles, his exuberant comic verse (in which, however, there are many words "which a gentleman would not use"), and in a poem like "Love," which has suffered as much indiscriminate praise as Raphael's Madonnas, which it resembles in technique and sentiment, and in its exquisite perfection of commonplace, its _tour de force _of an almost flawless girlishness. But in "Christabel" the technique has an incomparable substance to work upon; substance at once simple and abnormal, which Coleridge required, in order to be at his best.

It has been pointed out by the profoundest poetical critic of our time that the perfection of Coleridge's style in poetry comes from an equal balance of the clear, somewhat matter-of-fact qualities of the eighteenth century with the remote, imaginative qualities of the nineteenth century. "To please me," said Coleridge in "Table-Talk," "a poem must be either music or sense." The eighteenth-century manner, with its sense only just coupled with a kind of tame and wingless music, may be seen quite by itself in the early song from "Robespierre":

"Tell me, on what holy ground May domestic peace be found?"

Here there is both matter and manner, of a kind; in "The Kiss" of the same year, with its one exquisite line,

"The gentle violence of joy,"

there is only the liquid glitter of manner. We get the ultimate union of eighteenth and nineteenth century qualities in "Work without Hope," and in "Youth and Age," which took nine years to bring into its faultless ultimate form. There is always a tendency in Coleridge to fall back on the eighteenth-century manner, with its scrupulous exterior neatness, and its comfortable sense of something definite said definitely, whenever the double inspiration flags, and matter and manner do not come together. "I cannot write without a _body of thought_," he said at a time before he had found himself or his style; and he added: "Hence my poetry is crowded and sweats beneath a heavy burden of ideas and imagery! It has seldom ease." It was an unparalleled ease in the conveying of a "body of thought" that he was finally to attain.

In "Youth and Age," think how much is actually said, and with a brevity impossible in prose; things, too, far from easy for poetry to say gracefully, such as the image of the steamer, or the frank reference to "this altered size"; and then see with what an art, as of the very breathing of syllables, it passes into the most flowing of lyric forms. Besides these few miracles of his later years, there are many poems, such as the Flaxman group of "Love, Hope, and Patience supporting Education," in which we get all that can be poetic in the epigram softened by imagination, all that can be given by an ecstatic plain thinking. The rarest magic has gone, and he knows it; philosophy remains, and out of that resisting material he is able, now and again, to weave, in his deftest manner, a few garlands.

Chapter 9

Critical Essays

COLERIDGE'S ANCESTRAL VOICES

WE all know now that Samuel Taylor Coleridge's poem Kubla Khan is a masterpiece. But how do we know this? And has it always been known?

Kubla Khan was first published in 1816 in a booklet that also contained Christabel and The Pains of Sleep. Looking back at the first reviews, it is clear that the poem's importance was at first in some doubt. The Monthly Review of January 1817 is typical — its review felt the poem was 'below criticism' — and the opinion of the Critical Review of May 1816, in its entirety, was that it was 'one of those pieces that can only speak for itself'. As for the British Lady's Magazine of October 1816, it rounded off five and a half columns on Christabel with the words: 'Kubla Khan, or a Vision in a Dream, Mr Coleridge describes as the real production of sleep: it is wild and fanciful'.

Most of the reviews adopted the same strategy as the British Lady's Magazine, and concentrated on Christabel to the near-exclusion of Kubla Khan and The Pains of Sleep. There were of course reasons for this. Christabel was the first and far and away the longest of the three poems, so it seemed natural to treat it as the central part of the book. And it had been read and talked of in admiring terms by the literati for quite a few years before it was actually published, whereas Kubla Khan was little known even among Coleridge's friends.

But perhaps the main reason for the neglect of Kubla Khan was Coleridge's notorious preface, in which he claimed that the poem was composed during a profound sleep. 'Perhaps a dozen more such lines', suggested the Edinburgh Review in September 1816, 'would reduce the most irritable of critics to a state of inaction'. The Academic was equally scathing in September 1821: '...all his works appear to have been composed in a sort of day-dream; and in this he has the advantage over his readers, who must exert themselves to keep awake'.

Perhaps surprisingly, no-one seemed especially intrigued at the idea of involuntary composition. In June 1816 the Eclectic Review found nothing strange in the idea that people who wrote a lot of poetry should dream in it as well, while a month later the Literary Panorama agreed and the Augustan Review recalled tales of Milton waking from sleep and writing down 'twenty or thirty verses, inspired during the night'. But while the role of unconscious processes in artistic creation was taken for granted, art was considered admissible only if it was tempered and controlled by conscious thought and technique: 'There seems to be no great harm in dreaming while one sleeps's the Augustan Review concluded, 'but an author really should not thus dream while he is awake, and writing too'.

Coleridge was writing at the tail end of the Age of Reason. The conscious mind was the key to progress and enlightenment; unbridled self-expression had yet to become fashionable; tradition and continuity were valued more than novelty; and artifice in art was still a sign of quality. With few exceptions the reading public adhered to critical standards based on experience and reason, and there was little room in either for unadorned dreaming. Indeed, it wasn't until the Surrealists and their popularization of Freud and Jung that the idea of dreams as somehow intrinsically artistic became even remotely respectable. Before then, the automatic writing of an Andre Breton or the admission by a Samuel Beckett that he didn't know what his works meant would have been met with blank looks and derision.

Coleridge was of his time. He made no attempt to claim that Kubla Khan should be valued more highly or read more carefully because of its supposed dream origin, but presented it instead 'rather as a psychological curiosity, than on the ground of any supposed poetic merits'. With no reason to doubt Coleridge's word, the Augustan Review was understandably impatient: 'it was poetry, and not psychology, which the public were likely to expect from him'.

After Freud, we modem readers can if we wish recuperate Kubla Khan as a poem by claiming that it shows the poetic unconscious at work. But this isn't the only strategy open to us. In these times of textuality and author-functions and the so-called death of the author many readers feel free to ignore the preface and the author's psychology with equal aplomb. And the empiricists can do the same thing, on other grounds, thanks to the discovery in 1934 of a draft of the poem which showed traces of revision, traces which hardly supported the poet's claim that composition had happened 'without any sensation or consciousness of effort'. Since this discovery the main drift of the reasonable and experienced inheritors of the Age of Reason has been to praise the poem for the amount of controlled and conscious artistic effort it displays.

In recent years a further way has opened up for the determined critic: that of questioning the truth of the famous story of opium, sleep and the person from Porlock, while accepting its presence in the name of a kind of poetic truth. Readers can treat the preface as an integral part of the poem, a kind of restatement of the main argument, which is that the vision has passed and left the poet with nothing but a fragment that would amaze the onlooker if it could only be completed. This is part of a broader movement that seeks to make the 'romantic fragment' a literary genre in its own right. By pulling in the preface and making a perceived lack of conclusion part of the message, this approach has the advantage of forging greater unity in the work. As readers generally demand unity in literary texts, this strategy appears peculiarly satisfying.

Wordsworth and Coleridge: Emotion, Imagination and Complexity

The 19th century was heralded by a major shift in the conception and emphasis of literary art and, specifically, poetry. During the 18th century the catchphrase of literature and art was reason. Logic and rationality took precedence in any form of written expression. Ideas of validity and aesthetic beauty were centred on concepts such as the collective "we" and the eradication of passion in human behaviour. In 1798 all of those ideas about literature were challenged by the publication of Lyrical Ballads, which featured the poetry of William Wordsworth and Samuel Taylor Coleridge. Wordsworth and Coleridge both had strong, and sometimes conflicting, opinions about what constituted well-written poetry. Their ideas were centred on the origins of poetry in the poet and the role of poetry in the world, and these theoretical concepts led to the creation of poetry that is sufficiently complex to support a wide variety of critical readings in a modern context.

Wordsworth wrote a preface to Lyrical Ballads in which he puts forth his ideas about poetry. His conception of poetry hinges on three major premises. Wordsworth asserts that poetry is the language of the common man:

To this knowledge which all men carry about with them, and to these sympathies in which without any other discipline than that of our daily life we are fitted to take delight, the poet principally directs his attention.

Poetry should be understandable to anybody living in the world. Wordsworth eschews the use of lofty, poetic diction, which in his mind is not related to the language of real life. He sees poetry as acting like Nature, which touches all living things and inspires and delights them. Wordsworth calls for poetry to be written in the language of the "common man," and the subjects of the poems should also be accessible to all individuals regardless of class or position. Wordsworth also makes the points that "poetry is the spontaneous overflow of powerful feelings: it takes its origin from emotion recollected in tranquility" . These two points form the basis for Wordsworth's explanation of the process of writing poetry. First, some experience triggers a transcendent moment, an instance of the sublime. The senses are overwhelmed by this experience; the "spontaneous overflow of powerful feelings" leaves an individual incapable of articulating the true nature and beauty of the event. It is only when this emotion is "recollected in tranquility" that the poet can assemble words to do the instance justice. It is necessary for the poet to have a certain personal distance from the event or experience being described that he can compose a poem that conveys to the reader the same experience of sublimity. With this distance the poet can reconstruct the "spontaneous overflow of powerful feelings" the experience caused within himself.

Wordsworth's critical ideas are manifested in his writing. He uses the language and subjects of the common man to convey his ideas. As he writes in "The Tables Turned," "One impulse from a vernal wood / May teach you more of man, / Of moral evil and of good, / than all the sages can" . These lines show that Wordsworth places little stock in the benefit of education or institutionalized wisdom. He implies that any person with exposure to Nature can learn the secrets of the world, regardless of social or economic considerations. In "I wandered lonely as a cloud," Wordsworth uses the sonnet form to express his ideas about poetry being the spontaneous overflow of emotion recollected in tranquility:

For oft when on my couch I lie
In vacant or in pensive mood,
They flash upon that inward eye
Which is the bliss of solitude;
And then my heart with pleasure fills,
And dances with the daffodils.

This stanza comes after Wordsworth has described experiencing in the natural world the wonderment that the night creates. In the poem he meditates on the stars and the light bouncing off waves on the water. He is unable to truly comprehend the beauty and importance of the experience until he is resting afterward, and he is able to reconstruct the event in his mind. This remembrance brings him a wave of emotion, and it is out of this second flood of feeling that the poem is born. In Wordsworth's poetry, these ebbs of emotion are spurred on by his interaction with Nature. In "Tintern Abbey" he writes that "Nature never did betray / the heart that loved her". Indeed, Wordsworth is continually inspired and led into transcendent moments by his experiences in Nature. These experiences bring to his mind a wide variety of contemplations and considerations that can only be expressed, as he writes in "Expostulation and Reply," in "a wise passiveness" .

While Wordsworth's critical ideas obviously worked for his poetry, Coleridge differed in his take on the art. Coleridge did not agree that poetry is the language of the common man. He thought that lowering diction and content simply made it so that the poet had a smaller vocabulary of both words and concepts to draw from. Coleridge focused mainly on imagination as the key to poetry. He divided imagination into two main components: primary and secondary imagination. In Biographia Literaria, one of his significant theoretical works, he writes:

The primary imagination I hold to be the living power and prime agent of all human perception, and as a repetition in the finite of the eternal act of creation of the infinite I AM. The secondary I consider as an echo of the former, coexisting with the conscious will, yet still identical with the primary in the kind of its agency, and differing only in degree, and in the mode of its operation.

It is the imagination involved in the poetry that produces a higher quality verse. The primary imagination is a spontaneous creation of new ideas, and they are expressed perfectly. The secondary imagination is mitigated by the conscious act of imagination; therefore, it is hindered by not only imperfect creation, but also by imperfect expression. To further subdivide the act of imagination, Coleridge introduces his concept of fancy. Fancy is the lowest form of imagination because it "has no other counters to play with but fixities and definite". With fancy there is no creation involved; it is simply a reconfiguration of existing ideas. Rather than composing a completely original concept or description, the fanciful poet simply reorders concepts, putting them in a new and, possibly, fresh relationship to each other. Coleridge also writes that poetry "reveals itself in the balance or reconciliation of opposite or discordant qualities" .Through juxtaposition ideas, concepts, and descriptions are made clear. The more imaginative the juxtaposition is, the more exciting the poem becomes.

As with Wordsworth, Coleridge also combines his theoretical ideas in his poetry. He abandons Wordsworth's notion of poetry for the common man, and uses lofty language, poetic diction, and subject matter that is specialized. While he still holds a reverence for Nature inherent to romantic literature, his poems are not exclusively based around the natural. He makes use of primary imagination in his work; because it is the kind of imagination he values most, and avoids secondary imagination or fancy as much as possible. "Kubla Kahn" illustrates his use of primary imagination:

In Xanadu did Kubla Kahn
A stately pleasure dome decree:
Where Alph, the sacred river, ran
Through caverns measureless to man
Down to a sunless sea.

The poem is the manifestation of a drug-induced vision. The lines have come to Coleridge unbidden, and represent the creation of a previously nonexistent setting. He creates these instances throughout the poem. Especially notable is the vision he describes in the last stanza, "A damsel with a dulcimer / In a vision I once saw: / It was an Abyssinian maid, / And on her dulcimer she played" . Both of these segments create entirely new scenes in the reader's mind. Coleridge also uses highly imaginative images to create juxtaposition in the poem. He writes, "A sunny pleasure dome with caves of ice!", and uses this image twice in the poem. The "reconciliation of opposites" manifests itself in lines such as these. The adjective "sunny" implies warmth, while "ice" is cold. Together they hint at a darker side to the sacrificially idyllic pleasure dome. The simple fact that it is Kubla Kahn's pleasure dome is juxtaposition as well. The leader of the Mongols is not colloquially thought of as a kind or benevolent man. This discordance, too, hints at the underlying darkness of the poem, thereby exposing a truth that all is perfect in neither the pleasure dome nor Coleridge's hallucination.

Coleridge and Wordsworth valued artful poetry. Although they had some different theoretical opinions, both of them succeeded at making poetry that is complex and dense enough to withstand two centuries of analysis, and modern critical practice has not yet fully distilled the potential meaning to be found in their work. It is easy to see how their work places them firmly in the realm of the Romantics, but it is quite difficult to come up with a single form of modern criticism that can fully deal with these two poets. Mimetic forms of criticism, including contemporary Platonists and Aristotelians, could offer observations about how the poetry of Wordsworth seeks to imitate Nature and the effects of Nature on the individual. He works to reconstruct an experience for the reader. Likewise, these same critics could say that Coleridge's imitation of human beings in poems like "Christabel" and "The Rime of the Ancient Mariner" teaches us something about human nature and behaviour.

Unfortunately, purely mimetic criticism would miss much of the rhetorical devices and aesthetic qualities embedded in the work. Pragmatic forms of criticism, which focus on the rhetorical purpose of the author, could offer insight as to how the poetry of Coleridge and Wordsworth seek to instruct the reader, and could also elucidate the rhetorical structure of their works. Both of the poets seek to reinforce the individual, the glory and value of Nature, and induce revelations in their readers. Also, as with all of the Romantics, Coleridge and Wordsworth are constantly seeking the sublime. This period follows the rediscovery of Longinus' ideas about the sublime, which describe how rhetorical structure is used to gain the same feeling of transcendence as Nature promotes. The work of Coleridge and Wordsworth is also rhetorically constructed to express their critical theories, which a pragmatic reading of the text would pick up. The expressive forms of criticism could offer valuable insights into the poems of Coleridge and Wordsworth by focusing on the texts as products of the poets. Certainly forms of psychoanalytical criticism would have much to say about Wordsworth's constant overflow of emotion and Coleridge's chemically altered imagination. Objective critics like the New Critics and formalists could shed light on the synergy created by the interaction of the various parts of Coleridge and Wordsworth's poems.

In Biographia Literaria, Coleridge wrote that a poem must be a cohesive unit, with every part working together to build into a whole. Both poets pay close attention to form and diction in their work, and create poems that are independent units of thought. Especially the work of Wordsworth seems to precipitate Marxist criticism, which could provide insight about the elements of class in his poems, and could also discuss the connection between form and content in the poetry. Postmodern critics would especially enjoy looking at the fierce individuality of Coleridge and Wordsworth, who each create their own micro narrative of the world while rejecting the metanarratives of their time.

The complexity of Wordsworth and Coleridge's theoretical ideas leads to the complexity of their poetry. It is impossible to name one form of criticism that could sum them up entirely, because ultimately they are working with a large number of weighty concepts. This is why their poetry is still read and analysed. Since Aristotle claimed in his Poetics that the complexity of a work is directly proportional to the greatness of the work, we have sought out literature that withstands multiple intense readings. Because we can look at the poems of Coleridge and Wordsworth in a large variety of ways, we are constantly finding new meaning, which gives the poetry re-readability not found in lesser work. Re-

readability is the hallmark of good literature and of the sublime. Coleridge and Wordsworth knew this, and they wrote toward that goal.

Coleridge on Dreaming: Romanticism

A full-length study of Coleridge's concern with dreams has long been a desideratum. Select writings, especially the notebook entries recording dreams and commenting on them, have been studied for such varied purposes as elucidating Coleridge's poems, assessing the effects of his opium use, revealing his ambivalence about women, evaluating his psychological insight, and determining his place in the history of oneirology. But before the appearance of Coleridge on Dreaming, no book was wholly occupied with surveying and interpreting Coleridge's oneirological writings, and it looked as if Coleridge's inability to 'devote an entire work to the subject of Dreams' (a hope he expressed in The Friend) had extended to his critics. Hitherto the most comprehensive examination of Coleridge and dreams took the form of a special double-issue of the psychological journal Dreaming, edited by David Miall and Don Kuiken. But precisely because this was a collection of essays by divers' hands, it was not expected to demonstrate uniformity of approach or even of subject. A book by a single author, in contrast, may reasonably be expected to demonstrate one kind of uniformity or the other.

Let me define these terms for the present context. Uniformity of approach would consist either in interpreting Coleridge's recorded dreams themselves (whatever one conceives dreams to be) or in interpreting his comments about his dreams, but not in doing both. Uniformity of subject would consist in confining one's attention either to dreams, as products of the nocturnal mind, or to 'dreams', as products of the waking mind (i.e. poetic constructs), but not in treating both as if they were the same.

A psychoanalytic study, because it is uniform in approach and assumes that both dreams and poem can reveal the contents of the unconscious, may neglect the formal differences between the texts it studies. But an 'historical exploration', which seeks to investigate 'Coleridge's responses to his dreams and to contemporary debates on the nature of dreaming' (I quote from the dust-jacket blurb of Coleridge on Dreaming), needs to adhere to both uniformities, so to speak. It has no business interpreting Coleridge's dreams for him or interpreting his poems as if they were dreams, for neither kind of interpretation contributes to an understanding of his relation to contemporary oneirology.

By these criteria of assessment, Coleridge on Dreaming is a disappointment. The problems begin on the title page with the concepts of dreams and medical imagination, neither of which is sufficiently defined in the book. The failure to distinguish between the literal and metaphorical use of the word dream, for example in the discussions of drama and Christabel, permits in turn a more serious confusion between different senses of the word imagination. Thus on the one hand imagination is identified with association, as when we are informed that in 'Dugald Stewart's Elements of the Philosophy of the Human Soul (1791), dreams are seen as the product of the imagination, which is the tendency in the 'human mind to associate or connect its thoughts together'' , while on the other it is identified with the formative power that Coleridge theorized in explicit rejection of associationism. Admittedly, Coleridge himself confused the issue by occasionally using the word imagination indiscriminately, and by falsely opposing imagination (conceived in German idealist terms) to fancy (conceived in British empiricist terms). But these facts make it especially imperative for the critic to sort out, rather than to reproduce, the confusion.

If there is one respect which Coleridge is perfectly consistent, it is in his insistence on the suspension of volition, or will, in sleep and nocturnal dreaming. Ford acknowledges this and correctly notes Coleridge's agreement on the matter with earlier oneirological writers, including Andrew Baxter and Erasmus Darwin, but she underestimates the importance of the fact, which is the key to understanding Coleridge's fundamental differentiation of poetic creations from oneiric aggregations. His definition of poetry as a 'rationalized dream' is quoted several times, but without due consideration of the adjective: because reason, for Coleridge, presupposes the presence of will, a rationalized dream is no dream at all, at least according to his usual description of dreams as phenomena produced during sleep by an unrestrained process of association. And just as the presence of will distinguishes poetry from dreams, so the absence of it prevents dreams from containing symbolic meaning.

It is one thing to assert that Coleridge's recorded dreams are symbolic, as Ford does, but quite another to assert that he considered them to be so. (To make both assertions, and to interpret the dream-texts accordingly, is to violate the principle of uniformity of approach.) Coleridge was certainly capable of entertaining the possibility that dreams have a language distinct from but analogous to spoken languages, but it is an exaggeration to say that he was 'firmly convinced' of it. In fact the notebook entries in which he recorded his dreams are remarkable not only for their detailed accounts of the content of the dreams, but also for their refusal to interpret those contents. The extent to which Coleridge was unable or unwilling to relinquish the associationist view of dreams as meaningless is revealed in his dismissive comments on precisely that book which, if he had attributed symbolic significance to dreams, he should have embraced: G. H. Schubert's Symbolic des Traumes, which he read in the second edition of 1821. Coleridge could hardly have failed to notice the similarity between Schubert's concept of the symbol and his own (as formulated in The Statesman's Manual), so why did he reject Schubert's argument that dreams can reveal to modern man the cosmic harmony which nature had revealed to ancient man—and on the grounds that Schubert's symbolic dreams 'ought not to have been confounded with those of proper sleep' .The answer is not, as Ford argues, that Coleridge believed there were 'many different dream languages', but rather that he was unwilling to attribute symbolic significance—which would imply the operation of the rational mind—to phenomena whose rationality he steadfastly denied. The thought that dreams might be meaningful could only increase their terror to someone who, even while explaining them in mechanist and associations terms, often kept himself awake at night to avoid them.

There is much of value in Coleridge and Dreaming, not least in its diligent assembly of Coleridge's scattered writings on dreams and its extensive attention to the Enlightenment contexts of those writings, particularly associations' psychology; but the book's methodological faults militate against its conclusions and prevent it from being considered a 'definitive' treatment of its various subjects.

Beres, David, "A Dream, a Vision, and a Poem

Beres' psychoanalytic reading of The Mariner's symbolism suggests that Coleridge's psyche was characterized by an oral fixation resulting from a repressed conflict between love and hatred for his mother. His unending search for love was expressed in his "memories of food and hunger, fantasies of satiation, and unconcealed demands for love and admiration." He sought and found the protecting love of a mother in other women, Mary Evans' and Poole's mothers, for instance. This continuing and conflicted need was also expressed in the figures of Life-in-Death and Christabel's Geraldine, both of which Beres interprets as representations of the "ambivalently loved preoedipal mother."

Coleridge's guilt is the symptom, Beres claims, of his "aggressive, murderous impulses against an object associated with food and protection." As such, the Albatross is a symbolic expression of his guilt. Beres reads the Mariner's vision of the water snakes phallically, as an attempt to come to terms with the maleness of mother and his own female qualities; the vision is Coleridge's attempt, he maintains, "to resolve his inner conflict and to gain absolution." Coleridge's addiction to laudanum cannot account for the symbolism of the poem; rather, its use is another symptom of Coleridge's other psychic woes. Beres suggests that Wordsworth's suggestion of an appropriate crime is an expression of his own sense of guilt over deserting Annette Vallon and child. His subsequent rejection of the poem can then be seen as his repudiation of his own crime. While Coleridge's defences were oral — attempting to incorporate the object of guilt — Wordsworth's defence was to retreat into "conservatism and forgetfulness, to isolation and repression"

Bostetter, Edward E., "The Nightmare World of The Ancient Mariner," Studies in Romanticism

Bostetter's article is New Critical and psychological, and examines the moral nature of Coleridge's vision of the universe as expressed in the poem. Bostetter's thesis is that the poem's vision is morally meaningful only within the nightmarish universe created by human fears. Bostetter considers two previous arguments on the subject. Lowes argues that the poem is a dream, and therefore the poem's moral is meaningful only within the poem.

Warren argues that the poem expresses a sacramental vision of the universe controlled by a benevolent God; that the poem's moral, which obtains in the world outside the poem also, is that of sin, punishment, repentance, and redemption. Bostetter points out that Warren ignores all the places in the poem in which the universe is presented as being controlled by a hierarchy of capricious, merciless, supernatural beings. Bostetter argues that the poem expresses Coleridge's fears that the universe is capricious and merciless.

The poem is a nightmarish parody of a dream, fulfilling fears rather than wishes. Coleridge countered those fears in his prose by asserting therein that the universe is benevolent. The poem's concluding moral tag is an assertion of this type (akin to whistling in the dark). Thus, contrary to Lowes, Bostetter argues that the poem's moral functions outside the poem itself in Coleridge's universe of fears. Bostetter extents the range of the moral's functioning by speculating that the reason for the poem's power is that it expresses a nightmare not peculiar to Coleridge but shared by all modern, rational poeple: an irrational, magical universe. Bostetter quotes to refute Warren's argument and support his own.

Brisman, Leslie, "Coleridge and the Supernatural,"

Brisman approaches the poem from a theological and, somewhat implicitly, a biographical point of view. Brisman endeavors to apply Coleridge's own hermeneutics to the poem. Brisman's thesis can be broken into several parts: Coleridge's distinction between Reason and Understanding is the basis for a hermeneutic framework which exploits the tension between signifier and signified; Coleridge elaborates his hermeneutics within the sphere of Biblical criticism; within the context Coleridge thus establishes, a reading of the poem can be produced. Coleridge distinguishes between Reason, which he equates with the primary and secondary Imagination, and Understanding, which he equates with fancy. Understanding is the natural faculty of sense-perception.

Reason is the supernatural light which illumines the mind of all humans, the ability to perceive the whole of which the parts are the manifestation, the faculty by which we participate in the divine Idea. This distinction becomes the basis for Coleridge's hermeneutics. Sensory phenomena such as miracles are signs which are incomplete in themselves and need to be referred to the realm of the idea in order to be interpreted: miracles are authenticated by doctrine, rather than authenticating doctrine.

The interpretation of signs as possessing authority in and of themselves Brisman labels preternatural. The interpretation of signs by referring them to an already established spiritual realm Brisman labels supernaturalism. Typology and allegory are the two ways by which the material signifier is referred to its spiritual signified. Typology closes the gap between the two and asserts the co presence of the signifier and the signified: every disciple is Christ. Allegory introduces historical speificity into the static scheme of typological equivalence, and thus opens the gap between the signifier and the signified, asserts their non-identity: Coleridge is not Christ, even though the two may be manifesting the same moral precepts. Coleridge resolves the tension between allegory and typology by making history itself typological, the historical analogue to the development of mind from matter, the emergence of Reason from Understanding, supernaturalism from preturnaturalism. Allegorical non-identity is therefore accounted for by the typological per iodization of history. After illustrating the operation of Coleridge's hermeneutics within the field of biblical criticism, Brisman interprets the poem as an enactment of the development from preturnaturalism to supernaturalism: the Mariner gains salvation by reinterpreting the albatross as an allegorical figure referring to the Christian values embedded in divine Reason but previously clouded over by his superstitions. Nonetheless, the Mariner's supernatural vision does not last. He exists at an intermediate stage in the development of Reason. Brisman compares him to a first-century Christian.

Cooke, Michael G., "The Will in English Romanticism: The Will in Romantic Poetry,"

Cooke argues that the will is a prime topos in the emergence of romanticism, one which permeates many of the issues central to a study of romanticism. He reads The Mariner, "Prometheus," "Tintern Abbey" and "The Solitary Reaper" as manifesting this central interest in the will and in its presence behind nothing less than "all emotions and passions." In analyzing The Mariner in these existential terms, Cooke isolates three "decision points" in the narrative to show the emergence of the will from silence "under chastisement, into a compulsive and impracticable mode of prophecy." The early reference to the Mariner's will (he "hath his will") demonstrates the centrality of the concept to the poem.

The first decision point is present in the Mariner's statement: "I shot the Albatross." In Cooke's view, this act is the Mariner's individuating response to finding himself in an arbitrary, random, impersonal world. Though the motive is ambiguous, the cause is easily identified: "I shot." The Mariner's act is "spiritually purposive . . . undertaking the adventure of individuality." The consequence of this self-enacting act is his discovery of "the implacable isolation and exposure of identity," meaning that his choice brings about his curse: he permanently becomes "a puzzled ontological adventurer."

The second decision point occurs within the new set of circumstances created by the first. The blessing of the watersnakes is an expression of "the basic will or state of his being." In this new expression and therefore perception of self, the Mariner's view of external reality changes. This change is not moral, but ontological, altering the Mariner's relationship to his world and to himself, but not expiating his earlier act. Cooke reads the Mariner's guilt as an indication that he recognizes himself in the his act; he never tries to escape blame. His need to retell his story is his way of keeping himself aware of his act. He tells his tale in response to the question "What manner of man art thou?" as a self-identifying act. The narrative's third decision point is the Mariner's "invocation of his ideal world," which expresses the Mariner's self looking beyond itself, to an inaccesible realm. No reformation is possible, according to Cooke, because ultimately the Mariner wills his own curse. The Mariner, Cooke concludes, depicts the will curtailing the theoretical possibilities of the world.

Davidson, Graham, "The Supernatural Poems: The Ancient Mariner,"

Davidson reads The Mariner as a supernatural poem, in which the representation of the real or material world is secondary to the representation of spiritual realities. Davidson argues that Coleridge then is not primarily concerned to create an independent and consistent physical world: The Mariner's "physical inconsistencies represent moral consistencies." The Mariner's condition, then, is revealed through his changing relationships with the various aspects of nature. His condition — the state of his conscience and his consciousness — also determines his perceptions of his reality, so that inner reality determines outer. The Mariner perceives the same creatures variously as "slimy things," "creatures of the calm" and "happy things"; Davidson gathers then that the poem presents the mind as sense-making rather than sense-made. Davidson sees The Mariner as depicting the need for the coördination of Reason and Understanding. Understanding provides a structure for comprehending sensation. Reason's ideas and principles disclose to us "our distinct but invisible humanity." Davidson refers to Beer's interpretation of the killing of the albatross as related to the Egyptian symbols of Sun, Serpent and Wings. The Mariner's crime removes the mediating agent between Sun and Serpent, between divine Reason and human Understanding. The Mariner is trapped between the wrath of conscience and the loathing of the flesh. Davidson agrees with this interpretation to a point, but sees the Mariner's plight as his being caught in a harsh and joyless reality which has been created by his own Understanding, which is no longer illuminated by Reason. His crime, however, Davidson sees as a kind of happy fall, which makes him aware of the need for Reason to inform Understanding, for sensation to be informed by more substantial principles; it is this insight which eventually forms the basis for the Mariner's new consciousness. Davidson also thinks that the poem's moral stanzas constitute a reasonable summary of the poem, reminding the reader of the poem's moral basis.

Ferguson, Frances, "Coleridge and the Deluded Reader: The Rime of the Ancient Mariner,"

In her post-structuralist analysis, Ferguson argues neither that the poem is "pure imagination" and therefore without rational meaning nor that it is a fairly clear moral allegory. Rather, her claim is that Coleridge is problematizing moral decisions, particularly insofar as our inability to anticipate consequences, that is, our incomplete knowledge, handicaps our ability to make any morally meaningful act. She thinks that most critical readings of The Mariner reflect "a craving for causes," which Coleridge may not have intended the poem to satisfy. Critics have tended to read the gloss, for example, as an unproblematic guide to the poem. But it offers "a strange kind of clarity and unity." For example, when the Mariner sees "a something," the Gloss calls it "a sign"; that is, the Glossist has decided that the something is significant because it assumes that "things must be significant and interpretable."

The gloss, like most criticism, shapes the poem's contradictory moral evidence into cause and effect patterns which the text itself never directly defines. The moral causality found by critics and the gloss in The Mariner is what Ferguson calls a "Barbauldian morality." Mrs. Barbauld wrote for children, to teach them to read for meaning, to supply them with the preconceptions that would enable them to find the right meaning. Her Lessons for Children, for instance, contains two moralistic stories illustrating unmistakeably the consequences of cruelty to birds. Ferguson argues that Coleridge possessed a more sophisticated understanding of the epistemological problems involved in both reading for meaning and making moral judgments.

In The Mariner, for example, he implies "that every interpretation involves a moral commitment with consequences that are inevitably more far-reaching and unpredictable than one could have imagined." The poem's moral seems to be that morality is permanently problematized, that it "appears to involve certainty only if you can already know the full outcome of every action before you commit it." His revisions to The Mariner shift the emphasis away from cause and effect morality toward the process of arriving at morals. For instance, the addition in 1817 of the gloss provides a moral line of interpretation but the new epigraph works against its certainty. The epigraph circles around knowledge and wavers between "belief and self-cautionary gestures," refusing to be certain. Far from ironic, as cause-seeking critics have thought it, the epigraph is a more fitting "key" to the poem than the gloss. This same tension is reflected in Coleridge himself in the conflict between his desire to be understood and to understand comprehensively and his understanding that our information is always incomplete.

Fulford, Tim, "Poetry of Isolation: The Ancient Mariner," Coleridge's Figurative Languages.

Fulford analyses the composition of the poem's discourses in the context of the assumptions of the historical biblical hermeneutics with which Coleridge was familiar. Fulford argues that the poem's discourses disrupt the hermeneutic circle of believers posited by biblical hermeneutics, and illustrate the isolating freedom provided by an exegesis discontinuous with tradition. Historical biblical hermeneutics attempts to deal with the problem posed by the finitude and historicity of interpretation. By positing a grand unity of perspective in God, historical biblical hermeneutics can deny the inerrancy of scripture (an embarrassingly untenable notion) while placing each sacred text in a cirle with other spiritual interpretations of existence authority, a circle which progresses toward though never reaching the circumscription of truth. Spiritual authority thus rests in a continually reinterpreted tradition of spiritual texts. McGann and Butler argue that Coleridge organizes the multiple levels of discourse in his poem to create such a hermeneutic circle: the Mariner interprets his own experience; his interpretation is affirmed but reinterpreted by the poem's narrator, the balladeer; the narrator's reinterpretation is deepened by the scholarly author of the gloss, who typologically integrates the poem into the tradition of Christian hermeneutics; critics such as Warren perpetuate the circle with their interpretations of the poem, which are modernizations and expansions upon the gloss. Fulford argues that the poem is more problematic than either McGann or Butler perceive it to be. The poem brings together, not in unity but in collision, radically discontinuous hermeneutic discourses; the poem breaks the hermeneutic circle.

The Mariner's interpretation of his experience cannot be reduced to the narrator's moralizing or the glosser's typological interpretation. As in "The Wanderings of Cain," in "The Mariner" traditional interpretations of guilt and punishment are destabilized by the poem's sypathetic treatment of the Mariner. The tension thus created between the Mariner's tale, the narrator, and the gloss is left unresolved. Furthermore, the Mariner himself breaks with hermeneutic tradition when he denies the Christian interpretation of the albatross and shoots it. His interpretation of the consequent events disconfirms the hermeneutic circle: through imagination the Mariner creates an interpretation of reality as chaos which is incompatible with the unifying assumption of the hermeneutic circle. His fate as a misunderstood prophet outside of society expresses the radically isolating consequences of the dissolution of the hermeneutic circle into the babble of competing discourses. Even the glosses are fissured by the incompatibility of the various interpretive discourses the glosser draws from the hermeneutic tradition and puts into play in the poem. The unity of the poem's hermeneutic circle is on the verge of collapsing into the fragments of a forced appearance. The poem does not capitulate entirely to radical discontinuity, but suffers intensely from the strain, created by the movements toward unity on the one hand and dissolution on the other, which is inevitable in all hermeneutic endeavors.

Haven, Richard, "The Ancient Mariner in the Nineteenth Century,"

Haven surveys nineteenth-century criticism of The Mariner in order to make the case that criticism of the poem says as much about the critics as it does about the poem. Formalist critics generally failed to appreciate the poem. It was critics such as Lamb, who took a more impressionistic approach, basing his criticism on the effect the poem had on him, who were able to overlook The Mariner's unconventionality and sees its value. By describing his own response, Haven claims, Lamb avoids subjecting the poem to his expectations. Lockhart's essay in Blackwood's (1819) Haven calls the "first serious and sympathetic attempt" to analyse Coleridge's poetic achievement. He seems to have recognized that The Mariner demanded a different kind of criticism than had been brought to the poem; he focused on the experience of the Mariner and of the reader. This approach allowed Lockhart to acknowledge one of the continuing problems of criticism in general and of The Mariner criticism, namely, that

"If a critic admits objective criteria do not have much to do with what happens when he reads a particular poem ... he may find himself without a language to talk about the poem." Therefore, he tries to make the reader feel what he has felt, forming his observations from his own impressions. Haven credits Lockhart with introducing several of the continuing themes in the criticism of the poem, perhaps the most significant of which is the notion that the poem's meaning is in "the psychological, or perhaps spiritual, validity of the experience which the Mariner has, and which the reader shares and may therefore understand."

Margaret Oliphant (Blackwood's 1871) also emphasizes the juxtaposition of the familiar and the unfamiliar, claiming that in experiencing the "visionary voyage," the reader "cross[es] the borders of the unseen." Charles Johnson (Temple Bar 1886) also speaks of the conjunction of realms, noticing how Coleridge uses the moral to bring his readers back to their "own countree." Haven concludes that the common concern of these and other nineteenth-century critics is with the poem's depiction of experience "beyond 'the limits of understanding.'" Haven feels that it is this aspect of the critical response to the poem which saved it from being "buried" by its early, unappreciative criticism and which demanded further consideration from readers.

However, Haven sees in these critics the general tendency to translate the poem's "unconscious allegory" into the reader's conscious allegory, describing this critical move as "not so much the discovery of 'meaning' inherent in the poem as an adaptation of the experience of the poem to the language and beliefs of the reader and critic." Twentieth- century criticism of the poem, he asserts, displays not so much an advance in understanding but a change in the language and belief structures to which the poem is being adapted, so that when modern critics find these early interpretations unsatisfying it is not because the interpretations are inadequate but because they interpret human experience differently.

Kitson, Peter, "Coleridge, the French Revolution, and 'The Ancient Mariner': Collective Guilt and Individual Salvation,"

Kitson looks at the political element of The Mariner, his basic premise being that even an absence of political content is political. He reads The Mariner as "an early attempt to enrich the world with a transcendent ideal forged, like Paradise Lost, from the wreck of his political aspirations." Specifically, his argument is that Coleridge no longer has faith in the ability of political action to effect significant improvement; he has internalized and naturalized his notions of change, crediting the imagination with restorative powers and perceiving not a political paradise but something like Milton's "paradise within." In Kitson's view, The Mariner depicts one man's moral revolution. Kitson argues that Coleridge's political disillusionment is specifically the result of his observations of the French Revolution.

Though Coleridge was an early and lasting supporter of the Revolution, he argued as early as 1795 that a moral revolution needed to precede successful political revolutions, a notion similar to Milton's that outward freedom depends on inner virtue. Coleridge believed at this time that the preaching of the Gospel and political action could bring about change. In his early reflection on the French Revolution, he regrets its excesses, but sees them as "unavoidable conditions of the establishment of the 'blest future state.'" However, a poem like "Ode to the Departing Year" belies the fragility of his optimism and feelings of guilt about the terrors of the Revolution. Here the guilt is perceived as national, England's shared responsibility for its crimes against France. Kitson argues that by 1798 Coleridge had abandoned his hopes for improvement through political action, beginning to develop instead "an inward process of redemption achieved through the contemplation of the divine presence in nature." Kitson finds this change expressed in "France: An Ode," "Fears in Solitude" and in The Mariner and argues that Coleridge specifically has Milton in mind in developing this notion that "freedom is a state of the virtuous mind." Viewing The Mariner as expressing Coleridge's change of heart about political reform, Kitson states that the significant elements of the poem are redemption and guilt but he undertakes almost no direct analysis of the poem. He asserts that The Mariner demonstrates "the progress from motiveless sin to individual redemption achieved through the agency of natural forces 'impregnated' with the divine."

Knight, G. Wilson, The Starlit Dome: Studies in the Poetry of Vision

Knight provides an impressionistic interpretation of the poem that focuses primarily on the symbolism of the imagery. He suggests that the albatross, hailed by the crew as a "Christian soul", symbolizes a Christ like force that guides humanity from "primitive and fearful origins", the latter symbolized by the snow and fog. Knight reviews the circumstances surrounding the slaying of the albatross and suggests that the moral significance of the Mariner's unmotivated act is indicated in the contrast of imagery in the poem. Water corresponds to the "primitive layer in the psychology of man", and the Albatross, the natural guiding force of instinct. The parching heat and dryness that follows corresponds to man's present mental state of agony. Thus, Knight views the crime as symbolic of the Fall from innocence. It is a "thwarting of some guiding purpose by a murderous self will", the consequence of which is the emergence of a "self-consciousness that leads to agonies and high aspirations." This new mode of being, suggests Knight, is accompanied by a knowledge of evil, as symbolized in the imagery of the "rotting sea" and the "slimy creatures". The fem-harlot of the death ship wins the soul of the Mariner and casts a spell that causes the crew to drop one by one. Thus, the Mariner, now soulless is left to endure a knowledge of death and a loneliness in which "God himself seemed absent". In the midst of his extreme despair the Mariner in an "unpremeditated and instinctive charity" blesses the sea snakes. The act symbolizes the momentary return of his natural instincts and elicits an "unforced forgiveness from God", symbolized by the slipping of the albatross from the Mariner's neck. "Purity", symbolized by water, this time in the form of refreshing rain, and "freedom", in the form of a vital and helpful breeze, replaces the "horror and sin" of the Mariner's previous state. Knight suggests that the kirk and the figure of the hermit represent "homely earthly qualities" of "unstriving peace". The Mariner is now on solid ground again after the "Nightmare and transcendent vision." His return symbolizes the embracing of agape, or Christian love, and the rejection of Eros. Knight suggests that the final lesson of the narrative is "total acceptance of God and his universe through humility, and love of man towards beast".

Magnuson, Paul, Coleridge's Nightmare Poetry

According to Magnuson, Coleridge's central aim in the Mariner poem was to render as accurately as possible a vision of a mind in the throes of a delirium. The poem depicts a state in which the"imagination modifies incoming sensation in terms of some predominant emotion", in this instance, fear. He suggests that as Coleridge's own sense of depression and isolation increased towards the end of 1803, so too did his familiarity with nightmares and his identification with the Mariner of the poem. Examination of the revisions to the final 1817 version of the poem reveal Coleridge's increased capacity to render a more realistic enactment of the mode of perception associated with the Mariner's nightmare state. Magnuson suggests that it is this mode of perception that underlies the source of evil and consequent guilt inherent in the Mariner's actions. The mind in the nightmare state is cut off from the "stabilizing external realities", and "forsakes the familiar world for the freely associating and uncontrolled imagination." He suggests that the well known interpretive problems the poem raises can be accounted for by highlighting the absence of any clear cause and effect pattern between the Mariner's sense of guilt and the punishment he is made to suffer. Magnuson argues, for example, that the initial storm that drives the ship and its crew into the unfamiliar lands of the ice and snow is associated in the Mariner's mind with a malevolent spirit . The implication is that the Mariner feels himself persecuted by a tyrannical God prior to committing the act with which his punishment is most directly linked. This suggests to Magnuson that, prior to killing the albatross, the Mariner has already entered a kind of twilight state. His fear and detachment from the stabilizing influences of external reality leads him in a distorted fashion to identify the bird with the malevolent storm.

In support of his interpretation, Magnuson draws from Notebook entries that suggest Coleridge believed there to be an "essential evil in day dreams and imaginings". The subjective random trains of association that occurred during these states could not be innocent because "the passive mind dissolves into a chaotic phantasmagoria of images and feelings". To "emancipate itself from the tyranny of association" was viewed by Coleridge as requiring "the most arduous effort of the mind", an act of will. Magnuson concludes that, in the case of the Mariner, the will has been overwhelmed by "the strong currents of fear". The loss of the will, along with the loss of external support, leads to a destruction of a sense of personal identity. He argues that the common interpretation that the blessing of the water snakes represents the Mariner's redemption is inconsistent with the fact that the central problem for the character, the "abdication of his will", still remains.

McGann, Jerome J., "The Meaning of the Ancient Mariner,"

In his somewhat new historicist article, McGann criticizes the state of Mariner criticism in order to understand not only the meaning of The Mariner but also how it means. Most of this criticism has been carried out, he argues, within the tradition that is "licensed and underwritten" by Coleridge and expressed in The Mariner, namely a Christian, hermeneutic tradition which developed out of and in response to the Higher Criticism. Coleridge sees Scripture as a "living and processive organism" that comes into existence and continues to develop in a historical sphere. Scripture is interpreted in the light of the "recorded history of those who read and interpreted the Scriptures in the enthusiasm and the faith that was peculiar to their age and circumstances."

Scripture should be approached then with one eye to the fact that "the received documents . . . report historically mediated materials" and with the other to the reader's own time-specific, culturally delimited perspective. McGann contends that The Mariner incorporates into itself layers of historical accretion which function as "'levels of authority' or points of view in terms of which the poetic events were to be experienced and narrated." McGann argues that with his revisions Coleridge made the poem into his "imitation of a culturally redacted literary work"; he finds four historical strata in the poem: 1/ the pre-Enlightenment Mariner's tale, 2/ the version passed down by balladeers, 3/ the seventeenth-century glossator's editorial comments and 4/ the post-Enlightenment poet's point of view on "his invented materials." He maintains that this self-contained textual history "exhibits in a concrete way the process of continuous spiritual revelation."

McGann claims that the poem's "events" are actually interpretations of events carried out in terms of the pagan, Catholic and Broad Church Protestant ideologies represented by the historical levels of the poem. Criticism that does not historicize the poem will merely reify this interpretive tradition: if there is no prior disbelief, no reaction to the pre-Enlightenment vision of reality expressed by the Mariner, there can be no suspension of disbelief. McGann considers the current critical interaction with the poem to be something like this.

He understands the poem to encourage diverse readings but thinks that "Since this encouragement is made in terms of the Christian economy, the interpretations have generally remained within the broad spiritualist terms . . . which

Coleridge's mind had allowed for." To gain true critical distance from and insight into the poem, McGann argues that it must be thoroughly historicized, a process that The Mariner itself initiates with its internal strata of text reception. McGann concludes that a historicizing, critical approach, rather than a hermeneutic approach allows "the meaning of the 'Rime' [to emerge] as the 'dramatic truth' of Coleridge's intellectual and religious commitments." This approach takes the poem beyond its current status as little more than an object of faith to the status of "a human — a social and a historical — resource."

Miall, David S., "Guilt and Death: The Predicament of the Ancient Mariner,"

Miall's biographically and psychologically informed reading of the poem is an attempt to return "questions arising from the poem's strangeness" back to the primary experience of the poem itself. The poem's strangeness and power, Miall argues, is the result of an unresolvable conjunction of guilt and the encounter with death. This ambivalence results from the poem's raising "questions about the adequacy of our moral categories for interpreting our place in the world" . The Mariner struggles to understand his experience by means of his moral framework but cannot, with the result that his experience seems irrational. However, if the experience were wholly irrational or random, it would not be so disturbing. Miall links this ambivalence to a prevailing sense of guilt or dread felt by Coleridge throughout his adult life. He suggests the root of this emotion is the death of Coleridge's father when Coleridge was eight.

He presents psychological evidence to the effect that children who encounter death before the age of nine are likely to repress their memories of grief and to develop a sense of guilt, as if they had somehow brought about the separation from their loved one. Coleridge's sense of dread found an outlet in the story of the Albatross. Miall also examines the

Mariner's experience of the death of his crewmates in psychological terms, likening the resulting emotional response to that of survivors of catastrophes. As the lone survivor, the Mariner becomes closed-off psychically and experiences a profound sense of guilt and an irreparable psychic wound. Though ultimately unsuccessful, the Mariner's attempt to deal with his wound, which parallels Coleridge's own search for the source of his dread, is a "heroic failure" which deeply affects the poem's reader, who recognizes the obduracy of meaning in an arbitrary world.

Modiano, Raimonda, "Words and 'Languageless' Meanings: Limits of Expression in The Rime of the Ancient Mariner,".

Modiano argues that The Mariner generates its dramatic action from the Mariner's effort "to reconstruct a painful episode of his past." Coleridge, she says, seems to be exploring "the discrepancy between actual experience and the recounting of experience by a character with a 'most believing mind.'" Modiano uses post-structural assumptions about language to examine this discrepancy, paying particular attention to the way in which the Wedding Guest influences the Mariner's retelling and the effect of that influence on the Mariner's attempts to understand his experience. She is fundamentally arguing two points: first, that the Mariner is attempting to put into words an unspeakable experience; and second, that he is attempting to put it into words comprehensible to his auditor. On the first point she argues that language itself "finally binds [the Mariner] to an inaccurate view of [his experience]." The paradox of the Mariner's situation is that he is compelled to retell his story in spite of the fact that the events which make up that story had deprived him of words when he first experienced them. In this retelling, he inevitably "endows his past with a coherence and meaning which it did not originally possess." Modiano argues that Coleridge uses the gloss to illustrate "what can happen to a work if clarity and secure moral explanations [replace] its vastly nebulous universe." As such it duplicates a central part of the poem's action: the Mariner attempts to retell his experience to a "conventionally-minded auditor" and the glossator tries to shape these same data for a reader with biases similar to the Guest's. The Mariner needs the Guest and this dependency will shape the telling of the tale.

Modiano finds two modes of discourse in the Mariner's tale: "the language of self" which she describes as a concrete and primarily sensorial mode of description and "the language of social discourse" which does not simply record sensations "but assigns them meanings dependent upon a system of shared mythology." Modiano finds in the Mariner's recounting of the tale an initial move from the second mode toward the first; that is, as he moves away from land "his tale gradually empties itself of metaphors which link him to the safe public world he has left behind." After the Guest's interruption in Part IV, however, which resensitizes the Mariner to his audience, he begins to use the second, public mode again, assigning meanings, specifically Christian meanings, to his experience.

While making his tale accessible to the Guest and holding his attention, these meanings also begin to shape his telling — shape, that is, and limit his attempt to understand his experience. Modiano describes this shift between modes of discourse in detail, arguing that "the Mariner erects orthodox structures out of unorthodox experience," to restate the point. She concludes by claiming that "the search for an adequate medium of expression that could accommodate the deepest demands of self without sacrificing either the authenticity or the intelligibility of the artistic product" is one of Coleridge's life-long concerns. Throughout his writings one finds his belief in the power of language, in words as "the wheels of intellect," tempered by his "gloomy awareness of the abstractness of words and their power to chain, distort, and impoverish the experiences of the self."

Prickett, Stephen, "The Living Educts of the Imagination: Coleridge on Religious Language,"

Prickett's primary purpose is to examine Coleridge's developing philosophy or theology of language. He argues that Coleridge's interest in the possibilities and limitations of language begins with an interest in religious language. Prickett begins by noting some religious elements of The Mariner, pointing out the difficulty of interpreting them using either a psychological or a religious framework. Analysis in one of these sets of terms is not satisfactorily complete and forces one back to the other set of terms, so that the reader is held in tension between two unsatisfactory alternatives. This is an example of Coleridge's stereoscopic view of language, which Prickett argues, Coleridge develops from his view of religious language. Coleridge sees scripture as having "a twofold significance": by being particular and concrete it is symbolic of universal truth. Additionally, religious language is not different in kind from other language, but in degree and mode. Coleridge sees it as openly symbolic, tensional, and stereoscopic; once religious language is seen in this way, ordinary language can be too. Prickett traces this developing notion in The Statesman's Manual, Biographia Literaria and Church and State, and concludes by suggesting the importance of Coleridge's dialectic view of language to the religious thinkers who followed him, even into this century.

Sitterson, Joseph C., Jr., "'The Rime of the Ancient Mariner' and Freudian Dream Theory,"

Sitterson attempts to reconcile formalist interpretations of The Mariner with contemporary psychoanalytic theory, suggesting that the formalist consensus that the poem is "structurally and thematically coherent," while incompatible with Freudian thinking about the meaningfulness of dreams, is compatible with current views of primary process thinking as it involves the self's attempt to integrate with its world. Sitterson disputes Freudian interpretations of the poem which almost universally read the poem as dream. While many critics have disputed Freudian interpretations, none have found the central weakness in the existing attempts at a psychoanalytic reading of The Mariner. The lack of agreement in readings of the albatross (for instance) is not the problem with applying this method to the poem, since dreams are always overdetermined. Neither is the problem that the method is a kind of procrustean bed: on Freudian assumptions, the interpreter has great latitude in seeking the latent content, provided he works in collaboration with the dreamer.

The flawed assumption, as Sitterson sees it, is that the poem can be treated as a dream, Coleridge's or the Mariner's, and that its coherent meanings can be disregarded. Freud started with the notion that dreams are meaningful; they are, however, rationally coherent only at the level of latent content, all apparent coherence in the manifest content being an "unessential illusion." Formalist criticism, says Sitterson, has unanimously concluded that there is an "ostensible continuity" to the Mariner's experience; it is, that is to say, unlike dream: its coherence is not the thinly concealed composite of fragments that Freudian analysis would expect to discern in manifest content.

Psychoanalytic interpretations have ignored the poem's coherence and merely assumed the poem to be a conglomerate of infantile fantasies and "the day's residues." Because of the regressive manner in which the Mariner recounts his tale, they have assumed the content to be regressive and any philosophical, moral or aesthetic coherence to be illusory. Sitterson claims that recent psychoanalytic theory recognizes the "nonregressively significant" place of primary process thinking in art and the fact that primary and secondary process thinking are closely conjoined in the healthy self's encounter with the world.

Sitterson works out these concepts in his own interpretation of The Mariner, claiming that the Mariner's account of his experience is not infantile or regressive, but rather "concerned with the affective significance of the world as it impinges upon the self" — the world not being limited here to the infantile world but including aspects besides the pyschological. The Mariner himself is aware of the moral's inadequacy, though he does not understand its insufficiency to order his experience. From a psychoanalytic perspective, its inadequacy is evidence of his pyschic disintegration, the lack of continuity between his primary and secondary process thinking. His moral, then, can be read as a measure of the adequacy of his method of assimilating his experience. The moral illuminates neither a flaw in the poem nor Coleridge's psychological problems, but a lack in the Mariner. His retelling of the tale and its moral are a result of his inability to fully assimilate the experience to the self. The poem implies that there is value in such disintegration, namely, in making the Mariner aware of a spiritual depth to life. It illustrates, then, the mixed blessing of self-consciousness and the fact that psychic disintegration is not always regressive.

Twitchell, James B., "The World Above The Ancient Mariner," Literature and Language

Twitchell reads The Mariner as an expression of Coleridge's Neoplatonism, which links the hierarchical structure of visible and invisible realms with inner, psychological reality. He thinks that the triviality of the crime is Coleridge's cue to the reader to notice "the mysteries of the world within and beyond," so that the poem leads its readers, as the Mariner is led, to a vision "of the unity of life both internal and external." Twitchell establishes from historical evidence (primarily his request to Thelwall to be sent several neoplatonic books) that Coleridge was inclined toward the Neoplatonists. Coleridge saw man as occupying a middle position in a hierarchical chain of life, distinct and separate from those beings above and below him. Between man and the gods, Coleridge placed a realm of neoplatonic and Christian daemons. Twitchell describes the poem's rendering of this hierarchy from the subaquatic Polar Spirit through the aerial or ethereal "fellow-daemons" to the angels above these and to "my kind saint" below only God. Twitchell claims that this hierarchy of spirits is an analogue for the Mariner's psyche, a "system of personified states" representing the "psychological layers leading down to an unknowable deep 'Truth.'" The poem then is seen as more of a psychodrama than a story. Twitchell argues that the gloss and epigraph show Coleridge "struggling to clarify" The Mariner's psychological significance.

Revisions to the epigraph and the addition of gloss and motto attempt to turn the poem from external to internal. Reading the gloss as the key to interpretation, Twitchell argues that the Mariner's crime is in breaking this hierarchical chain, violating the laws of hospitality and bringing himself into conflict with the daemons occupying the realm above man. The Mariner comes to see the connection between inner reality and outer reality. When he blesses the watersnakes, he is learning to see with the "inward eye." He joins the ranks those aware of the realms above; "by connecting himself not only to Nature but also to the invisible powers of life, [the Mariner] reweaves the filaments between the cosmic and microcosmic world." He reconnects what he has separated.

Watkins, Daniel P., "History as Demon in Coleridge's The Rime of the Ancient Mariner,"

In his new historicist reading of The Mariner, Watkins argues that "the narrative is a symbolic formulation of the contradictions and struggles within history, and that these historical pressures are antecedent to, and indeed are the primary source of meaning behind, all plot-level representations." He argues that "the Christian structures of authority governing the Mariner's world . . . are in vital conflict with antagonistic and apparently demonic forces which refuse to remain in the obscurity into which they have been cast." These demonic forces undermine "the idealized and uncritical assumptions of love, God, family, and community that prevail in the Mariner's world." Watkins argues that this conflict is best explained in historical or political rather than psychological terms since "it is produced in the very forms and relations . . . of social reality itself." The Mariner embodies this demonic force, "steadily follow[ing] a course that . . . subtly and brilliantly co-opts the vocabulary of Christian value for the sake of undermining and redefining that value."

His destructiveness is evident in the three interactions the poem depicts: between the Mariner and the albatross, the Hermit and company, and the Wedding Guest. He destroys the Guest and the Hermit and company by means of his story-telling just as he has destroyed the albatross by means of his impulsive action. Watkins sees this process of destruction as the Mariner's defining quality.

The hearers of his tale are doomed precisely because they think that it "can be placed safely within the scheme of things as set down by Christianity." Watkins sees the demonic in the Mariner in the reaction of the Pilot's boy ("'The Devil knows how to row'"), in the poem's images of death, rot, slime, etc., and in his sucking his own blood. His blessing of the watersnakes is also a demonic "redefinition of Christian vocabulary and of Christian ritual." The blessing is motivated by the same carelessness and impulsiveness that drove him to shoot the albatross.

Furthermore, the blessing is of a creature associated with the biblical serpent. On this reading, Watkins does not have to explain how the symbolic significance of sun and moon reverse after the blessing as Warren must. Rather, he thinks that the images of night and dark following the blessing reinforce the fact that the Mariner has converted to a demonic system of power. He sees in the Mariner's affirmation of Christian and traditional values at the end of the poem evidence of his demonic role. Watkins considers this demonism to be an expression of Coleridge's reaction to the social change and political changes at the end of the eighteenth century.

The poem incorporates, he thinks, aspects of social and political realities which Coleridge found threatening. His desire to believe in a benevolent God who leads society toward goodness had to meet the ideological shifts of his own time. Watkins sees Coleridge's conservativism as a response to his unsettled historical situation: Coleridge had to "address the various elements of that situation, to explain them and, if possible, to defuse them by integrating them into a larger and more palatable scheme."

He therefore could not deny history, so history remains present, undermining his vision of "ideal Christian goodness." Watkins attributes the power of Coleridge's poetry to the disjunction between his attempt "to create a world picture that is larger than mere history" and the unavoidable "presence of historical change" which conflicts with that vision.

Bibliography

Ashton, Rosemary. A review of Rosemary Ashton's The Life of Samuel Taylor Coleridge. (Blackwell, 1995) reviewed by Michael John Kooy.

Burgoyne, Daniel. "Coleridge's 'Poetic Faith' and Poe's Scientific Hoax." Romanticism On the Net 21 (February 2001)

Fulford, Tim. "Mary Robinson and the Abyssinian Maid: Coleridge's Muses and Feminist Criticism." Fulford considers gendered poetics and Coleridge, in Romanticism on the Net, 13 (February 1999).

Gibson, Matthew. A review of Yeats, Coleridge and the Romantic Sage. (St. Martin's, 2000). Reviewed by Mark Sandy. In Romanticism on The Net, Issues 32-33 (November 2003-February 2004).

Haney, David. A review of The Challenge of Coleridge. Reviewed by Nicholas Reid in Romanticism on the Net, 29 (2003).

Harper, George McLean. Reprint of an older critical article, "Coleridge's Conversation Poems" from English Romantic Poets M.H. Abrams, ed. (1960).

Hogsette, David S. "Eclipsed by the Pleasure Dome: Poetic Failure in Coleridge's 'Kubla Khan,'" in Romanticism on the Net 5 (February 1997).

Kneale, J. Douglas. A review of Romantic Aversions: Aftermaths of Classicism in Wordsworth and Coleridge. Reviewed by Brennan O'Donnell in Romanticism on the Net, 18 (2000).

Koenig-Woodyard, Chris. "A Hypertext History of the Transmission of Coleridge's 'Christabel,' 1800-1816." Romanticism On the Net 10 (May 1998).

Koenig-Woodyard, Chris. "Sex-text: 'Christabel' and the Christabelliads." On contemporary parodies of "Christabel." Romanticism On the Net 15 (August 1999).

Mahoney, Charles. "The Multeity of Coleridgean Apostasy." In Romantic Circles edition on Irony and Clerisy, August 1999.

Miall, David S. Notes and critical commentary on Coleridge's poem "Frost at Midnight," from Professor Miall, Univ. of Alberta.

Newlyn, Lucy. A review of The Cambridge Companion to Coleridge. Ed. Lucy Newlyn. (Cambridge UP, 2002). Reviewed by Nicholas Reid. Romanticism on the Net, Issues 36-37 (November 2004-February 2005).

Perry, Seamus. "Coleridge, the Return to Nature, and the New Anti-Romanticism: An Essay in Polemic," in Romanticism on the Net, 4 (November 1996).

Priestman, Martin. "Temples and Mysteries in Romantic Infidel Writing." Romanticism On the Net, 25 (February 2002).

Reid, Nicholas. "Form in Coleridge, and in Perception and Art More Generally," Romanticism on the Net, 26 (2002).

Rzepka, Charles J. "Re-collecting Spontaneous Overflows: Romantic Passions, the Sublime, and Mesmerism." [Coleridge] Romantic Circles edition on Romantic Passions, April 1998.

Roman, Laura. "Daniel Sanjiv Roberts, Revisionary Gleam: De Quincey, Coleridge and the High Romantic Argument." Romanticism On the Net, 20 (November 2000).

Saintsbury, George. An older critical article on verse form in Coleridge and other Romantics, in The Cambridge History of English and American Literature in 18 Volumes (1907-21).

Scott, Matthew. "The Circulation of Romantic Creativity: Coleridge, Drama, and the Question of Translation." Romanticism On the Net, 2 (May 1996).

Shaffer, E.S. "Ideologies in Readings of the Late Coleridge: Confessions of an Inquiring Spirit." Romanticism on the Net 17 (February 2000).

Smith, Christopher. "Southey and the Emergence of Lyrical Ballads." Romanticism On the Net 9 (February 1998).

Vallins, David. A review of David Vallins, Coleridge and the Psychology of Romanticism. Reviewed by Mary Perkins in Romanticism on the Net, 18 (2000).

Wendling, Ronald C. A review of Wendling, Ronald C. Coleridge's Progress to Christianity: Experience and Authority in Religious Faith (Bucknell University Press, 1996). Reviewed by Neil Vickers in Romanticism on the Net, 14 (1999).

Wallace, Catherine M. The Besetting Sins of Coleridge's Prose from Coleridge's 'Biographia Literaria,' Text and Meaning, 1989.

Wallace, Catherine M. Coleridge's Biographia Literaria and the Evidence for Christianity, Interspace and the Inward Sphere: Essays on the Romantic and Victorian Self, 1978.

Wallace, Catherine M. Coleridge's Theory of Language, in Philological Quarterly, 59 (1980).

Wallace, Catherine M. The Function of Autobiography in Biographia Literaria, from The Wordsworth Circle, 12 (1981).

Wallace, Catherine M. Teaching the Preface/Biographia Dispute, on Wordsworth's Preface and Coleridge's Biographia Literaria, from The Wordsworth Circle, 9 (1978).

Wallace, Catherine M. Unlikely Theologians and the Coleridgean Imagination in the Anglican Theological Review, vol. 86, no. 1 (Winter 2004).

Weinberg, Alan. "'Yet in its depth what treasures': Shelley's Transforming Intellect and the Paradoxical Example of Coleridge." Romanticism On the Net, 22 (May 2001).